Hume

on Religion

David Hume's *Dialogues Concerning Natural Religion* is arguably the most important book on the philosophy of religion. *Hume on Religion* is a stimulating and accessible guide to this classic work. It guides students through the central questions in Hume's philosophy of religion: Does the world exist by chance or by design? Is there a god? If so, is it a god who cares about us, and what are we to think of the abundance of evils in the world? These are amongst the deepest, most enduring and contested questions that arise in human experience.

David O'Connor discusses these questions and others in this clear and accessible GuideBook. He provides a background to Hume's life and the *Dialogues* and a careful exploration of each section of the text. The *Dialogues* play a central role in understanding Hume's philosophy as a whole and this GuideBook will provide an excellent introduction to Hume and his continuing importance in philosophy and religion today.

Hume on Religion will be essential reading for all students of philosophy and religion and all those coming to Hume for the first time.

David O'Connor is Professor of Philosophy at Seton Hall University. He is the author of *God and Inscrutable Evil* and *The Metaphysics of G.E. Moore*.

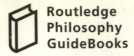

Routledge Philosophy GuideBooks

Edited by Tim Crane and Jonathan Wolff
University College London

Berkeley and the Principles of Human Knowledge
Robert J. Fogelin

Aristotle on Ethics   *Gerard J. Hughes*

Hume on Religion   *David O'Connor*

Leibniz and the Monadology   *Anthony Savile*

The Later Heidegger   *George Pattison*

Hegel on History   *Joseph McCarney*

Hume on Morality   *James Baillie*

Kant and the Critique of Pure Reason   *Sebastian Gardner*

Mill on Liberty   *Jonathan Riley*

Mill on Utilitarianism   *Roger Crisp*

Wittgenstein and the Philosophical Investigations
Marie McGinn

Plato and the Republic   *Nickolas Pappas*

Locke on Government   *D.A. Lloyd Thomas*

Locke on Human Understanding   *E.J. Lowe*

Spinoza and the Ethics   *Genevieve Lloyd*

LONDON AND NEW YORK

Routledge Philosophy GuideBook to

Hume
on Religion

ROUTLEDGE

■ David O'Connor

First published 2001
by Routledge
11 New Fetter Lane, London
EC4P 4EE

Simultaneously published in
the USA and Canada
by Routledge
29 West 35th Street, New York
NY 10001

*Routledge is an imprint of
the Taylor & Francis Group*

© 2001 David O'Connor

Typeset in Times by Florence
Production Ltd, Stoodleigh, Devon
Printed and bound in Great Britain
by TJ International Ltd, Padstow,
Cornwall

*British Library Cataloguing in
Publication Data*
A catalogue record for this book is
available from the British Library

*Library of Congress Cataloging
in Publication Data*
O'Connor, David, 1949–
Routledge philosophy guidebook to
Hume on religion/David O'Connor.
    p.   cm. — (Routledge philosophy
guidebooks)
    Includes bibliographical references
and index.
    1. Hume, David, 1711–1776.
Dialogues concerning natural religion.
2. Natural theology.   I. Title: Hume
on religion.   II. Title.   III. Series.
B1493.D523 O36 2001
210–dc21   00-051836

ISBN 0–415–20194–2 (hbk)
ISBN 0–415–20195–0 (pbk)

Contents

v

CONTENTS

Preface

Hume's *Dialogues concerning Natural Religion* may be the single most important and influential book of philosophy on the subject of religion. In it, Hume examines some of the most vexing, enduring, and profound questions that arise in human experience: Is there a god?; If so, is it a god who cares about us?; If there is a god, what are we to think of the abundance of evils in the world?; Does the world exist by chance or by design?; Is religious belief rational? These questions are in the vanguard of our efforts, throughout history, to make sense of the world and our place in it.

Taking up these questions in his *Dialogues*, Hume sifts and probes, in great detail, some of the strongest arguments for and against the idea that the ultimate source of the world is an intelligent, benevolent being who cares about us. But the idea withers under his examination, leaving only a trace behind, a hollowed-out deism with no religious significance. Hume's friends advised suppressing the book. They feared for his good name and peace of mind in the event

of publication. Hume took their advice, and the book was never published in his lifetime. It first appeared in print in 1779, three years after his death.

My aim here is to provide a reliable and interesting guide to this controversial book, the centrepiece of Hume's philosophy of religion. But Hume's philosophy of religion occupies a central place in, and provides excellent access to, his philosophy overall. Consequently, I hope this book will also be a useful introduction to Hume's general philosophy.

The *Dialogues* is not at all a difficult book to approach, even for a beginner in philosophy. It is interesting and rewarding on a first reading, and it remains so through multiple readings. Since I first read it as an undergraduate in Ireland in the 1970s I have gone back to it several times, and it has always held my interest. The reason, I think, is that its topics are perennially interesting and the writing excellent. It is a remarkably good book, among the best philosophical dialogues we have, and I say that mindful of the dialogues of Plato.

But, you may now be wondering, if the *Dialogues* is so accessible, why does it need this guide? A good question. The answer is that it does not. Yet, welcoming though Hume's book is in its own right, I think some illumination here and there may be helpful, especially to a reader approaching the book, and perhaps its author, for the first time. Think, for instance, of how, sometimes, our appreciation and enjoyment of a painting that we already find interesting and attractive is enhanced by an unintrusive interpretation. I hope to provide something akin to that here.

The *Dialogues* was controversial in its own time, as I said, and it remains so today. It is controversial in two ways. In the first place, it offers, and perhaps endorses, ideas that, in fundamental ways, run counter to various religious orthodoxies. But second, it was and is controversial in the sense that, on crucial points, the right interpretation of the book is contestable. For instance, there continue to be serious disagreements among Hume scholars even on such a basic question as which character in the book best represents the views of the author. Thus, while Hume's book is welcoming, it does not wear its meaning on its sleeve, so to speak. But that is a strength, not a weakness. Especially in a dialogue. For thereby it engages us in its drama of ideas and characters in conflict, and requires us to be diffident in drawing final conclusions. And that is also, I think, part of the reason that Hume's *Dialogues* continues to be rewarding through multiple readings. In a spirit of diffidence, then, without laying claim to the last word on any of the topics I discuss, I offer in this book what I hope is a clear, consistent, illuminating, and, of course, correct line of interpretation of Hume's text.

But no book is neutral; every book reflects a point of view, and mine is no exception. The point of view you will find here is sympathetic to Hume. I think his philosophical approach to religion is by and large right, and that he is far more right than wrong in his assessment of the main arguments for and against religious belief.

Almost a year ago, shortly after I had finished a first draft of this book, I realized that it would have to be recast in a subtle, yet profound, way. The problem was that my voice in the book was less a guide's than a commentator's. I saw the problem clearly enough, but, perhaps like an actor having difficulty 'finding' a character he or she is going to play, I was far less clear about how to fix it. Then, quite by chance, I found the solution. Casting about for a suitable text to use in my Introduction to Philosophy course, I read *Think* by Simon Blackburn. Reading his book, I found my voice, such as it is, in this book. I do not know how to explain the happy accident of the one thing begetting the other, and I am not telling this story of serendipity to invite comparison to Professor Blackburn's excellent book or somehow to make him responsible for mine. My reason is simply to acknowledge a curious debt of gratitude to him for helping along a book he does not even know exists (at least at the time I am writing this Preface).

I have incurred other debts of gratitude that I wish to acknowledge too. I am grateful to Jonathan Wolff, University College London, for the opportunity to write this book in the first place, as well as for his encouragement, patience, and advice from start to finish. I am grateful to Adrian O'Connor and to Anna Muster for reading portions of the text, through several drafts, and for their respective criticisms, interest, and encouragement. I am grateful to J.C.A. Gaskin for valuable criticism of my penultimate draft and for his many suggestions on improving it. This book is much the better for his generous help. I also thank Routledge's other (this time, anonymous) reader for useful criticisms of the same draft. I am indebted to Sarah O'Connor for smoothing away my software difficulties, as well as for her continuing interest in this project. I am grateful to John Ranieri, chairman of the philosophy department at Seton Hall University, for a similar ongoing interest, and, on the same account, to James Abruzzo. I thank the Dean of the College of Arts and Sciences at Seton Hall University, James VanOosting, for supporting my application for sabbatical leave in the Fall term of 1998, and the (then) Acting Provost of the university, Peter Ahr, for granting it. During that period of leave I wrote much of the first draft, and its not having survived in the final version of this book in no way lessens my gratitude. Stacey Colter, secretary of Seton Hall's philosophy department, provided valuable secretarial help, for which I thank her. I am grateful to Muna Khogali for patiently and efficiently (or so it seems at an ocean's distance) steering this work through production at Routledge. In the end, however, the help in various ways of all the people mentioned notwithstanding, I alone am responsible for errors and shortcomings that remain.

Maplewood, New Jersey
September 2000

A note on the edition of the *Dialogues* used

My page references to the *Dialogues concerning Natural Religion* are to J.C.A. Gaskin's 1998 edition for Oxford University Press. This edition includes several of Hume's other writings on religion. They are, his book, *The Natural History of Religion*, an autobiographical essay, 'My Own Life,' Section XI from the *Enquiry concerning Human Understanding*, and his 1751 'Letter concerning the *Dialogues*'. Because I cite these texts in this book, it is useful to have them available with the *Dialogues* itself.

Abbreviations

Works of Hume referred to in the text

DNR   *Dialogues concerning Natural Religion*, ed. J.C.A. Gaskin (New York: Oxford University Press, 1998). 'Oxford World's Classics' edition.

EHU   *Enquiry concerning Human Understanding*, ed. L.A. Selby-Bigge, third edition, P.H. Nidditch (New York: Oxford University Press, 1995). Gaskin, in his 'Oxford World's Classics' edition of the *Dialogues* and *The Natural History*, includes Section XI of Hume's *Enquiry*. Accordingly, when I make reference to EHU: Section XI, I give two citations, first to the Gaskin edition, designated by addition of 'G' to the page reference, and second to the Nidditch edition.

LCD   'A letter concerning the Dialogues, 10 March 1751' in J.C.A. Gaskin, 'Oxford World's Classics' edition of the *Dialogues*.

MOL   'My own life', in Gaskin's 'Oxford World's Classics' edition of DNR and NHR.

NHR   *The Natural History of Religion*, ed. J.C.A. Gaskin (New York: Oxford University Press, 1998). 'Oxford World's Classics' edition.

NYRB   *The New York Review of Books*, Vol. XLVII, Number 11, 29 June 2000.

THN   *A Treatise of Human Nature*, ed. L.A. Selby-Bigge, second edition, P.H. Nidditch (New York: Oxford University Press, 1978).

Chapter 1

Introduction

Hume's life, his philosophy of religion, and his influence

Life

David Hume was born in Edinburgh, Scotland, on 26 April 1711, and died there sixty-five years later, on 25 August 1776. In an autobiographical essay, 'My Own Life', written shortly before his death, Hume tells us that, on both sides, he came of a 'good' family (MOL: 3). The family was related to the earl of Home, although not itself of the aristocracy. The Humes were country gentry, fairly comfortably off, but 'not rich' (MOL: 3). Upon their father's death, in 1713, Hume's older brother, John, inherited the family estate, while Hume himself and his sister, Katherine, each received a modest annuity. Knowing from an early age that his inheritance would not be enough to support him, Hume saw that he would need to earn a living, and money was to worry him on and off until he was almost forty.

The family estate, Ninewells, which was not large, was in Berwickshire, near Berwick-on-Tweed, close to the English border. Hume spent much of his childhood there, receiving a good education by tutors

hired to teach his brother and himself. As a boy, Hume was well read: 'I . . . was seized very early with a passion for literature, which has been the ruling passion of my life, and the great source of my enjoyments' (MOL: 3). By his own description, he was a sober and industrious boy, with a 'studious disposition' (MOL: 3). Hume was raised in the Presbyterian Church, the established Church of Scotland, which, at the time, represented a severe and censorious form of Calvinism. His biographer, E.C. Mossner, tells us that the young Hume was quite religious and that he accepted without question such doctrines as original sin, predestination, and the total depravity of human nature.

Despite this early devotion, Hume lost his faith quite young, either as a student at the University of Edinburgh, 1722 to 1725–6, or shortly thereafter. A few months before his death, Hume told James Boswell, the biographer of Samuel Johnson (1709–84), that 'he never had entertained any belief in religion since he began to read Locke and Clarke' (Boswell 1947: 76). That was in his early teens, while enrolled at the University of Edinburgh. It may be a bit of an exaggeration that reading those philosophers – John Locke (1632–1704) and Samuel Clarke (1675–1729) – was the sole or principal cause of Hume's loss of faith, yet reading them at a time when his religious conviction was wavering undoubtedly both sped and shaped the collapse of his faith. But, possible overstatement notwithstanding, the remark to Boswell also shows us that Hume's abandonment of religious belief had a pronounced intellectual dimension. Mossner puts the two points together as follows:

> it is abundantly clear that the youthful Hume relinquished his religious beliefs gradually over the course of years rather than immediately upon reading Locke and Clarke. And it is also clear that those religious beliefs were relinquished under philosophical pressure – that Hume reasoned himself out of religion.
>
> (Mossner 1954: 64)

There is also an ironic aspect to Hume's point that it was upon reading Locke and Clarke that he lost his faith, inasmuch as both of those philosophers believed a convincing case could be made out for the existence of a deity. At any rate, in spite of his loss of faith, Hume remained very interested in religion, and, in the words of the Hume scholar, J.C.A. Gaskin, 'wrote more about religion than about any other single philosophical subject' (Gaskin 1988: 1).

Hume's mature attitude to religion was not benign. From his adolescence onwards he had a strong antipathy to the grim and rigid Presbyterianism that had prevailed in Scotland during his youth and in which he had received his own religious upbringing, as well as to Catholicism, which he saw as a superstition (EHU: 51). In addition, he had a lifelong distaste for, and distrust of, what he saw as a mixture of zeal and hypocrisy widespread among the devout, or at least among those professing to be devout. His particular term of disparagement for this phenomenon, borrowed from Locke, was 'enthusiasm'. In Boswell's last conversation with Hume, the biographer quotes him to say that, 'when he heard a man was religious, he concluded he was a rascal, though he had known some instances of very good men being religious' (Boswell 1947: 76).

In his late teens, with university life already behind him, Hume had an insight that would change his life. It was the concept of a new, comprehensive, and fundamental system of philosophy. The corner-stone of this new system would be Hume's introduction of 'the experimental method of reasoning into moral subjects,' as the sub-title of his first book, his *Treatise of Human Nature* (1739), tells it. In essence, Hume believed he had discovered a radically new way of understanding human nature. As he would develop his theory, first in the *Treatise*, and then subsequently in the *Enquiry concerning Human Understanding* (1748), a human being is less a creature of reason than of feeling and habit. It was a theory having the potential to cause an intellectual revolution. For, if true, it would overturn the basis of self-understanding that had prevailed from ancient times, namely, human nature understood as first and foremost rational.

This turn to experimentalism in the human and social sciences – our present-day equivalent of Hume's 'moral subjects' – was modelled on Isaac Newton's (1642–1727) great success the previous century in providing a fundamental and comprehensive experimentalist account of physical nature. It was the opening up to Hume's imagination of what he called a whole 'new scene of thought'. In a letter, he later described his vision as follows:

> after much study and reflection on this [new medium by which truth might be established], at last, when I was about 18 years of age, there seemed to be opened up to me a whole new scene of thought, which transported me beyond measure, and made me, with an ardour natural to young men, throw up every other pleasure or business to apply entirely to it.
>
> (Mossner 1954: 65)

Presently, we will see something of the Newtonian influence on Hume's thinking in the *Dialogues concerning Natural Religion*.

Hume entertained very high hopes for his *Treatise of Human Nature*, expecting it would both be well received and revolutionize philosophical thinking. The expectation that it would, indeed that it could, be both of those things is, perhaps, testimony to some naïveté on Hume's part, for intellectually revolutionary works are rarely welcomed by those whose thinking they deem, or show, to be obsolete. His expectations so high, the book's reception was a bitter disappointment. In a passage that is often quoted, Hume described the book's initial impact this way: 'Never literary attempt was more unfortunate than my Treatise of Human Nature. It fell *dead-born from the press*; without reaching such distinction, as even to excite a murmur among the zealots' (MOL: 4).

Indeed, in one respect, response to the book was even worse than that. Not only did it not change the philosophical outlook of its readers at the time, but, six years after publication, it was the basis for significant harm to its author's interests.

That came about as follows. In 1745, Hume was a candidate for a professorship of philosophy at the University of Edinburgh. But he was accused by the principal of the university, William Wishart, also professor of divinity there, of heresy, scepticism, and atheism, charges based on Wishart's reading of the *Treatise*. To his very great disappointment, Hume did not get the job. Six years later, in 1751, Hume would try again for a professorship, this time of logic at Glasgow University, but he was denied then too. Thus it was that Scotland's greatest philosopher never succeeded in winning appointment to a university professorship in his own country, or, for that matter, anywhere else.

Hume had a second career as a diplomat and government official, in addition to his life of scholarship. This began in 1746, not long after his rejection at the University of Edinburgh, when he was offered, and quickly accepted, the post of secretary to General St Clair who, at the time, was planning a military expedition to the eastern provinces of Canada. Hume spent the next three years as a diplomat in General St Clair's service, first in his military campaign in France, the plan to fight against French forces in Canada having been called off, and then in a diplomatic mission in Italy. One effect of Hume's second career was to solve his hitherto chronic financial problem. Returning to England in 1748, he pronounced himself financially secure: 'my appointments, with my frugality, had made me reach a fortune, which I called independent, though most of my friends were inclined to smile when I said so: in short I was now master of near a thousand pound' (Mossner 1954: 220). Hume's second career thus aided his first in an important respect, for he was now free, at the age of thirty-seven, to devote himself to a life of reading and study, without worrying over-much about how to maintain a sufficient income.

In the early 1750s, Hume circulated portions of his recently-drafted *Dialogues concerning Natural Religion* among his friends, and was widely advised in strong terms to suppress the book. Fearing the effect upon his life and reputation of an anticipated hostile reaction to the book, Hume took the advice. He returned to the manuscript ten years later in 1761, and revised it again in 1776, shortly before his death. Although withheld from publication for prudential reasons, Hume was eager that his *Dialogues* appear in print, and to that end he specified in his will that, within two years of his death, the book must be published. It was eventually guided into print by Hume's nephew and namesake, as both Hume's long-time publisher, William Strahan, and his long-time friend, Adam Smith (1723–90), the famous economic theorist, were, for their own reasons of prudence, reluctant to arrange for publication.

In the early 1760s, approximately fifteen years after his diplomatic service on the staff of General St Clair, Hume returned to that second career. For three years, until 1766, he served as secretary to the British Embassy in Paris, a period in which he enjoyed many contacts with French intellectuals, notable among them Voltaire

(1694–1778) and Jean Jacques Rousseau (1712–78). Hume returned to London in 1766 to be Under Secretary of State, a post he held for two years. Recalling his rejection, twenty years before, for a professorship at the University of Edinburgh, and recalling especially the reasons for that rejection, we may see a measure of poetic justice in his appointment now to be Under Secretary of State, for among Hume's responsibilities was appointment and promotion of church authorities in Scotland. In 1768 Hume retired to Scotland, famous, prosperous, his ambition to be a man of letters and, in that respect, of 'reputation', realized.

What kind of person was David Hume? By all contemporary accounts, his mind was quick, nimble, sharp and subtle, traits that at first, apparently, struck many as surprising. This was because, in body, by early middle age, he had become heavy and fat, with a face and eyes that, in repose, were dull and lifeless. For, then as now, we tend to associate sharpness of mind with sharpness of features, and clumsiness of body with that of mind. Hume was gregarious, funny, witty, by every account a splendid conversationalist, and he was popular among his friends and acquaintances. He enjoyed good conversation, the company of both sexes (although he never married), food, and wine. Hume described himself as, 'a man of mild dispositions, of command of temper, of an open, social, and cheerful humour, capable of attachment, but little susceptible of enmity, and of great moderation in all my passions' (MOL: 9). Adam Smith, in a letter written shortly after Hume's death, described him this way,

> his temper, indeed, seemed to be more happily balanced . . . than that perhaps of any other man I have ever known . . . I have always considered him . . . as approaching as nearly to the idea of a perfectly wise and virtuous man, as perhaps the nature of human frailty will permit.

> (Smith 1947: 247–8)

Hume's demeanour and behaviour in the months before his death are a good illustration of Adam Smith's description. In the first half of 1776, suffering greatly from colitis, and possibly cancer, Hume knew that he would not live long. Despite that, Boswell detected in him no terror of death, no trace of the fear of the unknown that, twenty years earlier, in his *Natural History of Religion* (1757), Hume had identified as a chief source of religious belief. In Boswell's words, 'it surprised me to find him talking of different matters with a tranquility of mind and a clearness of head which few men possess at any time' (Boswell 1947: 78). In short, it seems that, in both good times and bad, Hume embodied many of the pagan virtues he so admired; temperance, prudence, courage, rectitude untied to any kind of super-naturalism, sympathy, and cheerfulness in the face of the inevitable. Consistent with this, at the end of his life no less than before, Hume appears to have had none of the grim joylessness of the strict Presbyterianism in which he was raised.

Hume on religion

Philosopher, historian, psychologist, anthropologist of religion

It is principally for its seminal contributions to the philosophy of religion that Hume's thinking on religious topics occupies an important place in the world of ideas today. His most extensive philosophical examination of fundamental religious ideas occurs in the *Dialogues concerning Natural Religion*, thus making that book his major contribution to the philosophy of religion. But the *Dialogues* is not Hume's only philosophical work on the subject of religion. In addition, two famous sections of his *Enquiry concerning Human Understanding*, published just three years before the first draft of the *Dialogues* in 1751, deal with important topics in the philosophy of religion and one of them anticipates aspects of Hume's thinking in the *Dialogues*. Furthermore, several of Hume's essays, 'Of Suicide' and 'Of the Immortality of the Soul', for instance, also deal philosophically with religious questions.

But Hume's philosophical writings on religion do not comprise the whole of his work on the topic. For he was also a psychologist, anthropologist and historian of religion, as his book, *The Natural History of Religion* (1757), clearly shows. Furthermore, his six-volume *History of England* (1754–62) emphasizes the role of religion at important points in English history. Parenthetically, Hume was more famous in his own time for that *History of England* than for any of his philosophical books, and it was to remain the standard work in its field until well into the nineteenth century.

The principal topic in *The Natural History of Religion* is the origin of religious belief, with Hume's approach combining history, psychology, and anthropology, as I said. Essentially his thinking is that the monotheistic religions such as Christianity, Judaism, and Islam all derive from polytheistic religions (NHR: 135, 159). The effect was to suggest, controversially, that the single-deity religions are further removed from original religious feeling than those countenancing multiple gods, the pagan religions of ancient Greece and Rome, for instance. In addition to that historical claim about the origins of religion, in the same book Hume makes a controversial psychological point on the subject. It is that religious belief, whether polytheistic or monotheistic, traces in the end to dread of the unknown (NHR: 176), a point he repeats in the *Dialogues* (DNR: 128). It is a point in which we may see a foreshadow of an idea that would be made famous over a century later by Sigmund Freud (1856–1939).

From time to time in this study of the *Dialogues*, we will see that Hume's other writings in the philosophy of religion, and also his non-philosophical writings on the subject, shed a useful sidelight on aspects of his thinking in the *Dialogues*. But, by and large, it is the *Dialogues* alone and in its own right that we will concentrate on here.

Hume's philosophy of religion

The main theme in Hume's philosophy of religion is the relationship between faith and reason. Is religious belief supported by reason, and, if it is, how well? Or does the weight of evidence go against it? And if it does, how decisively? Or is the subject matter of religious belief beyond the scope of reason altogether? Due largely to Hume's influence, these questions shape philosophy of religion to this day.

Basic features of Hume's philosophy of religion: evidentialism, deism, irony, and scepticism

Evidentialism

There is an important assumption in Hume's philosophical thinking on religion. It is that religious belief is rational if and only if there is sufficient evidence to support it, and that, otherwise, it is not. In a more general form – *any* belief is rational only in direct proportion to the balance of evidence in its favour – the assumption is fundamental in Hume's approach to all philosophical inquiry. He puts the point best himself: 'A wise man . . . proportions his belief to the evidence' (EHU: 110). This view is often called evidentialism, and because of his commitment to it we may classify Hume as an evidentialist.

But while he is among the philosophers most associated with evidentialism, Hume neither originated the theory nor brought it to prominence in modern philosophy, which is to say, philosophy during the seventeenth and eighteenth centuries. For instance, it underlies René Descartes's (1596–1650) policy of accepting no belief whatsoever, not even the belief that physical objects exist, without first having an iron-clad assurance of sufficient evidence for it. Furthermore, among British philosophers who influenced Hume, the evidentialist position was emphasized by Locke as a basic principle of any belief system worth taking seriously: 'he governs his assent right and places it as he should who, in any case or matter whatsoever, believes or disbelieves according as reason directs him' (Locke 1961, Vol. 2: 280).

There are significant differences among the three philosophers just mentioned, Hume, Locke, and Descartes, including differences in their respective versions of evidentialism. But those differences need not detain us here, as, for purposes of our discussion of the evidentialist strain in Hume's philosophy of religion in the *Dialogues*, the generic description of evidentialism that I gave above will suffice.

Evidentialism, the proportioning of assent to evidence, has a lot to recommend it. It reflects our deep intuition that we ought to be able to back up our knowledge-claims with evidence, and it is a good safeguard against superstition. Bertrand Russell (1872–1970), Karl Popper (1902–94), and A.J. Ayer (1910–89) immediately come to mind from among the many prominent and important recent philosophers committed to it. But there is also serious opposition to the position. In Hume's own day, it was strongly contested by his fellow Scottish philosopher, Thomas Reid (1710–96), although evidentialism continued to be the majority view among philosophers at the time. More recently, it has been attacked by such analytical philosophers as G.E. Moore (1873–1958) and Ludwig Wittgenstein (1889–1951), by the phenomenological philosopher, Martin Heidegger (1889–1976), and by various theistic philosophers, for instance, the American philosopher of religion, Alvin Plantinga (1932–). But other prominent philosophers of religion continue to take an evidentialist approach to their subject; for instance, J.L. Mackie (1917–81), William L. Rowe (1931–), and Richard Swinburne (1934–). In short, evidentialism is a controversial subject in philosophy nowadays, and perhaps nowhere more so than in the philosophy of religion.

Hume weighs the evidence for and against religious belief in three interlocking ways: first, he considers whether the subject matter of religion comes within the scope of reason at all; second, he tests the strength of the case for religious belief; and third, he examines religion's ability to defend itself against a potentially fatal line of criticism. As these three subjects are our principal topics in this book, a preliminary word now about each one: first, the question whether religious belief belongs to reason at all introduces the wider question of scepticism, a subject that is omnipresent in the *Dialogues*, and about which more in a moment; second, the principal theistic supporting argument that Hume examines is the design argument for the existence of a deity, and the bulk of the *Dialogues* is devoted to that topic; and third, the main argument against the rationality of religious belief is an argument from the existence of widespread horrendous evil in a world that is supposedly made by a supremely good, knowing, and powerful deity, this argument being discussed in Parts X and XI of the *Dialogues*.

Deism

The outcome of the whole discussion, and Hume's final position in the philosophy of religion, is both deflationary and ironic. It is deflationary in that the strongest religious position he is prepared to accept on the total evidence is a very weak form of deism. But even his acceptance of that is hedged with conditions. Briefly, deism is the view that there is an original supernatural source of the universe, but, while this source is perhaps a personal agent of some sort, with a mind somehow resembling ours, there is not sufficient reason to think such a being is all good, or even overall good, or cares about us.

But Hume does not accept even as much as this generic form of deism. For he is convinced that the facts of evil in the world give us good reason, not just to not endorse, but to *reject* the idea that the supernatural source of the universe, if any, is good or cares about us. Furthermore, deism gives us no particular reason to believe in any kind of life after death for human beings, or in any divine plan for goodness to triumph over evil in the end. Lastly, it gives us no reason to engage in religious practices of any kind, to make prayers, or to worship.

Irony

Hume's final, weakly deistic, position is deeply ironic. This is because, while inclining towards a weak form of deism, he seriously doubts that we can ever find a sufficiently favourable balance of evidence to justify accepting *any* religious position. His irony, then, is that at the same time that he tends to weakly accept a weak form of the religious hypothesis, a slim and conditional deism, 'attenuated deism' as J.C.A. Gaskin aptly describes it (Gaskin 1988: 7), he undercuts that very tendency itself. And that is the essence of irony, namely, stating something in such a way as to be deliberately self-defeating; that is, to propose something in such a way that, at the very same time it is put forth, the proposition undercuts itself. Thus Hume, on the one hand, inclines to a weak form of deism, yet, as we will see, at the same time he gives us good reason to think that the very debate within which he inclines to deism is incapable of answering its own fundamental questions. What he gives on the one hand, he takes back with the other. That irony, the self-undercutting of the positive side of his philosophy of religion, reflects one of the deepest, most important, and far-reaching aspects of Hume's philosophical thinking, namely, his scepticism. Briefly, then, an introductory word about scepticism, a topic central to my tale in this book.

Scepticism

Scepticism, which comes in different forms and strengths, is essentially the view that, apart from the merely formal truths of logic and mathematics, on the one hand, and the indubitable contents of our own immediate consciousness, on the other, we are incapable of knowledge. The core of it is the view that all claims to knowledge of the physical universe are either false or unjustified. The particular form of it that Hume comes to in his mature work, which he calls 'mitigated scepticism' (EHU: 161), holds that, in the last analysis, it is not reason or evidence that sustains our most basic beliefs about what is real, but custom and habit (EHU: 159). On that point, recall 'the whole new scene of thought' that, as a young man, opened up to Hume, and which both contained the essence of his proposed revolution in ideas and foretold the direction of his life's work as a philosopher.

According to the mitigated form of scepticism that Hume espouses, we cannot provide good evidence for our basic beliefs about the world or for our system of such beliefs, but that does not mean that we should, or, for that matter, could, abandon them. On Hume's theory, such beliefs, for instance our belief that material objects exist, are 'instinctual', by which he means that they belong to our very nature. Hume puts the point this way in his *Treatise of Human Nature*:

> nature breaks the force of all sceptical arguments in time ...
> [We] must assent to the principle concerning the existence of
> body, tho' [we] cannot pretend by any arguments of philo-
> sophy to maintain its veracity. Nature has not left this to [our]
> choice.
>
> (THN: 187)

Hume does not mean our specifically rational nature. Instead, his idea is that such beliefs belong to our very nature as beings who walk and eat and play, that is, to our animal nature, and we could not function in the world at all without them. Such beliefs lie too deep for evidence, and they are presupposed in all searches for evidence: 'we must take [them] for granted in all our reasonings' (THN: 187). We hold such beliefs pre-conceptually and pre-reflectively; that is, instinctively, as do other animals (EHU: 106). The framework of such basic beliefs marks the limits of evidence, and thereby of Hume's commitment to evidentialism. And by the same token it is an important reminder of the limits of sceptical doubt.

An obvious question to ask at this point is whether some *religious* beliefs are natural or instinctual too, after the fashion of our unbreakable conviction that physical objects exist or that there are causal connections among them. And some theistic philosophers *do* maintain this, or something very close to it, about certain fundamental religious convictions. The aforementioned Alvin Plantinga is a case in point. For Hume, though, the answer to the question is unequivocally 'no'. On that, more later.

Scepticism comes up right at the start of the *Dialogues*, where the two main characters, the theist Cleanthes and the sceptic Philo, the latter being the principal spokesman in the *Dialogues* for Hume himself, clash over it. That initial disagreement is about the very genuineness of scepticism, whether it is a serious position or just a sham, that is to say, only a mischievous pretence by clever but shallow naysayers; and this initial disagreement frames the whole subsequent conversation about religion in the book. It would be hard, then, to overstate the importance of scepticism to Hume's thinking about the rationality of religious belief. And so it would be hard to exaggerate its importance in his *Dialogues concerning Natural Religion*.

Hume's scepticism is often grouped with the kind of scepticism that, ironically, came to prominence in the mid-seventeenth century largely as a consequence of Descartes's efforts to refute it, yet a better ancestral home for Humean scepticism is in Cicero's (106–43 BC) conception of the position. And Hume himself says as much in Section XII of the *Enquiry*, where he provides a useful taxonomy of sceptical positions (EHU: 149–65). For present purposes, it is unnecessary to examine that taxonomy, yet the Ciceronian model of scepticism that Hume uses for his own position is a useful reminder that, while indeed a modernist, he also has deep intellectual and cultural roots in the ancient world, especially ancient Rome. Gaskin puts the point well in the 'Introduction' to his edition of the *Dialogues*: 'To an unusual extent, Hume's intellectual home is the humanism of the great classical authors rather than what he came to regard as the narrow and life-contorting dogmas of Christianity' (Gaskin 1998: xxi–xxii).

An evidentialist, sceptical, ironic deist

Evidentialism, scepticism, irony, and deism are the keys to Hume's philosophical thinking about religion. But there are different ways of finding a balance among them, and those differences will affect the nuance, although perhaps not the substance, of the interpretation we put on Hume's philosophy of religion. For instance, if we say that, in the last analysis, he is an evidentialist, sceptical, ironic deist, that shades in a somewhat different direction to saying of him that he is an evidentialist, ironic, deistic sceptic, although the differences are not profound. And so it would go for other combinations.

My own view is that, considered specifically as a philosopher of religion, the first of the two characterizations just given is a better fit than any other. This aligns my reading of Hume as a philosopher of religion with Gaskin's and with Norman Kemp Smith's, two of the most renowned scholars of Hume's philosophy of religion, both of whom see him as having been, in the last analysis, a deist of a certain, albeit very weak, kind. But my representation of Hume as a sceptical deist raises a question as, at face value, scepticism and deism pull against each other. After all, deism is a substantive position, whereas scepticism seems to undercut commitment to substantive positions as a matter of principle. In Chapter 10, though, when I come back to this characterization of Hume's final position, we will see that, if there is tension between his deism and his scepticism, it is low-level tension.

There is disagreement among Hume scholars about another aspect of his final position as a philosopher of religion as well, and serious arguments are available to support the idea that Hume is not a deist at all, but a theist, or an atheist, an agnostic, or a fideist. Briefly, let us look at those possibilities.

Theism, atheism, agnosticism, and fideism

The deistic conception of a supernatural designer and creator of the world falls a long way short of what many religious believers in the Judeo-Christian tradition think of as God, belief in whom is the essence of theism.

Theism

According to theism, there exists, and could not possibly not exist, a personal creator and designer of the universe. This creator is good, indeed perfectly good, in his or her essential nature, and cares about us individually. Furthermore, this being has power, intelligence, and knowledge without limit. The capitalized form of the word 'god' is reserved for this being, the God of theism. From time to time, I will refer to this position as standard theism, in order to differentiate it from a weaker, narrower variation on it that Hume discusses in the *Dialogues* (Part XI especially, but the ground is readied in Part II). I shall refer to this narrower version as limited theism.

Limited theism commits to a personal deity who is good and cares about us, who is immensely powerful and knowledgeable, but whose goodness, power, and knowledge are less than perfect or infinite. The fundamental difference between this limited theistic conception of divinity and the deistic conception is that neither goodness (to any degree) nor caring about us are attributed to the god of deism. This does not mean that those properties are necessarily denied of the deistic concept of god, but, rather, that the evidence is insufficient to warrant their attribution. Thus, as we saw before, to *deny* such attributes to the deity, as Hume will in the context of the problem of evil, would be a further weakening of the already weak concept of deity to be found in deism. More importantly, perhaps, that denial means that Hume's version of deism is not open to theism. That is, it could not, even in theory, be self-consistently developed into either limited or standard theism. Thus, Hume is no theist.

Atheism

Atheism comes in different forms, the strongest denying *any* kind of deity. But the term is also commonly used to mean denial of the God of theism specifically, thereby relativizing atheism to standard theism. By virtue of his acceptance of a weak form of deism, Hume is no atheist in the strongest sense of the term. Thus it would be false and misleading to call him an atheist, plain and simple. But neither is that the last word on the subject.

In Parts X and XI of the *Dialogues*, we see Hume prepared to grant that there is no formal contradiction between evil and the God of standard theism, '[their] consistence is not absolutely denied' (DNR: 107). None the less, he is convinced that the facts of evil in the world warrant denying various moral attributes to the deity, for instance, perfect goodness and benevolence, or caring about us individually. But those are attributes that, in standard theism, are essential to God. Thus, as he denies those of any deity that might be warranted on the total evidence, Hume *is* an atheist in the sense of the term reserved for denying the God of standard theism. In that context, Gaskin aptly describes him as a 'moral atheist', by which he means that Hume rejects the standard theistic attribution of moral qualities to the deity. The distinguished English philosopher, Bernard Williams (1929–), puts the point well: 'he . . . was certainly an atheist by, say, Christian standards: about the non-existence of the Christian God, it seems clear that he felt no doubts' (Williams 1963: 77).

We may extend the point to cover limited theism too, for, as I said above, Hume is no theist. Standard theism sees the moral attributes of the deity as infinite, thereby giving one kind of meaning to the terms 'perfect goodness', 'perfect justice', and so on. But the limited theism that Cleanthes advocates interprets those terms more narrowly than that. Thus, for instance, in Part XI Cleanthes will portray the deity in limited theism as 'finitely perfect, though far exceeding mankind' (DNR: 105). But Hume's moral atheism covers finite perfection as well as infinite. In short, he is an atheist relative to all forms of theism; that is the significance of his moral atheism.

In sum, then, Hume is a deist, in one sense of the term, and at the same time an atheist, in one sense of that term. Both of those terms, along with 'sceptic', 'evidentialist', and 'ironist' are needed to do justice to Hume's thinking on religion.

Agnosticism

Agnosticism is another term that is used in different senses by different thinkers. However, it is best and most commonly understood relative to both standard theism and atheism, as a position equidistant between them. As such, agnosticism neither affirms nor denies God, on the grounds that the evidence is insufficient to justify a verdict either way. Among Hume scholars, James Noxon, the author of a well-respected book on the development of Hume's philosophy, classifies him as an agnostic (Noxon 1966: 361).

Because agnosticism is the view that we do not, or cannot, know or justifiably believe whether God exists or not, it would not be unusual to see it as, in practice, dovetailing with scepticism with regard to religious belief. So understood, I do not object to calling Hume an agnostic. But, notwithstanding that, there are two good reasons to resist classifying Hume as agnostic. The first is that, while agnosticism is equidistant from both standard theism and atheism, Hume's thinking is not. As we saw, he sees the balance of evidence to be distinctly unfavourable to standard theism in particular. The second reason not to classify Hume as an agnostic is his acceptance of a very limited form of deism. And agnosticism, with its connotations of a position that is essentially and strictly non-committal insofar as the existence of a deity is concerned, is likely to mislead us in regard to Hume's final position on that.

Fideism

Lastly, there is fideism, a position that draws some strength from Hume's work, but that is not endorsed or intended by him, notwithstanding Philo's seeming profession of it at the very end of the *Dialogues* (DNR: 130). Fideism is the view that religious belief, although unable to be justified by reason, is justified by faith alone. It is a position often associated with the Danish theologian, Sören Kierkegaard (1813–55) and, on a certain interpretation of Wittgenstein, with some of his religious followers too. Fideism is proposed by the theist, Demea, at the start of Part II of the *Dialogues* (DNR: 43–4) and reiterated by him towards the end of Part III (DNR: 57–9), but then, at face value oddly, he offers a proof of God's existence in Part IX, thereby adopting a position seemingly incompatible with his initial view. In Chapter 8, I will suggest a way of possibly reconciling these seemingly conflicting aspects of Demea's position. As noted, Philo, the principal representative in the *Dialogues* of Hume's own thinking, claims to endorse a fideistic position at the very end of the book. We will see in Chapter 10, though, that the claim is insincere.

Without intending to do so, Hume's thinking aids fideism, inasmuch as he subjects the rational basis of religious belief to severe criticism, without, in the end, refuting it. The effect is that faith, of some sort, is left standing, but without much rational or evidential support, thus opening the door to a fideistic interpretation of it. If Hume is right in his attacks on religion's philosophical support, we may see fideists as, in a sense, making a virtue of necessity.

How can we be sure that Hume was not himself a fideist? The reason is that fideism presupposes faith, an existential commitment either to the God of standard theism or to a deity of some other kind, and Hume did not have faith in that sense. He accepted a very weak form of the deistic hypothesis, but solely as a 'plain philosophical . . . proposition' (DNR: 129), heavily hedged. What remains of religion for Hume is reason, together with a feeling that order in nature may not be accidental, but no faith. Hume's deism is completely without significance for morality or anything else bearing on the conduct of life; there is no existential dimension in it at all (DNR: 129).

A final, and I hope not complicating, word about fideism. While Hume is no fideist in the usual sense of the term, there is something to be said for thinking of his work on knowledge and belief at large – his epistemology, that is – as amounting in the end to a kind of secular fideism. I am suggesting that a strictly metaphorical use of the word 'fideism' may be useful to characterize Hume's view that certain fundamental beliefs, not including any religious beliefs, hold independently of any evidence, whether for or against them. But this is secular fideism, not religious. It is a suggestion to drain the word 'fideism' of all religious connotations and, thus purged, to then extend its use to those 'instinctual' or 'natural' beliefs that we earlier saw to represent the mitigating factor in Hume's scepticism. At any rate, whatever the merits of taking licence with the word 'fideism', back now to the subject at hand.

If we ask whether Hume believed in God, the answer is 'no, but'. He did not believe in the God of standard theism, or in any variation thereon in limited theism, but he did not rule out all concepts of deity, and neither was he non-committal on the subject. But let us remember that Hume was not eager to make his religious views crystal clear, that ambiguity suited his purposes, and this creates difficulty in definitively pinning down his final position on religion. I will come back to this deliberate ambiguity in the Afterword.

A basic distinction: Hume's Fork

Hume draws a fundamental distinction between two kinds of propositions or beliefs that he regards as mutually exclusive. The distinction is crucial in his philosophy of religion, and so it will be useful to have it before us from the outset. In the *Enquiry concerning Human Understanding*, he makes the point this way;

> All the objects of human reason or enquiry may naturally be divided into two kinds, to wit, *Relations of Ideas*, and *Matters of Fact*. Of the first kind are the sciences of Geometry, Algebra, and Arithmetic; and in short, every affirmation which is either intuitively or demonstratively certain . . . Propositions of this kind are discoverable by the mere operation of thought, without dependence on what is anywhere existent in the universe . . . Matters of fact . . . are not ascertained in the same manner . . . The contrary of every matter of fact is still possible.
>
> (EHU: 25)

Propositions of the former kind are known to be true or false *a priori*, that is, prior to any experience, and in that sense they are completely independent of all experience. By contrast, the truth or falsity of the latter kind of propositions are known *a posteriori*, that is, after (posterior to), or on the basis of, experience. And Hume believed that the best available model of *a posteriori* reasoning was Newton's.

But what would it mean to know something absolutely and completely apart from any experience whatsoever? It may be useful to think of that along the following lines. Suppose that, in addition to its operating program, we load into a computer a set of logical and mathematical truths, and no more. That is, we load no empirical data whatever into its memory, no information about what exists in the actual world of our experience. As an example of a mathematical truth, think of the proposition, '7 + 5 = 12', while an example of a purely logical truth would be the inference rule called *modus ponens*, namely, '*p* is true; if *p* is true, then *q* is true; therefore *q* is true'. Now, with the basics of mathematics and logic in its memory, suppose we ask the computer whether means-end order exists on purpose or whether it just happens to exist. The computer will be powerless to answer; no match will be found in its data bank for the terms 'means-end', 'order', or 'on purpose'. The computer has only *a priori* knowledge; all it knows are so-called truths of reason. It knows no matters of empirical fact, and it has no empirical 'expectations'. Nothing existing in actual reality, or, apart from contradictions, not existing there, could 'surprise' it. If we ask our computer for the sum of 7 and 5, it will answer 12. But if we ask it if there are twelve apostles, or seven seas, or five fingers on my daughter's left hand, it will be clueless. For, to answer those questions, it must know something about what exists in fact, for instance, five-fingered humans with left hands. And so, too, it would be with us if all that we knew were *a priori* truths.

Hume's point is not that, in actual practice, a human being ever has only *a priori* knowledge and no more. His point is that a human being, just from his or her store of *a priori* knowledge, would never know what to expect to happen in real life; indeed such a person would have no idea even what *could* happen in real life. Quite simply, such a person would have no notion there even *was* a real life, that is, things above and beyond mathematical and logical truths. So far as such a person would be concerned, anything at all that did not involve an outright contradiction could be true or could occur.

This distinction between the domain of the *a priori*, the world of pure mathematics and formal logic, on the one hand, and, on the other, the domain of the *a posteriori*, which is everything else, is often referred to as Hume's Fork. The name was coined by the contemporary English philosopher and Hume scholar, Antony Flew (Flew 1997: 53). The distinction between *a priori* and *a posteriori* matters is fundamental in Hume's philosophical methodology and in his philosophy of religion, and it will come up at crucial points in this book.

Hume's influence

To use a slang term for it, Hume's fingerprints are all over contemporary philosophy of religion. Theism's ability to cope with the problem of evil and, both related to that as well as more broadly, its ability to defend its own rationality, are central topics in philosophy of religion today. In the former case, Hume's distinction between logical and empirical forms of the problem of evil, together with his view that the latter present more vexing difficulties for theism than the former, are orthodoxies among philosophers of religion today. (We will discuss these topics in Chapter 9.) In the latter case, Hume's discussion of theism's rationality comes down to the status of evidentialism. And although, as we saw earlier, that theory has come under severe criticism of late, it remains the point of reference for much philosophical thinking about faith and reason.

A third area in contemporary philosophy of religion where Hume's legacy is strong is the traditional proofs for the existence of God. But his influence there is largely negative. By and large, the design argument has never quite recovered from Hume's attacks upon it, nor from the effects of Charles Darwin's (1809–82) theory of evolution by natural selection, roughly a century after Hume's *Dialogues*. Essentially, Darwin undercut design theorists' most important assumption, namely, that brute nature could not be self-ordering. Interestingly, in Part VIII of the *Dialogues*, we will see Hume anticipate the theory of evolution, inasmuch as we will find him there sketching out an embryonic version of just such a theory.

Although a scarcer commodity in philosophy nowadays than in pre-Humean times, design arguments are not altogether extinct. For instance, the prominent English philosopher of religion, Richard Swinburne offers one. However, no version of the design argument that neglected Hume's criticisms would now be taken seriously, or deserve to be. Granting that, however, theistic strategies to deal with

Hume vary. Some current versions of the design argument address Hume head on, attempting to defeat, or at least to rebut, his criticisms, while others try largely to avoid those criticisms by modifying the ground on which the argument stands. Swinburne's argument is a good example of the former approach, while Mark Wynn's book, *God and Goodness* (1999), provides a clear instance of the latter.

In his *Dialogues concerning Natural Religion*, Hume puts religious belief on trial for its intellectual life. And religious belief has been in the dock ever since, facing essentially the same case that Hume develops in that book. That is the core of his influence in the philosophy of religion. While there is disagreement among Hume scholars about various aspects of his thought, as I mentioned, I think there would be wide agreement on his influence.

Chapter 2

An overview of the *Dialogues*

Introduction

The centrepiece of Hume's philosophy of religion is *Dialogues concerning Natural Religion*. The model of philosophical dialogue writing followed in it is Cicero's. Cicero, whose form of scepticism is reflected in Hume's, as we saw in the previous chapter, wrote several philosophical dialogues, including two in the philosophy of religion, *De Natura Deorum* and *De Divinatione* (*Concerning the Nature of the Gods* and *Concerning Divinity*, respectively). The first of them was especially influential for Hume. It is not, then, Plato or Hume's contemporary among philosophers who wrote famous dialogues, George Berkeley (1685–1753), whose dialogues influenced Hume in writing his own.

There are three main characters in Hume's book: two theists, Cleanthes and Demea, who do not subscribe to the same version of theism, and a sceptic, Philo, who, in the end, acquiesces in a weak form of deism. Although there is disagreement among scholars, the

23

consensus seems to be that Philo is the principal spokesman for the author. That is how I represent him here. There are two minor characters as well, Pamphilus and Hermippus.

The conversation among the three main characters is presented to us as a flashback. Pamphilus is telling Hermippus what took place the previous summer when he was present in Cleanthes' library throughout a discussion there among Cleanthes, Demea and Philo. We, for our part, suspend our disbelief about Pamphilus's word-for-word recall of a long, detailed, and often subtle conversation.

In preparation for his tale, Pamphilus gives a sketch of each participant in the discussion. He tells Hermippus that Cleanthes, who, for a reason we are not told, is responsible for Pamphilus's education, has an 'accurate philosophical turn' of mind (DNR: 30). Furthermore, it is Cleanthes who, at the end, Pamphilus declares the winner in the argument (DNR: 130). Pamphilus represents Philo as manifesting a 'careless scepticism' (DNR: 30), but, none the less, as getting 'nearer to the truth' about religion than the theistic Demea, although less close to it than Cleanthes (DNR: 130). He describes Demea as a defender of a 'rigid inflexible orthodoxy' (DNR: 30).

We must take Pamphilus's scorecard with at least a pinch of salt. For, as we will see in the next chapter, Hume subtly, but effectively, undermines his narrator's credibility as a judge of the outcome. And that is but one of several devices that Hume uses to disguise, at least partially, his true thinking on religious belief.

Before beginning a detailed examination of the argument in the *Dialogues*, let us here trace it out in broad outline.

The *Dialogues* in outline

The title

As announced in the title, the subject of Hume's book is natural religion. But what is that? The first thing to note is that natural religion is not religion at all, but philosophy. Its name notwithstanding, natural religion belongs to reason, not to faith. Sometimes, the enterprise is called natural theology, for instance by Demea in Part I (DNR: 32) and by Philo in Part XII (DNR: 129), but that name is misleading too, although less so, inasmuch as theology does obviously belong to reason.

Essentially, natural religion is the enterprise of supporting religious belief by reason and argument. How much of religion is actually supported, that is, successfully supported, in this way? That is the basic question about religion that Hume is asking, and, as we shall see, he thinks the answer to it is 'not much'. In short, then, the subject of the *Dialogues* is the extent to which religious belief is upheld (or is able to be upheld) by reason and evidence.

The Prologue

It is in the Prologue that we first meet Pamphilus and Hermippus. In addition to the aforementioned character sketches of the three participants in the discussion, Pamphilus offers two reasons for the particular suitability of dialogue to natural religion. They are, first, the sheer obviousness (as he sees it) of 'the being of a God' (DNR: 30), together with, second, the obscurity in our understanding of the nature of that deity. Assuming for the moment that the existence of the deity is obvious and that our concept of divine nature is obscure, why are these good reasons? In the first place, we are told that the dialogue form, with its different voices, and its twists and turns as conversation develops, will enliven a subject – the existence of the deity – in which, allegedly, there is no room for serious disagreement. Then, second, with the concept of the divine nature so allegedly obscure, the multiple strands and layers of thinking that a dialogue, as opposed to a linear narrative, can simultaneously keep before us will help to capture the subject's inherent complexity.

We will see in the next chapter that, at best, the distinction between our knowledge (as well as our capacity for knowledge) of the existence and of the nature, respectively, of the deity is dubious. Furthermore, if our ignorance of the divine nature is really as complete as Demea will initially depict it, the distinction is also incoherent, as we shall see. But this dubiousness does not compromise the development of the argument in the *Dialogues*, for, when the distinction comes up among the principal characters in the book, as it does in Part II, Cleanthes, the advocate of natural religion, rejects it, and Philo, the main voice of the author, while saying at that point that he subscribes to it, subsequently ignores it in practice, until, in Part XII (DNR: 119), with the ulterior motive of advancing the cause of scepticism, he sketches out a version of it. Insofar as this distinction is concerned, Philo's motive in Part XII reflects Hume's throughout the book. For Hume, thus for Philo too, the main virtue of the distinction is that it facilitates a smooth and natural introduction of scepticism into the conversation, while maintaining the option of denying it as his own view of religion in real life, should the need to do so arise.

Before leaving the Prologue for the main body of the text, let us note an oddity in Pamphilus's praise of the particular suitability of the dialogue form of writing to the subject of the book. The oddity is that, supposedly, he is narrating, verbatim, a conversation among Cleanthes, Demea, and Philo. That being so, what form other than dialogue-form could his narrative take? Insofar as the action, so to speak, of the book is concerned, a discussion is being recounted; thus, within the 'reality' of Pamphilus's narration, there is no writing at all. Strictly speaking, then, his praise of 'dialogue-writing' (DNR: 29) seems a bit out of place. But this is not, obviously, a large or significant point, merely a curiosity, so let us go into Hume's book proper.

Part I

The root of the central conflict in the *Dialogues*, as well as in philosophy of religion in general, comes up early in Part I. It is the conflict between our tendency to try to answer ultimate questions, on the one hand, and, on the other, Hume's conviction that such questions far exceed the reach and power of our understanding. The clash of these two things, each initially plausible and attractive in its own right, is the centre of the *Dialogues'* drama, and the most fundamental theme played out in the book.

The basic issue here is scepticism in relation to our natural wonderment about such things as order throughout the universe. To Cleanthes, scepticism is an inherently absurd position, impossible, upon reflection, to hold. Philo counters with a distinction between extreme and mitigated scepticism. The latter, being 'thoroughly sensible of the weakness, blindness, and narrow limits of human reason'

(DNR: 33), resists definitive pronouncements 'upon objects, which . . . are too large for our grasp' (DNR: 37): for instance, in addition to the aforementioned order throughout nature, 'the creation and formation of the universe; the existence and properties of spirits; the powers and operations of [God]' (DNR: 36–7). Opposed to this, there is Cleanthes' confidence in a robust concept of reason, rooted in and reflecting our basic wonderment, and well able, he thinks, to establish 'the religious hypothesis' by 'the simplest and most obvious arguments' (DNR: 40).

In sum, Part I is about the powers of the mind, as, indeed, insofar as religious belief is concerned, is the whole book.

Parts II and III

Brushing aside Demea's distinction between the allegedly known existence of God and God's allegedly unknown (and unknowable) nature, Cleanthes introduces a design argument to 'prove . . . the existence of a Deity, and his similarity to human mind and intelligence' (DNR: 45). In Hume's terminology, the argument is *a posteriori*, not *a priori*. Recalling from the previous chapter the distinction between those two kinds of propositions and arguments, this means that Cleanthes' argument relies on experience and not relationships among pure concepts. The major premise in his argument is that means-to-end order in nature 'resembles exactly' the means–end order evident in man-made things (DNR: 45). Thus, 'by all the rules of analogy . . . the causes also resemble' (DNR: 45). Cleanthes' conclusion is rather modest, namely, that 'the Author of nature is somewhat similar to the mind of man' (DNR: 45). Philo responds by laying down the basic criteria of analogical arguments, by re-stating Cleanthes' argument, and by opening an attack upon it.

Cleanthes and Philo continue this discussion into Part III, where Cleanthes develops another form of design argument, also *a posteriori*, which he characterizes as 'irregular', in contradistinction to his argument in Part II (DNR: 57). Part III ends with Demea reiterating his fideistic conviction that, while we know the deity to exist, the divine nature is beyond our ability to discover.

Parts IV and V

Two of Hume's most damaging criticisms of the design theory come up in Parts IV and V. The first of them is that, to the extent the design theorist is successful in establishing a likeness between order in nature, especially the means-to-end order we find in organisms, on the one hand, and order in man-made things, on the other, the more the design hypothesis is being committed to an unwelcome anthropomorphism. In addition to means-to-end order, there is also, throughout nature as a whole, that is, throughout both biological and non-biological nature, order as sheer regularity. It is the former kind, though, the means-to-end order found in living things, that is principally in question in Hume's discussion of the design hypothesis. Briefly, now to return to the earlier point, anthropomorphism – the unwelcome fate that Hume suggests may be in store for the design hypothesis – is the view that various distinctively human attributes apply to non-human things as well. Thus, for instance, an anthropomorphic philosophy of religion models its description of divine nature on a description of human nature. Anthropomorphism comes in different strengths, and the question brought up in Part IV is, 'when does the modelling become too close?'

Philo's second criticism is a potentially very damaging regress argument. Specifically, if as Cleanthes, on behalf of design in nature, insists, a cause of order in nature must be sought outside of nature, in a supernatural mind resembling the human, then does this not trigger a legitimate question about the cause of order in that alleged mind itself? And is not that question just as legitimate and natural as the initial question about the cause of order in brute nature itself? But if this is right, then an important advantage that the design theory supposedly has over its naturalistic rivals, namely, its ability to finally answer the question about the ultimate source of order in the natural world, is lost. On the regress criticism, the supposedly divine mind itself, which, after all, presumably has an orderly structure, is left unaccounted for.

In his closing remarks in Part V, Philo, completely unexpectedly, and under no pressure from any arguments of Cleanthes, concedes there may, after all, be something to Cleanthes' design hypothesis (DNR: 71). He will repeat this in Parts X and XII, quite fulsomely in the latter, and the effect is to pose a serious problem of interpretation of the whole book.

Parts VI, VII, and VIII

The theme of order in nature and the extent, if any, to which a mind must be postulated as its original source is continued in these three Parts. In Parts VI and VII, the emphasis is on Philo's questions whether mind and matter are really distinct and whether a biological account of the physical universe could be as plausible as Cleanthes' mechanistic description. Back in Part II, in his first design argument, Cleanthes had proposed as an obvious truth that the universe is 'nothing but one great machine' (DNR: 45). The gist of the biological alternative now introduced into discussion is that, possibly, the universe could instead be justifiably regarded as a vast, self-organizing, self-perpetuating organism.

A further biological note is struck in Part VIII. It is Philo's speculation that the universe might be described in evolutionary terms. Specifically, his idea is that a process of purely natural selection might be operative throughout nature. A theory of natural selection would then account for both orderly processes and ordered structures in terms of the adaptiveness of organisms to environmental conditions. Philo introduces this hypothesis, but does not commit to it; the tone is conjectural and speculative throughout, and the discussion culminates in his recommendation of a 'total suspension of judgement [as] our only reasonable resource' (DNR: 88–9). Parenthetically, it is worth noting that the science of biology was still over a hundred years in the future when the *Dialogues* was written, and that so was Darwin's theory of evolution by natural selection. The result, as I observed in the first chapter, is an historically interesting anticipation of two important scientific developments.

Part IX

The design argument is now put aside and a different kind of theistic argument introduced, namely, Demea's *a priori* argument for the necessary existence of God. This is a version of the cosmological, or first-cause, argument, prominent in the history of natural religion/ natural theology. Unlike Cleanthes' probabilistic design arguments, Demea's aim is to prove solely from first principles, not from experience, and beyond any possible doubt, that God exists; indeed that God could not possibly not exist.

Demea's argument is severely criticized by Cleanthes, with its ultimate dismissal turning on the distinction between *a priori* and *a posteriori* propositions, another instance of the importance of that distinction in Hume's thinking about the rationality of religious belief.

Parts X and XI

The design hypothesis, temporarily set aside in Part IX, is brought back in Parts X and XI, at least the underside of it. In these two Parts the subject is the existence of vast amounts of seemingly pointless evil, including various malfunctions and other 'dis-orders' in nature. The facts of evil raise serious questions about the idea that the world was originally designed by a powerful, intelligent, good, just, benevolent, personal being.

Philo argues compellingly that the world's abundance of evils both blocks the design theorist's inference to a personal source of order who is all good, benevolent, and cares about us individually, and gives us good reason to think no such being exists at all. (The latter is the gist of the moral atheism that, in Chapter 1, I attributed to Hume.)

Part X ends on a startling note; Philo's second unprovoked concession to Cleanthes' design hypothesis (DNR: 104). The discussion in Part XI develops out of that concession, which is more strongly expressed than the version in Part V, and centres on two things, each a candidate-explanation of an orderly universe containing vast amounts of seemingly pointless evil. The first of these is Cleanthes' articulation of his final position in natural religion, namely, a limited version of theism, while the second is Philo's hypothetical explanation of the same basic facts. This is what the contemporary philosopher of religion, Paul Draper, aptly calls the hypothesis of indifference. It is the view that the originating source of order in the universe, if any, is completely indifferent to our lives and fate as individuals (DNR: 113–14). At this point in the conversation, Demea, unsettled by how things are turning out, departs, leaving Cleanthes and Philo alone in Part XII.

Part XII

Part XII is vexing and puzzling, and the occasion for serious differences of opinion about what Hume's attitude to religion is in the end. Simply stated, the problem is the one that surfaced at the ends of Parts V and X, now here in Part XII more fully and lavishly articulated than before, namely, Philo's claim that he agrees with Cleanthes' design hypothesis. It is a concession going against the run of Philo's thinking from the start, and for which he gives not just no supporting evidence but no reason to think his previous criticisms are no longer devastating.

That said, though, the problem of interpreting Philo's overall position in the light of his concession is diluted by the fact that, as Part XII develops, we see there is good reason to think there may be less, indeed a lot less, to Philo's about-face than meets the eye. In the end, while remaining first and foremost a sceptic on 'ultimate' questions, Philo's (and by extension Hume's) position is that the best of the substantive hypotheses is a minimal deism, a view that fits well with the moral atheism that surfaced in Part XI. That being said, it needs to be said also that there is so little substance to Philo's deism that it is scarcely different from scepticism, or, in its implications for worship and other religious practices, from naturalism. Briefly, in opposition to supernaturalism, naturalism is the theory that there exist no beings or forces outside the physical universe.

Other topics that come up in Part XII are the connection between religion and morality – a subject of much interest to Hume, whose thinking greatly advanced the cause of a purely secular morality – and the difference between true and false religion.

Hume brings the *Dialogues* to a close by having Pamphilus offer an assessment of the conversation, namely, the dubious scorecard previously mentioned.

Natural religion and religion in practice

To this point, we have been talking about the philosophy of religion, natural religion in particular, but what about religion as we find it day to day, religion in people's lives? The question that preoccupies Hume – 'What is the relationship between faith and reason?' – does not often come up for believers in their day-to-day lives of faith. And this naturally leads to the question of the connection, if any, between the issues that absorb philosophers of religion, on the one hand, and religious faith in everyday life, on the other.

Let us begin to answer this question by noting Hume's position that the religious hypothesis, to the narrow extent it is warranted by the evidence, 'afford[s] no inference that affects human life, or can be the source of any action or forbearance' (DNR: 129). For instance, on that position, religious morality, strictly understood, becomes an oxymoron. But, morality aside, many people find enormous comfort in their faith; it sustains them in an often painful existence in an often dread-filled world. Hume argues in his anthropological study of religion, *The Natural History of Religion*, and Philo observes in Part XII of the *Dialogues* (DNR: 127–8), that it is dread which originally inspires people to think, or wish, or hope, that there is a controlling personal agent, a supernatural being, behind the world who will, or at least may, heed their prayers and pleas; 'the first ideas of religion arose . . . from the incessant hopes and fears, which actuate the human mind' (NHR: 139), and 'terror is the primary principle of religion' (DNR: 128). So, in seeking the connection, if any, between natural religion (as well as the philosophy of religion in general) and religion in practice, let us focus on religion as a possible source of comfort against, for instance, the dread that what the future holds in store for us is complete personal annihilation in death. And let us look at the issue in terms of the relationship among the main characters in the *Dialogues*, beginning with the two theists.

Two sides of theism: two conceptions of deity

Cleanthes and Demea each represent one side of theism. Cleanthes upholds the idea that faith and reason coincide in fundamental and important respects, while Demea represents (perhaps inconsistently) the 'faith alone' or fideistic strain in theism. Notwithstanding that their respective theisms are quite different, there is an important similarity between them. It is that both seek to give support and comfort to religious practice, although in very different ways.

Cleanthes, by way of natural religion, proposes to underwrite an accessible deity. His is a god who resembles us, a personal god who, while greatly exceeding us in power, knowledge, and goodness, is yet, being 'finitely perfect' (DNR: 105), on a continuum with human persons. It is a deity who cares about us as individuals and whose caring seems plausible and natural to us; that is, it seems in character with the rest of Cleanthes' description of 'the Author of nature' (DNR: 45). By contrast, Demea's conception of the deity is very different. His is a god whose nature is 'adorably mysterious and incomprehensible' (DNR: 45). His deity is magisterial, exalted, supreme, a 'necessarily existent Being . . . who cannot be supposed not to exist without an express contradiction' (DNR: 91). It is a deity worthy of worship and awe; in Demea's words from Part II, '[f]inite, weak, and blind creatures, we ought to humble ourselves in his august presence, and, conscious of our frailties, adore in silence his infinite perfections' (DNR: 43). Demea's is the God of the Old Testament, while Cleanthes' is a scaled-back version of the deity of the New.

But it is in the very infinity, majesty, and remoteness of Demea's God that the believer's comfort lies. For to be the creature of such an almighty being is to be a part, albeit a small and uncomprehending one, of a whole that, given the perfection in every respect of its creator, can only be conceived of as for the good. We do not need to understand in order to be comforted by the thought. Demea expresses the point as follows in Part X:

> This world is but a point in comparison of the universe: This life but a moment in comparison of eternity . . . the eyes of men, being then opened to a larger view of things, see the whole connection of general laws, and trace, with adoration, the benevolence and rectitude of the Deity, through all the mazes and intricacies of his providence.

> (DNR: 101)

At the start of Part VI, Demea accepts Philo's characterization of Cleanthes' natural religion as vague and uncertain, and emphasizes its uselessness to faith (DNR: 72). His point is that something much stronger is needed. What he has in mind is an argument such as his own in Part IX for the necessary existence of the God of standard theism.

My point is that Cleanthes and Demea, in their different ways, offer a deity comforting to religious belief in actual practice. Implicit in this is my suggestion that, in the end, Demea's notion of the divine nature turns out to be less inscrutable to us than he made it seem initially. And then there is Philo, the principal voice of the author.

Natural religion, religion in practice, and 'true religion'

If we give in to our natural wonderment, notwithstanding our scepticism about the powers of the mind to begin with, then the upshot of Philo's examination of the case for religion is a weakly deistic view that both the world itself and any ultimate source it may have are completely indifferent to us as individuals (DNR: 113–14, 129). If nothing better than this can be made out, then, contrary to Cleanthes and Demea, religion is not a justified source of hope that the universe is meant for our sakes and that death is not the end. If Hume is right, the dread that initially turns people's minds to hope of a transcendent redeemer is left unrequited. And, on the other hand, if we do *not* give in to our natural wonderment, and instead adhere to scepticism about the powers of the mind, then again religion is not a justified source of hope that the end of life is not just death and personal annihilation. Either way, there is no justified hope for us in religion.

In sum: Hume, as a philosopher of religion, concentrates upon the cognitive or theoretical content of religion. That means his focus is the merits of theories like theism, deism, atheism. But while these do not come up as such in the daily lives of believers, they are not divorced from those lives either. The connection between the two is seen especially clearly, if, and when, the best that reason (natural religion) can uphold is a deity totally indifferent to us as individuals. For, with that outcome, a person's turning to religion in the face of a painful or dread-filled world ultimately makes no difference, and faith comes to no more than a believed fairy tale. Yet that is the heart of the position that, in Part XII, Philo will represent as 'true religion' (DNR: 125). It is a position that religious people, in the usual sense of religion, will surely find outrageous and offensive. And Hume surely realized that.

Chapter 3

The scope and legitimacy of natural religion

(Prologue, and *Dialogues*, Part I)

Introduction

Hume introduces the basic theme in his philosophy of religion, faith and the limits of reason, right at the start of the *Dialogues*. In the Prologue to the book, in Pamphilus's effort to set the scene for Hermippus, a distinction is proposed between our supposedly certain knowledge of 'the being of a God', on the one hand, and our doubt and uncertainty about the nature of that deity, on the other (DNR: 30). Within the *Dialogues* proper, Demea makes the same distinction, but in stronger terms. He does so at the start of Part II, building on his account at the start of Part I of the limits and weakness of reason. From now on, I shall refer to the distinction as Demea's Distinction.

Philo develops Demea's description of the weakness of human reason (DNR: 33). Cleanthes, rightly, sees this as amounting to scepticism, a position he views as obviously ridiculous. Yet, while insisting that scepticism is absurd, Cleanthes also thinks that, if taken seriously, it could be dangerous to religious belief

(DNR: 34). And, as the conversation develops, we see he is right in the latter point.

Agreeing with Cleanthes about one kind of scepticism (DNR: 36), Philo subscribes to a version that he regards as sensible and prudent. According to this, in theological matters we resemble 'foreigners in a strange country' (DNR: 37); that is, we do not know our way about.

In these early skirmishings, three views of natural religion come up. The first, which Pamphilus (mistakenly) assures us is reflected throughout the book, would limit natural religion to clarification of the concept of deity. The second, reflecting Philo's scepticism, would outlaw natural religion completely – the potential danger seen by Cleanthes. The third, and quite traditional, conception of natural religion is Cleanthes' own attempt to establish 'the religious hypothesis . . . on the simplest and most obvious arguments' (DNR: 40). Notwithstanding Pamphilus's announcement, Hume's *Dialogues*, at its core, is a contest between the second and third views of natural religion. That competition represents Hume's address to the fundamental philosophical question about religion, which is that of the role of reason in regard to faith. His answer to that question represents an exclusive endorsement of neither the second nor third views of natural religion just sketched, but it is very much closer to the second than to the third. We will see by the end of the *Dialogues* that his concession to the traditional idea of natural religion is a deism so weak and hedged, and so shorn of practical or religious implications, as to be scarcely different from the affirmation of no substantive position at all.

There is also another dimension to this rivalry between the second and third conceptions of natural religion just mentioned. It is that the contest between them reflects a struggle that was going on at the time among different interpretations of the significance of Newton's physical experimentalism for empirical or experimental method in philosophy. Cleanthes represents one side in that struggle, Philo another.

In Part I of the *Dialogues*, Cleanthes is explicit in his invocation of Newton against what he sees as the excessive restrictedness of Philo's sceptical view of the range of philosophical inquiries and beliefs that the empirical evidence permits, inquiries of a natural religionist sort in particular (DNR: 38). And a little later on, citing Locke's brand of natural religion, Cleanthes implicitly bids for a Newtonian endorsement of his own upcoming effort (in Part II) to establish the existence of a deity on empirical grounds (DNR: 41). By contrast, Philo, Hume to Cleanthes' Locke (and Clarke) insofar as cultivating natural religion along Newtonian lines is concerned, does not appeal openly to Newton at all. But he will make it unmistakably clear that he thinks an application of 'the experimental method' to natural religion has a very deflationary result. This aspect of the struggle between Cleanthes and Philo reflects an important sub-text in their discussion through most of the *Dialogues*.

There is another Newtonian aspect too. It will come up in Part IX of the *Dialogues* when Cleanthes strongly, and devastatingly, attacks the *a priori* argument for the existence of God that Demea introduces there. In so doing, Cleanthes will be speaking for Hume himself, and for Hume's Newtonianism in particular, in contrast to here in Part I, where he does not. We will take up that subject in Chapter 8.

The limits of reason

Setting (and missetting) the scene

Pamphilus's opening remarks supposedly set the scene for the conversation he is proposing to recount. But, in an important respect, they fail to do so. He tells Hermippus that, in the conversation, the existence of God is agreed to be beyond question, leaving only the nature of the deity to be discussed (DNR: 30). Pamphilus believes what he is saying, of course, but his sincerity does not make it so.

There are three good reasons not to accept his account of the discussion, thus three reasons to think Hume undercuts his own narrator. Each of these reasons reflects a practice followed by one of the main characters. First, take the agenda that is actually followed in the *Dialogues*, as opposed to the official one announced by Pamphilus. The actual agenda, coming from Cleanthes initially, takes in arguments for and against the existence of a deity (DNR: Parts II through VIII, and Parts X and XI; note that while Part IX also contains an argument for the existence of a deity, that argument does not trace to Cleanthes). But that agenda does not square with Pamphilus's announcement; indeed it would be impossible on the basis of it. Second, Philo participates in those arguments in full awareness of what is at stake. For that reason, Philo is only pretending to agree to Demea's Distinction (DNR: 44), whose point is to put the existence of the deity off limits in the discussion. Third, even Demea, the strongest advocate of his own distinction, gives us reason to be wary of it, inasmuch as, in Part IX, he too introduces an argument for the existence of God (DNR: 90).

The untenability of a strong version of Demea's Distinction

Quite apart from the fact that Demea's Distinction is not adhered to in the actual discussions comprising the *Dialogues*, no such distinction can be made in practice, at least not in the strong terms initially proposed by Demea (DNR: 43). That is because any argument for or against the existence of a deity is committed, of its very nature, to some particular conception of deity, a point made explicit by Cleanthes in his first version of the design argument (DNR: 45). The point can be generalized, for it holds true not just of gods but of anything at all. Without *some* account, no matter how vague or incomplete, of the nature or attributes of the thing in question, to say that the thing is known to exist will be vacuous. Consequently, when Demea tells us we can be certain that God exists, he is (rightly) taking it for granted that his claim differs in its meaning from the claim that, for instance, Dublin exists, or that the Atlantic Ocean exists, or that black holes exist. His claim has content; there is some account implicit (even if not explicit) in it of the nature of the affirmed thing.

Scepticism: introduced by Demea, seconded by Philo, ridiculed by Cleanthes

Whatever its merits, Demea's Distinction is Hume's first introduction in the *Dialogues* of the idea that there are severe limits to what we can understand and know, and that those limits are important in our philosophical thinking about religion. That is the note on which Part I begins, and it is held throughout the book.

Demea, talking about education, maintains that a person's exposure to questions about 'the nature of the Gods' should only come up after thorough study of logic, ethics, and physics. He gives two reasons; that the subject is inherently difficult, requiring 'the maturest judgment in its students', and that, before engaging with natural religion, the mind needs first to accept its own inherent limits (DNR: 32). Philo takes up this deflationary theme, emphasizing that we must first 'become thoroughly sensible of the weakness, blindness, and narrow limits of human reason' (DNR: 33). It is Cleanthes who first identifies this position as scepticism (DNR: 34). And he does so with undisguised hostile intent.

Philo makes two points. Each is important in the discussion that is now developing. The first is that, in all spheres, the 'limits' of human reason are 'narrow' (DNR: 33). But, second, the mind is especially limited in subjects 'so remote from common life and experience' (DNR: 33) as, for instance, 'the origin of worlds, or . . . their history from eternity to eternity' (DNR: 34). He repeats the second point two pages later in very similar terms.

The significance of the second point is that, should the at-large scepticism reflected in Philo's first point be disputed and shown to be overstated or even false, the second point would still hold good. For the second point is quite independent of scepticism as a general disposition or philosophical outlook; it is the modest and sensibly evidentialist point that our prospects of getting to the truth diminish the more we depart from life and experience. Philo's second point promises to be an especially potent antidote to Cleanthes' natural religionist argument. The reason is that Cleanthes commits himself and his argument to a strong evidentialism, inasmuch as he ties meaning, understanding, and knowledge to experience. It is not for nothing that the opening words in his design argument in Part II are '[l]ook round the world' (DNR: 45).

In reacting to Demea's and Philo's joint account of the limits of reason, Cleanthes addresses himself first and foremost to Philo, not Demea (DNR: 34). This is significant, for it shows us that the main line of argument in the book is between Cleanthes and Philo.

Cleanthes' response to Philo on the limits of reason is essentially a taunt. He is disinclined to take Philo seriously: 'You propose then, Philo ... to erect religious faith on philosophical scepticism' (DNR: 34). This is the remark in which Cleanthes first attaches the name 'scepticism' to the account of the powers and limits of the mind that Demea has just introduced and Philo seconded. To Cleanthes, it is obviously absurd to build faith on scepticism.

He proceeds, first, to translate into practical, concrete terms what he supposes Philo to be saying, and then, second, to propose the following way of measuring both Philo's sincerity and the merits of his position: 'Whether your scepticism be as absolute and sincere as you pretend, we shall learn bye and bye, when the company breaks up; We shall then see, whether you go out at the door or the window; and whether you really doubt, if your body has gravity, or can be injured by its fall' (DNR: 34). He will return to this tactic at the start of Part III. Cleanthes' point is that if self-proclaimed sceptics really believed what they say, then they would not survive long in the world. But if they are only pretending, if they are merely striking an intellectual pose, then we may justifiably disregard them and continue with the serious business of natural religion. He sums up his point in a way intended both to tie Philo to extreme or Pyrrhonistic scepticism and to dismiss him along with it: 'nothing could be more ridiculous than the principles of the ancient Pyrrhonians' (DNR: 35).

Pyrrhonism is a form of scepticism tracing to the ancient Greek thinker, Pyrrho (c. 365–c. 270 BC), although most of what we know about it today comes to us through the writings of the third-century AD Greek philosopher, Sextus Empiricus. Essentially, this ancient form of scepticism denies that we can know anything at all, apart from basic truths of mathematics and logic, on the one hand, and outside the immediacy of our individual experience, on the other. Thus it denies any knowledge of the supposedly objective world beyond experience.

Cleanthes insists that a Pyrrhonistic stance cannot be sustained in day-to-day living. As he puts it, '[t]he bent of his mind relaxes, and cannot be recalled at pleasure: Avocations lead him astray: Misfortunes attack him unawares: And the philosopher sinks by degrees into the plebeian' (DNR: 35). In a famous passage in his *Treatise of Human Nature*, Hume makes essentially the same point in very similar terms:

Most fortunately it happens, that since reason is incapable of dispelling these clouds, nature herself suffices to that purpose, and cures me of this philosophical melancholy and delirium, either by relaxing this bent of mind, or by some avocation, and lively impression of my senses, which obliterate all these chimeras. I dine, I play a game of back-gammon, I converse, and am merry with my friends; and when after three or four hour's amusement, I wou'd return to these speculations, they appear so cold, and strain'd, and ridiculous, that I cannot find in my heart to enter into them any farther.

(THN: 269)

And, from the *Enquiry concerning Human Understanding*, here is one of several passages that make the same point: 'The great subverter of Pyrrhonism or the excessive principles of scepticism is action, and employment, and the occupations of common life' (EHU: 158–9).

But while, in his disavowal of Pyrrhonistic scepticism, and especially in the manner of his disavowal – emphasizing scepticism's untenability in practice – Cleanthes reflects the thinking of Hume himself, this reflection is only good up to a point. That is because, for Hume, but not for Cleanthes, the foregoing dismissal of Pyrrhonism is not the last word on the subject. In order to find full expression in the *Dialogues* of Hume's thinking on Pyrrhonistic scepticism, we must look to Philo, not Cleanthes.

Philo's (and Hume's) mitigated scepticism

Philo agrees that extreme scepticism cannot be lived: 'To whatever length any one may push his speculative principles of scepticism, he must act, I own, and live, and converse like other men' (DNR: 36). But, unlike Cleanthes, who thinks this means that Pyrrhonistic scepticism has been shown to be false, Philo does not think so at all. To his way of thinking, as to Hume's, our inability to be extreme sceptics in actual practice tells us something important about our own pychological make-up, but it does not tell us that Pyrrhonistic scepticism is either false or succumbs to a superior argument. Philo makes that clear in the following lines:

But it is evident, whenever our arguments ... run wide of common life, that the most refined scepticism *comes to be upon a footing with them, and is able to oppose and counterbalance them. The one has no more weight than the other.* The mind must remain in suspense between them; and it is that very suspense or balance, which is *the triumph of scepticism.*

(DNR: 37–8, emphasis added)

That is, Philo's agreement with Cleanthes that we cannot be Pyrrhonistic sceptics for very long entails no agreement with Cleanthes' robust conception of the power of reason.

Furthermore, even Philo's agreement with Cleanthes about the untenability in practice of Pyrrhonistic scepticism is only good up to a point, because Philo emphasizes that taking Pyrrhonistic scepticism seriously has the trickle-down effect of making us cautious 'when [we] turn our] reflection on other subjects' (DNR: 36). For instance, it will innoculate us against superstition, and make us aware that, 'when we look beyond human affairs ... When we carry our speculations ... into the creation and formation of the universe ... we have ... got quite beyond the reach of our faculties' (DNR: 36–7). In this context, it is important to note that Philo, speaking for Hume, sees religion as it exists in actual practice as superstition: in Part XII, 'popular religions" (DNR: 125) and 'vulgar superstitions' (DNR: 121) are terms he uses synonymously.

Agreeing with Cleanthes on the unliveability of pure Pyrrhonistic scepticism, Philo none the less adheres strongly to a variation on it, what Hume himself calls 'mitigated' scepticism (EHU: 161). The principal difference between the two is the aforementioned point that a general doubt cannot be sustained in the face of life itself. But we saw too that, for Hume, this is not taking reason's side against Pyrrhonism. It is the force of our animal nature, nothing else, that keeps our capacity to doubt in check; even the sceptic 'must act ... and live, and converse like other men' (DNR: 36). Philo goes on as follows: 'and for this conduct he is not obliged to give any other reason than the absolute necessity he lies under of so doing' (DNR: 36). Furthermore, in a footnote in Part XII, which may be Hume speaking in his own voice or through Philo – there is a scholarly difference of opinion on the point – we read this: 'No sceptic denies, that we lie under an absolute necessity ... of thinking, and believing, and reasoning with regard to all kinds of subjects, and even of frequently assenting with confidence and security' (DNR: 121, note 1).

Nature does not leave it to our decision to doubt or not doubt certain things in practice; for instance, that the ground is solid or that there is a world of things all about me; ''tis in vain to ask, Whether there be body or not? That is a point, which we must take for granted in all our reasonings' (THN: 187). And a few lines earlier in the same passage in the *Treatise*: 'Nature has not left this to [the sceptic's] choice.' Such basic beliefs are instinctual and natural. They are convictions stronger than any evidence that could be used either in their support or against them. They are, then, immune to refutation.

Of course, circumstances can (and sometimes do) cause us to doubt that this particular ground is solid, or that this particular dagger is real. However, they are the exceptions, not the rule. But the rule is not a rational rule; it is not dictated by reason, but by the 'necessity' of our animal nature. We can no more be full-time doubters than animals can.

Hume and existentialism

This suggests a way in which Philo is a forerunner of the contemporary hero of some existentialist literature. My suggestion here is that, unlike Shakespeare's Hamlet, for whom 'conscience [reflection] does make cowards of us all' (Act III, Scene I), Hume's Philo engages no less robustly with the world than you or I, or his opponent in debate, Cleanthes. In that respect, Hume, in Philo, gives us a character who acts, and continues to act, while fully aware that there is no rational basis or ultimate justification for his actions. And that is an essential trait of the existentialist hero. In that regard, Philo is a good representative of what Hume, in his *Enquiry concerning Human Understanding*, describes as, 'the whimsical condition of mankind, who must act and reason and believe; though they are not able, by their most dilligent enquiry, to satisfy themselves concerning the foundation of these operations, or to remove the objections, which may be raised against them' (EHU: 160). Along those lines, think, for instance, of Albert Camus's Bernard Rieux in *The Plague* or of Jean-Paul Sartre's Roquentin in *Nausea*.

But I make the suggestion about Hume's Philo and certain heroes (or anti-heroes) of existentialist fiction cautiously. For it must be said on the other side that Hume's Philo is unlike the figure of the contemporary existentialist hero in an important respect, namely, that Philo has no choice in the matter. In going on with life in the face of recognizing that there is no ultimate justification to do so, he is acting from habit; he is a creature of our common human nature. In that fundamental respect, Philo is more a-rational than such heroes of existentialist fiction as Camus's Rieux or Sartre's Roquentin. The likeness I am suggesting, then, is partial and qualified.

Pyrrhonistic and mitigated scepticism: a summary, and an agreement with Cleanthes

Getting back now to the two forms of scepticism that Hume puts before us, here is a brief summary. The mitigated sceptic, Philo for instance, agrees with his Pyrrhonistic counterpart on all of the following points: it is not reason, but the habit of everyday pre-reflective living, that restricts sceptical doubt; within the sphere of reason and argument, Pyrrhonistic scepticism has the better of the dispute with non-scepticism; our powers of understanding are in general weak and limited; and, in matters beyond the scope of our experience, our minds are especially unreliable. In those matters, mitigated scepticism simply *is* Pyrrhonistic scepticism. Thus, in an important sense, Cleanthes is right in accusing Philo of Pyrrhonism, inasmuch as Philo thinks that the subject matter of natural religion lies, in principle, beyond the reach of our minds.

Two alleged inconsistencies and a prejudice

Cleanthes refuses to grant any significant difference between Pyrrhonistic and mitigated scepticism, and he accuses Philo of intellectual inconsistency, perhaps even dishonesty, in his profession of scepticism, especially insofar as the subject of natural religion is concerned. Cleanthes develops his accusation, 'your doctrine and practice are as much at variance in the most abstruse points of theory as in the conduct of common life' (DNR: 38), as follows.

In the sciences, we find numerous examples of well-established theories that go beyond common experience and thinking; for instance, 'Newton's explication of the wonderful phenomenon of the rainbow' (DNR: 38), or 'the arguments of Copernicus and Galileo for the motion of the earth' (DNR: 38). And he returns to the point about Copernicus two pages later, to develop it further. In such cases, thinkers like Philo do not withhold their acceptance on 'the general presumption of the insufficiency of human reason, without any particular discussion of the evidence' (DNR: 39). And it would be silly to do so. Cleanthes' point to Philo is that, in such matters, '[w]herever evidence discovers itself, you adhere to it, notwithstanding your pretended scepticism' (DNR: 38). Furthermore, in such matters, sceptics like Philo 'are obliged, in every question, to consider each particular evidence apart, and proportion their assent to the precise degree of evidence which occurs' (DNR: 39). And, as we saw in the first chapter, this is a fundamental tenet of the very evidentialism that Hume himself (and both Philo and Cleanthes in the *Dialogues*) advocates.

The alleged intellectual inconsistency here is that Philo's general sceptical disposition does not fit with his own responses to scientific theories, and so is conveniently suspended in regard to them. But Cleanthes also opens up a darker possibility. It is that it is not just practical and intellectual inconsistency that Philo is guilty of, although those are serious enough, but perhaps dishonesty too. However, on that score, Cleanthes tells us he is not yet ready to agree with some other (unnamed) critics that sceptics like Philo are 'only a sect of liars' (DNR: 39). Despite the last disclaimer, though, I think we must suspect that, in fact, he is quite ready to embrace the moral dimension of his charge, and that here he is simply indulging in the common rhetorical practice of making a negative point while posturing otherwise.

An additional layer in Cleanthes' taunting of Philo is his reminding him that, among 'the vulgar', there is 'a general prejudice against what they do not easily understand' (DNR: 38). As a result, such un-, or anti-intellectual people approach the world with an at-large sceptical outlook that makes them suspicious, at best, and dismissive, at worst, of advances into new areas of scientific knowledge. And the point of this unfriendly reminder is to liken this kind of suspicious outlook to Philo's own. In making this accusation, the new advance in knowledge that Cleanthes has in mind is his own project in natural religion. Not content with this, Cleanthes further baits Philo by pointing out to him that scientific illiteracy and suspiciousness of reason among 'the vulgar' commonly go hand in hand with religious credulousness and superstition, attitudes and outlooks that he knows are repugnant to Philo ('your abhorrence of vulgar superstition', Part XII, DNR: 116). As Cleanthes says, '[t]hey firmly believe in witches; though they will not believe nor attend to the most simple proposition of Euclid' (DNR: 38).

There is more than a grain of truth in this description of an attitude widespread among the so-called 'vulgar', both in the eighteenth century and today. For instance, think of how, nowadays, many people take seriously the idea that Elvis is alive, or JFK, or that the Queen had Princess Di murdered, or that the US government (on its own or with the connivance of the UN) is hiding captured space aliens; or fall for the most fanciful claims of pop psychology or of televangelists, while deeply suspicious all the while of the views of serious thinkers in various fields.

In addition to the foregoing accusations of inconsistency, Cleanthes charges Philo and his 'sect' with dismissing natural religion as part of their blanket description of the limits of reason. In this, he is charging Philo with what logicians call the fallacy of division. This is the fallacy of supposing that just because something obtains in general, it also obtains in each particular situation. Thus, as Cleanthes sees it, Philo is assuming that just because of 'the general presumption of the insufficiency of human reason', reason is insufficient in questions of religion in particular (DNR: 39).

But, Cleanthes goes on, unlike those scientific theories that Philo and his 'sect' *do* scrutinize, and then accept or reject in proportion to the balance of the evidence, for instance the Copernican theory which 'contains the most surprising paradox' (DNR: 40), 'the religious hypothesis . . . is founded on the *simplest and most obvious* arguments' (DNR: 40, my emphasis). Thus, he sees it as sheer prejudice on Philo's part to treat theological and religious theories as automatically inferior to theories offered up in other areas of human science, as well as in the natural and social sciences. Very briefly, the Copernican theory holds that, contrary to the way it looks, the sun does not rotate around the earth; that is the essence of the so-called 'paradox' that Cleanthes refers to. This will come up again later on.

An important counterpoint to scepticism underlies the foregoing criticisms. It is Cleanthes' implicit refusal to play the game on the sceptic's terms. In effect, Cleanthes is refusing to agree that, before any claim to knowledge can be justified, whether in common life or in the sciences, we must *first of all* prove that our senses or our reason could not be wrong in such instances. This point's importance is its recognition that nothing could satisfy this sceptical demand for such a proof in advance. But Cleanthes thinks that we need not be worried about this, for, as he sees it, this demand by the sceptic is finessed by the fact that the sceptic's 'own conduct . . . refutes [his] principles' (DNR: 39), that is, his own conduct both in responding to various scientific theories and in the practicalities of daily living.

Cleanthes' common cause with Locke, and Hume's irony

Against the scepticism that Philo brings to natural religion, Cleanthes makes common cause with John Locke's conviction 'that a chain of arguments, similar to that which established any truth in morals, politics, or physics, was always employed in discovering all the principles of theology, *natural* and revealed' (DNR: 40–1, my emphasis). But, in having Cleanthes so identify himself with Locke, and thus with Locke's brand of Newtonianism, Hume is being doubly ironic.

The first irony is that Locke's argument for the existence of a deity is a cosmological or first-cause argument, but Cleanthes strongly opposes such an argument when it comes up in the *Dialogues* (Part IX, DNR: 91–2). The second irony is that, as Hume must have known many contemporary readers of his *Dialogues* would recall, Locke was powerfully criticized by the Irish philosopher, George Berkeley, for, among other things, opening the door to atheism (as well as to scepticism and materialism). Thus, Cleanthes' making common cause with Locke could be expected to raise the same question about him as Berkeley raised about Locke himself, especially if Cleanthes' arguments were to run into trouble. And Hume, through Philo, is determined to see that they do.

In addition to that ironic insinuation of atheism and scepticism, there is an explicit charge of atheism in Part I. Cleanthes is the accuser. He insists that the religious case is 'obvious' (DNR: 40). Accordingly, sceptical opposition to it is tantamount to denial of the deity altogether. As he puts it, in the face of such obviousness, 'atheist and sceptic are almost synonymous' (DNR: 41).

While we are noting ironies, the following is worth filing for later reference. It is Philo's classification of deism as a heresy, stemming from presumptuousness about the powers of reason (DNR: 41). This is ironic, because, at the end of the *Dialogues*, Philo himself endorses a form of deism, albeit very weak and limited.

Who is the truer evidentialist, Cleanthes or Philo?
And the wider implication of the question

Cleanthes' accusations open up an interesting question, namely, who, between Cleanthes and Philo, is the truer, more committed, and more consistent evidentialist? Or, to put the same question another way, which of them is the truer Newtonian? Recall from the first chapter that, for Hume, the essence of evidentialism is that 'a wise man . . . proportions his belief to the evidence'. So, by that light, which of our two main protagonists in the *Dialogues* is the wise, or at least the wiser, man?

Both would maintain that they are following the evidence, and only the evidence, to wherever it leads. And in this, each one, by his own measure, would be right. Their fundamental difference is in their respective understandings of just what is to be counted as evidence, with Cleanthes taking a more expansive view of it than Philo.

But the question can be re-cast as the wider and deeper question, whether scepticism is warranted in regard to religious belief, and, if it is, to what extent? If Cleanthes is the truer evidentialist, then, proportionately, scepticism is not warranted in regard to religious belief. But if it is Philo, then, proportionately, it is. Of course, here at the beginning of the *Dialogues*, we are not in a position to decide which of the two characters is the truer evidentialist. So, recognizing what is at stake in the question, let us put off answering it until we have worked our way through the whole of Hume's book.

Negative connotations of the word 'scepticism'

In addition to accusing Philo of inconsistency and prejudice, and perhaps dishonesty too, Cleanthes enjoys the rhetorical advantage of being able to paint his opponent as an extremist. The advantage comes from the largely negative connotations of the word 'scepticism'. Briefly, a word's connotation is the set of associations that comes with it. By contrast, a word's denotation is whatever the word picks out or refers to.

Commonly, the word 'scepticism' connotes the outlook of the naysayer, the intellectual obstructionist who, having nothing positive to contribute, is content to be a nit-picking spoiler of the attempts of other, more intellectually serious, people to solve difficult and important problems. More than once in the course of their discussion, Cleanthes will so address Philo. For instance, in Part II, he refers to him as a 'caviller' (DNR: 52), that is to say a quibbler; in Part III as 'obstinate' and trafficking in 'sceptical play and wantonness' (DNR: 55), as well as dealing in 'ambiguity', 'evasion', 'perverse, obstinate metaphysics', and 'blind dogmatism' (DNR: 56); in Part IV he points to Philo's 'abstruse doubts, cavils, and objections' (DNR: 65); in Part V his accusation is that Philo has nothing to offer beyond 'the utmost indulgence of your imagination' (DNR: 71); in Part VII he describes Philo as trying only to raise 'doubts and objections', a task to which he says Philo is especially well-suited, that Philo is only stirring up 'out-of-the-way difficulties' that fly in the face of 'common sense and reason' (DNR: 83), and so on. In short, Hume is well aware of the rhetorical power of the word 'sceptic', and he gives it to Cleanthes to put to effective use.

His doing so raises the following question; considering that Hume himself was a sceptic by philosophical temperament and practice, that the sceptic Philo is the principal mouthpiece for Hume's own views in the *Dialogues*, and that readers of the book will so regard him, why does Hume create a character, Cleanthes, who so persistently (and perhaps damagingly) exploits the negative associations of the word 'sceptic'? It is a good question, and I will suggest an answer in the Afterword.

Chapter 4

Cleanthes' first design argument

(*Dialogues*, Part II)

Introduction

Rejecting Demea's Distinction as a misguided and misleading 'circumlocution', Cleanthes does the very thing the Distinction rules out; he introduces an argument to prove the existence of a deity, 'somewhat similar to the mind of man' (DNR: 45). The basic premise in his argument proposes a close analogy between order and regularity in the natural world, on the one hand, and in the world of human affairs, on the other. But much of the order in the human world is means–end order that traces back to purposes and intentions, thus, ultimately, to a mind of a certain kind. Cleanthes concludes that the universe too, in virtue of the allegedly similar means–end order manifest in it, traces to a similarly intelligent source. That is the essence of Cleanthes' thinking in Part II, and throughout the book.

In responding, Philo lays down two criteria of analogical arguments, thereby establishing a framework within which to evaluate Cleanthes' position.

The first criterion emerges as part of an initial criticism of Cleanthes' argument (DNR: 46), while the second comes up in the course of Philo's re-statement of that argument (DNR: 48). Through the remainder of Part II, Philo and Cleanthes contest the merits of Cleanthes' analogy, with Philo having the upper hand, and Cleanthes seeming to be on the defensive.

Cleanthes' first design argument

Dismissing Demea's fideistic idea that we can (and do) know with certainty, but without relying on evidence or reasoning, that God exists, Cleanthes offers the following, experience-based argument to prove the existence of a deity:

> Look round the world: Contemplate the whole and every part of it: You will find it to be nothing but one great machine, subdivided into an infinite number of lesser machines, which again admit of subdivisions, to a degree beyond what human senses and faculties can trace and explain. All these various machines, and even their most minute parts, are adjusted to each other with an accuracy, which ravishes into admiration all men, who have ever contemplated them. The curious adapting of means to ends, throughout all nature, resembles exactly, though it much exceeds, the productions of human contrivance; of human design, thought, wisdom, and intelligence. Since therefore the effects resemble each other, we are led to infer, by all the rules of analogy, that the causes also resemble; and that the Author of nature is somewhat similar to the mind of man; though possessed of much larger faculties, proportioned to the grandeur of the work, which he has executed. By this argument *a posteriori*, and by this argument alone, do we prove at once the existence of a Deity, and his similarity to human mind and intelligence.
>
> (DNR: 45)

The analogy

If the world is a 'great machine', there has to be a design plan behind it. Machines do not just come about; they are made. Cleanthes' basic idea is thus an alleged likeness between artefacts, man-made things such as sewing machines, bicycles, and motorways, on the one hand, and the world described in mechanistic terms, on the other. At the time, largely under the influence of Isaac Newton, mechanistic conceptions of the natural world were in vogue, and so Cleanthes' argument would have been judged timely on that account. Given that man-made things reflect intention and purpose, and claiming a significant likeness between them and natural processes, Cleanthes aims to prove that natural processes do too.

Examples of intentional order in human life are such things as my heating the oven to 175 degrees Celsius in order to bake a cake, your drinking a cup of tea to relieve your thirst, the musician's practising the piano in order (she hopes) one day to play at Carnegie Hall, and so on. In all these situations, the antecedent action is done in anticipation of its either bringing about, or contributing to bringing about, some consequent state of affairs. Sometimes the antecedent (the means) is a necessary pre-condition of the desired consequent (the end), but other times it is not. You could have relieved your thirst by drinking a glass of beer, for instance, or by eating a snowball. But I could bake my cake only by heating the oven to a temperature not much less than 175 degrees, even though that precise temperature surely is not necessary; 173 degrees would work fine too, I'm sure. At any rate, the thing to notice here about means–end ordered things in human life (and primate life generally) is that they reflect intelligence, a mind of a certain sort.

But means–end order does not seem to be confined to the human world. Throughout the natural world, but particularly where life in any form is involved, there are regular occurrences that reflect order strikingly similar to means–end order in human affairs. Plants bend towards the light, and photosynthesis occurs; if our optical nerve system were not more or less as it is, we would be sightless; without the intricate arrangement of bones, muscles, and sinews in our wrists and hands, we would not have the dexterity crucial to human life; were their bones not hollow, birds could not fly, and were they unable to move their tails laterally, they could not turn in flight; were the particular mix of gases in our atmosphere not almost exactly what it is, then life as we know it could not exist; and so on.

The natural world is a vast complex of regular, repeating, orderly structures and occurrences, and Cleanthes is proposing a two-step way of making sense of the overall patterns in them. His first, and most important, step is to liken some of those patterns – patterns of means-to-end order in living things, both vegetable and animal – to means–end order in man-made things. His second step is to propose, on the basis of the alleged likeness, a source of means–end order in living things like that in artefacts, namely, a mind something like ours. The fundamental idea is that when the effects are similar – means–end order in living things and in man-made things – then, proportionately, their respective causes will be similar too. Like effects imply like causes (DNR: 48). That is a basic principle in Cleanthes' argument, as it is in all our interpretations of what happens, both in biological nature and in the world of human affairs. It is a principle borne out again and again in our experience.

The relative modesty of Cleanthes' conclusion

Cleanthes commits himself to less than standard theism, as described in the first chapter. Specifically, the so-called Author of nature is not presented as an infinite being, the omnipotent, omniscient, morally perfect, supernatural God of standard theism, who cares about us. Relative to that conception of the deity, Cleanthes' inference is modest, being limited to the existence of a very powerful being with intelligence similar in kind to ours, 'the Author of nature is somewhat similar to the mind of man; though possessed of much larger faculties' (DNR: 45). Furthermore, it is notable that no moral attributes, not even limited ones, are predicated of this being at this point. Of course, Cleanthes is not precluding the possibility that this so-called Author of nature might in fact be an infinite being, or even the God of theism. Nor, at this stage in his argument, does he commit to the idea that the Author of nature is only a finite being, although much more powerful and wise than we are. Later on, though, at the beginning of Part XI, he will make such a commitment (DNR: 105). When he does, I shall refer to his position as limited theism.

Is Cleanthes' conclusion too modest to be religiously significant?

Why should anybody interested in whether the God of standard theism can be proven from facts about the natural world bother with Cleanthes' argument at all? It is a good question. Without a good answer, a theist would be justified in dismissing Hume's thinking on natural religion as simply irrelevant to standard theism.

But there is a good answer. Suppose Cleanthes' design argument fails. Suppose also that there is no other supporting argument to shore up his (relatively modest) conclusion. His position would then fail the test of evidence. But the conclusion in Cleanthes' argument is implicit in standard theism, and a necessary part of it. After all, the God of standard theism is supposed to be a personal being, to be capable of plans, thus to have a mind, and so on. Consequently, any argument that fails to uphold Cleanthes' conception of the deity, must also fail to uphold standard theism. Here is an analogy: if this container fails to hold eighteen litres of water, it must fail to hold twenty.

What if we reverse the question? What if Cleanthes' design argument succeeds? Will it thereby uphold standard theism too? No. Standard theism would still remain in need of adequate philosophical support, support proportionate to its greater size. If we establish that this container does in fact hold eighteen litres, we have not thereby established that it holds, or could hold, twenty. But we would have established that it might, and so success in upholding Cleanthes' position would show that upholding standard theism was not out of the question, at least not on the evidence from which Cleanthes' conclusion is drawn.

In addition, and most important of all, if Cleanthes' argument succeeds, it will have justified a fundamental idea essential to the whole enterprise of natural religion. It is the idea that, in the last analysis, no merely naturalistic or this-worldly theory makes adequate sense of the natural world, thereby propelling us in the direction of a non-naturalistic, and, in particular, supernaturalistic, theory as necessary to do the job. Without justification of that idea, no theistic or deistic hypothesis whatever is warranted.

Thus, to dismiss Cleanthes' argument in Part II as too modest to matter to standard theism would be unwarranted.

First discussion of the design hypothesis

Demea's worry about leaving room for doubt

Demea is the first to respond to Cleanthes' argument. Noting that it is an *a posteriori*, thus a probabilistic, argument, he warns that it gives an advantage to atheists that they would otherwise not have (DNR: 45). What he has in mind is that, even if Cleanthes' argument works as promised, it will not (because it cannot) establish beyond all doubt that a deity exists. And so dissenters will not be silenced on pain of self-contradiction. Even if successful, Cleanthes' argument remains open to further debate. As such, it 'indulge[s] a rash curiosity' and 'excite[s], instead of satisfying, the doubts, which naturally arise from a diligent and scrutinous enquiry' (EHU: 13G/135).

Demea's worry reminds me of a joke made at the expense of the Jansenist sect, the so-called Port Royal Logicians, that, had they not attempted to prove the existence of God, nobody would have thought to doubt it. The sect, which flourished in France and in Holland in the middle of the seventeenth century, was influenced by the work of Descartes, although he did not belong, and its most famous member was the philosopher (theologian, and commentator on Descartes) Antoine Arnauld (1612–94). Very briefly, Jansenism held that morality, obedience to God in particular, is impossible without divine grace. It was condemned as a heresy by Pope Innocent X.

By contrast to what he sees as the licence to doubt issued by Cleanthes' argument, Demea himself wants to leave no room at all for either doubt or debate on the existence of the deity. In Part IX, we will see him try to make good on this. And let us note that both Demea's initial fideism (Parts II and III) and his eventual attempt to prove God's existence (Part IX) share that goal, namely, placing belief in the existence of God beyond debate or dispute.

Degrees of analogy

Unlike Demea, with whom at this point in the debate he is in alliance against Cleanthes, Philo does not object to the probabilistic nature of Cleanthes' argument. How could he? After all, he is himself committed to empiricism. Taking the argument on its own terms, then, Philo's first criticism goes directly to the heart of the matter. It is that the argument's basic analogy is too weak to support its conclusion. He appeals to a fundamental principle of analogical arguments, which he states as follows: 'wherever you depart, in the least, from the similarity of the cases, you diminish proportionably the evidence' (DNR: 46).

Philo agrees that, for instance, seeing a house fully justifies our certainty in concluding that it had an architect and builder. Houses are artefacts, and all our experience of artefacts points to their having designers and makers. But surely, Philo goes on, we are not entitled to suppose that the universe as a whole resembles a house to any extent that would justify a similar conclusion (DNR: 46).

Cleanthes strongly disputes this point, as he must, and goes immediately to the heart of their disagreement: 'But is the whole adjustment of means to ends in a house and in the universe so slight a resemblance? The oeconomy of final causes? The order, proportion, and arrangement of every part?' (DNR: 46). In essence, Cleanthes' whole case is packed into these lines, its key point being his invitation to compare means–end order in artefacts and in nature, in terms of their respective 'final causes'.

Final causation

What kind of cause is a final cause? The notion of 'final causation' traces, through Scholastic philosophers of the Middle Ages such as St. Thomas Aquinas (1225–74), to Aristotle (384–22 BC) in ancient times. The basic idea is that, sometimes, the cause of something occurring in the present resides in the future; the effect is here and now, but the cause does not yet exist. The idea seems false and counter-intuitive at first. None the less, in certain kinds of cases, it is plausible, even commonplace. For instance, suppose somebody asks you, 'what caused you to stay up all night last night?', and you answer, 'I have a philosophy exam today and I was studying for it'. We would accept that answer as perfectly sensible in the circumstances. But, when we examine your answer, we see right away that the cause of your studying, or at least one of the causes of it, was in the future. (There is a controversial philosophical theory implicit in my example, namely, that motives can be causes. But let us not sidetrack to pursue it. For, even if that idea is false, it is not obviously false, or absurd, and so the example can serve well to illustrate final causation.)

The basic idea is that certain things can best be understood in terms of our purposes in doing them, in terms of their anticipated consequences. Why did you, what caused you to, have solar panels installed in your new house? Your expectation that it will cut down on energy costs. And so on.

In these examples of final causation in the human world of plans, purposes, and expectations, we can easily see intention at work. But what about the non-human world of brute nature? Take photosynthesis. Why does this plant bend towards the light? So that, by the action of sunlight on the chlorophyll, carbohydrates necessary for life can form in it. At one level of explanation, this account of what is going on in the plant is not at all controversial. The key words in the explanation are 'so that'. They suggest final causation. The plant bends now, in order that carbohydrates can form later.

For the sake of argument, let us agree to accept a final-causation explanation of what happens in the plant. Have we thereby accepted that Cleanthes has made good on his analogy? No. Part of it, yes, but not the whole of it. Not the crucial part. For, even granting final causation in nature, it still remains for him to prove that final causation in nature, like final causation in the human world, reflects, or issues from, intention. And Cleanthes is fully aware that he must prove *that* point. Final causation in nature is not enough by itself, as final causation does not equal or entail intent. The plant bends towards the light. That is final causation. But the plant does not intend to bend towards the light, for the plant has no intentions at all. Cleanthes' case for intention's being reflected in nature is the alleged analogy between means-to-end order in man-made things and in natural things. That analogy is the make-or-break element in his entire argument.

Degrees of analogy again

The concept of final causation now in hand, let us go back to Cleanthes' and Philo's first skirmish over Cleanthes' analogy. Cleanthes concedes that inferring an architect or builder of the universe from our experience of means–end order in nature is not 'so certain' as our conclusion that a house has an architect or builder (DNR: 47). The former inference, unlike the latter, is not 'infallible' (DNR: 47). But Cleanthes does not intend this concession to go very far. It is a relative, not an absolute, concession. And in making it, Cleanthes remains fully convinced that his conclusion about the universe's having a designer is objectively strong and justified in its own right. Here is a parallel case. Tim Henman is not as good a tennis player as Pete Sampras, but, that comparative judgement aside, he is certainly a very good player in his own right, and to deny that he is would be grossly and obviously false. Nor is the comparison to Sampras grounds for denying that Henman is a very good player, objectively speaking. In the same way, Cleanthes believes the conclusion in his argument, when compared to the point about houses having architects, is less certain than it, yet it is well within the bounds of reasonableness none the less. In his words, '[s]teps of a stair are plainly contrived, that human legs may use them in mounting; and this inference is certain and infallible. Human legs are also contrived for walking and mounting; and this inference, I allow, is not altogether so certain . . . but does it, therefore, deserve the name only of presumption or conjecture?' (DNR: 46–7). Clearly, he thinks not.

Philo responds by emphasizing that, apart from experience, we know nothing at all of the world. Nor could we (DNR: 47). *A priori*, which is to say apart from all experience of the world, any non-contradictory state of affairs we might think of is as possible as any other. I might now blink and, upon re-opening my eyes, this laptop computer has vanished; or water might start to pour from that book over there on the desk; or you might click your fingers and I end up in the Quad at the University of Pennsylvania; or that goldfinch, now contentedly singing in her cage, just explodes; and so on. Insofar as pure *a priori* thinking is concerned, 'matter may contain the source or spring of order originally, within itself, as well as mind does . . . The equal possibility of both . . . suppositions is allowed' (DNR: 48). Unlike nowadays, this materialistic supposition – the first of two in Part II, the second coming two pages later – would have been seen at the time as an outrageous suggestion. With the point just quoted, essentially an application of Hume's Fork, Philo commences to re-state Cleanthes' argument.

Philo's re-statement of the design argument

Philo begins with a powerful and persuasive example of the kind of point Cleanthes wishes to make. It is this. Suppose we throw several pieces of steel together in a pile, and then wait for them to self-organize into a watch. Perhaps a watch is too complicated, so suppose instead that we wait for them to self-organize into a bridge, or at least a bridge-like structure, even one as simple as two upright pieces with a third, cross-piece, lying on top of them, spanning them. We would expect to wait a very long time for these things to just happen, surely forever in the case of the watch. To be sure, *a priori*, it is logically possible that a wind, say, could blow the pieces up in the air and that, upon descending, they would fall together in a bridge-like way, or even a watch-like way. But the mere fact that there is no formal contradiction in thinking that the wind could blow the pieces into a watch is no evidence at all that it will, or would, ever actually happen, or that it is even remotely reasonable to expect it. The logical possibility of its happening is not evidence that it might happen, not even very weak evidence that it might (DNR: 48).

With the foregoing example as the first step in Philo's re-stated version of the argument, I shall number the remaining steps in it.

2. We believe with as much certainty as we bring to any factual matter that, if these pieces of steel are to constitute a watch or a bridge, the intervention of something over and above mere brute nature is required (DNR: 48). And the same is true of all other artefacts.

3. What kind of thing? An agent like us in certain significant respects; specifically, an agent with a mind more or less like ours, an agent who can form and carry out plans.

4. Do we have any experience of self-organization of things into complex, functioning wholes? We appear to, for is not the coming together of our ideas to form a complex idea, a plan, say, an example of such self-organization? As Philo, in Cleanthes'

behalf, puts it: 'But the ideas in a human mind, we see, by an unknown, inexplicable oeconomy, arrange themselves so as to form a plan of a watch or house' (DNR: 48).

There is some ambiguity here. Do we experience an agent, presumably ourselves, doing the organizing of ideas into a plan? Presumably, sometimes at least, we do. That is, sometimes, we do seem, deliberately and with self-awareness, to organize our thoughts into something compound, a hypothesis, say. But equally, we seem to have experience of our ideas striking us in already-organized shape. For immediate purposes, it does not seem to matter which of these two possible models of organization of thoughts we choose to focus on, for the point that they both serve to support is approximately the same, namely, that '[e]xperience ... proves, that there is an original principle of order in mind, not in matter' (DNR: 48); or, more exactly, they seem to support the first part of that claim – there is an original principle of order in mind – not the second part, which is that there is no original principle of order in matter.

5.   Philo concludes his re-statement of Cleanthes' argument as follows: 'From similar effects we infer similar causes. The adjustment of means to ends is alike in the universe, as in a machine of human contrivance. The causes, therefore, must be resembling' (DNR: 48).

In re-stating the argument, Philo sharpens and tightens it in certain respects, and, in the 'pieces of steel' example, gives Cleanthes a powerful illustration of his basic point. Cleanthes, for his part, accepts that Philo has given 'a fair representation' of the argument (DNR: 48).

Beneath the surface of Step 4 in Philo's re-statement

Let us digress very briefly to note that Philo seems to be committing Cleanthes to a form of substance dualism. Substance dualism is a metaphysical theory, which is to say a philosophical theory of the ultimate constituents and nature of reality, according to which, in the last analysis, reality divides into two basic categories of things or substances, mental things and physical things, that is, mind and matter. A strong and influential version of such a dualism was held by Descartes in the century before Hume, and arguably Cleanthes' position reflects a dualism significantly akin to Descartes's. The main reason to think so is that Step 4 in Philo's version suggests a basic difference in kind between mind and matter, inasmuch as Step 4 stresses that an original principle or source of order is found in mind, but not in matter.

The criteria of good analogical arguments

The design argument now before us is at once a cause–effect argument and an analogical argument. Hume lays down four criteria, two that apply to it as a cause–effect argument, and two as an analogical argument. Let us bring these criteria together in one place, starting with those applying to cause–effect arguments.

Criteria to evaluate the design argument as a cause–effect argument

The first criterion: like effects, like causes

In his re-statement of Cleanthes' argument, following the point that experience shows us an original principle of order in mind but not in matter, Philo builds the following bridge to the argument's conclusion, '[f]rom similar effects we infer similar causes' (DNR: 48). Cleanthes himself had said the same thing in his original presentation of the argument, '[s]ince . . . the effects resemble each other, we are led to infer, by all the rules of analogy, that the causes also resemble' (DNR: 45). This bridging proposition is the first criterion of cause–effect arguments. Plainly, it also functions as a criterion of analogical arguments, for the primary evidence offered for the causal claim is similarity between the effects.

Cleanthes claims to reach his conclusion 'by all the rules of analogy'. In so doing, he relies on the principle that like effects imply like causes. But the principle has a price tag. And Philo is happy to point out just what it is: 'Unless the cases be exactly similar, [just reasoners] repose no perfect confidence in applying their past observation to any particular phenomenon. Every alteration of circumstances occasions a doubt concerning the event' (DNR: 49).

The second criterion: the proportionality of cause to effect

Hume's second criterion of cause–effect arguments is in the *Enquiry concerning Human Understanding*. There, in Section XI, he says this: 'When we infer any particular cause from an effect, we must proportion the one to the other, and can never be allowed to ascribe to the cause any qualities, but what are exactly sufficient to produce the effect' (EHU: 14G/136).

These two criteria are closely related to one another, but they are not identical. The first emphasizes the similarity we are entitled to expect between the causes of two (or more) similar effects; the second emphasizes our entitlement to project a cause that is adequate to produce a given effect, and nothing more than that. For instance, if all I know is that there is enough water in that drum to fill this eighteen-litre container, I do not thereby know there is enough in it to fill a twenty-litre container. Hume himself gives a powerful and famous example of the point, the 'weighing scale' example (EHU: 14G/136), that we will discuss later on.

Side-note: Hume's scepticism about cause–effect relations

Famously, notoriously, Hume's scepticism includes scepticism about the objective reality of cause–effect relations themselves. Very briefly, his thinking about causation is as follows.

Asking for the empirical or experiential content of the concept of causation, Hume breaks it down into three components; contiguity or proximity of two or more things, succession of one by another, and necessary connection between or among them. Take any occurrence; my letting go of this paperback copy of the *Dialogues*, and its immediate fall to the floor. What caused its fall? My letting go (in this atmosphere, with this gravitational pull, and such like). Once let go, the book had to fall, so to speak. Now extract the empirical content.

We see, or otherwise experientially detect, contiguity and succession. My hand is first seen in very close proximity to the book, indeed in direct contact with it. We then see the occurrence of the one event, my letting go, before the other, the book's fall to the floor. That is, we have experience of succession. We also believe with absolute conviction that, once let go, the book will indeed fall to the floor. It has no choice in the matter, so to speak. That is what is meant by necessary connection in this context; once let go, the book *has* to fall. Furthermore, we have no doubt at all on that score, given no reason to suspect any tricks. But, Hume insists, we have no experience at all of necessary connection itself; over and above the proximity of my hand to the book, and the sequence of my letting go and then its falling, there is nothing more in our experience. We never see (touch, taste, hear, or smell) causation. Thus we have neither knowledge of causal connections or justified belief in them.

The antidote to our lack of evidence supporting belief in the reality of causal connections is, as Philo says in Part I of the *Dialogues*, action, habit, custom (DNR: 36–7; see also EHU: 75). Believing in the objective reality of causal relations is among the things that nature has not left to our choice.

There are passages in which Hume seems to deny causation, but he does not. What he does deny is that there is ever any more to our concept of it than what experience gives, namely, proximity, succession, and the habitual expectation that constant repetition of those two generates in us. It is a controversial point in Hume scholarship, and some commentators maintain that Hume's scepticism includes denying the existence of causation.

But whether or not we think Hume's scepticism about causal relations includes denial of their actual existence, and not just denial of knowledge or justified belief in causation, there is no doubt that, for Hume, no design argument can prove the existence of a deity, and likewise no cosmological or first-cause argument. For Hume's scepticism rules out all causal *evidence*, thus both design and first-cause arguments too. And some readers of his *Treatise* saw that implication clearly; for instance, the professor of divinity at the University of Edinburgh, William Wishart, cited it as a reason for Hume's unfitness to be professor of philosophy there.

Hume's scepticism about causal relations does not come up in the *Dialogues*, but having it in mind may add depth and texture to our examination of the causal dimension of the design argument. Let us now go back to the criteria applicable to that argument.

Criteria to evaluate the design argument as an analogical argument

The third criterion: closeness of fit between the analogues

As a specifically analogical argument, Cleanthes' argument is bound by the two following conditions. The first of them comes up in Philo's initial response to Cleanthes. It is his point that, 'wherever you depart, in the least, from the similarity of the cases, you diminish proportionably the evidence' (DNR: 46). The evidence is weakened as we deviate from strict similarity between the analogues.

The fourth criterion: analogies obtain between types

A few pages after his re-statement of Cleanthes' argument, Philo states the second, specifically analogical, criterion, as follows: 'When two *species* of objects have always been observed to be conjoined together, I can *infer*, by custom, the existence of one whenever I *see* the existence of the other: And this I call an argument from experience' (DNR: 51). This condition is also stated in Section XI of the *Enquiry concerning Human Understanding*: 'It is only when two *species* of objects are found to be constantly conjoined, that we can infer the one from the other' (EHU: 23G/148). The point is that, strictly speaking, analogies obtain between things, not as strictly individual things, but as instances of types of things. I expect this tennis ball to be just like that one when I hit it. Why? Simply because they are the same kind of thing. The point is completely generalizeable, and we will see below that it has the potential not just to weaken Cleanthes' argument, but to defeat it altogether.

These four criteria shape Hume's examination of the design hypothesis. They are not, then, notes struck once, at the beginning of the *Dialogues*, and heard no more thereafter. Instead, we will see their influence throughout.

Philo's criticism and Cleanthes' rebuttal

Philo's attack

Immediately after Cleanthes agrees that Philo gives 'a fair representation' of the argument (DNR: 48), Philo makes a powerful, subtle, and multi-layered attack on it. Before Cleanthes next speaks, four pages later, Philo sets forth ten points, some of which are potent and seriously damaging to Cleanthes' theory. I shall number Philo's points for convenience.

1. Using the division of labour between pure reason and experience-based reason that is Hume's Fork, Philo emphasizes two points: first, that all factual inferences rely on experience; and second, that all experiential ('experimental') reasoning presupposes that the future will resemble the past. He puts the latter point, essentially the first criterion of cause–effect arguments, as follows: 'all experimental reasonings are founded on the supposition, that similar causes prove similar effects, and similar effects similar causes' (DNR: 49).

2. With all factual inferences thus tied to their roots in experience, we must be very careful, when constructing an argument, to adhere to this principle. Differences matter, and conclusions must be carefully calibrated so as not to outrun the supporting evidence; in effect, this point reflects both the second and third criteria of analogical arguments. Philo makes his point like this, in the process repaying Cleanthes' earlier taunt to him with one of his own: 'The slow and deliberate steps of philosophers, here, if any where, are distinguished from the precipitate march of the vulgar, who, hurried on by the smallest similitude, are incapable of all discernment or consideration' (DNR: 49).

The two foregoing points are generalities, applicable to any and all experiential inferences. Now Philo turns to the specific case at hand, Cleanthes' experimental inference from certain facts of order in nature to a personal, intelligent, supernatural source, allegedly resembling the mind of man.

3. Can we seriously suppose that the universe, the one and only totality of everything that is, was, and will be, has a cause that resembles the causes of houses, ships, furniture, and machines, because of some resemblances between the universe and such artefacts? Is this careful and deliberate reasoning? Or is it rash, impressionistic, and vague? (DNR: 49). There is no doubt that Philo thinks the latter. The first three criteria are evident in this objection.

4. It is true that, in the universe, thought and intelligence are causes of things: they are undoubtedly among 'the springs and principles' of various occurrences (DNR: 49). Experience plainly shows us that, and Philo has no wish to deny it. But he does seriously question the weight that Cleanthes places on it, while attempting to identify an ultimate cause of the universe's own orderliness. For, as Philo emphasizes, thought is but one of a multitude of causal and explanatory principles. There are 'a hundred others, [that] fall under daily observation'; among them, 'heat or cold, attraction or repulsion' (DNR: 49). On the following page, he goes further, stressing that, 'even from our limited experience, [nature] possesses an infinite number of springs and principles' (DNR: 50).

5. What is the significance of the foregoing point? It is that a serious doubt arises whether something that is true of a part or parts of a whole can be straightforwardly projected on to the whole itself. And the doubt is especially acute when, as in this case, there is a 'great disproportion' (DNR: 49) between the part and the whole. Students of logic will recognize Hume's point here as reflecting a justified worry that either the fallacy of hasty generalization or the fallacy of composition is committed by Cleanthes in thus inferring from part to whole. The two fallacies are not identical, but they border one another. Briefly, the basic point in them is that, without special circumstances, it is unjustified to conclude that something which is true of a sample must also be true of the wider population to which the sample belongs

(hasty generalization), or that something which is true of a part must also be true of the whole that contains it (composition) (DNR: 49).

6.   But even if we allow, for the sake of argument, that experience of the operation of a part is indeed a just basis for a conclusion about the origin of the whole containing that part, what justifies basing our analogy on 'so minute, so weak, so bounded a principle as the reason and design of animals is found to be upon this planet?' (DNR: 50). In particular, why focus on *thought* as the part of the universe especially suited to shed light on the origin of the whole? Why this partiality in our own favour? In Part IV, Philo will develop this as one of his most damaging criticisms.

7.   Continuing to think about parts and wholes, and reiterating his point that there are many principles at work in nature, Philo asks two questions, the first covering part-to-part analogies, the second covering part-to-whole analogies: 'When nature has so extremely diversified her manner of operation in this small globe; can we imagine, that she incessantly copies herself throughout so immense a universe?' (DNR: 50), and 'if thought, as we may well suppose, be confined merely to this narrow corner, and has even there so limited a sphere of action; with what propriety can we assign it for the original cause of all things?' (DNR: 50). He concludes with the jibe, 'the narrow views of a peasant, who makes his domestic oeconomy the rule for the government of kingdoms, is in comparison a pardonable sophism' (DNR: 50).

8.   But again, even if thought and intelligence *were* the rule throughout the whole of the universe, how would that justify projecting them backwards in time to the *origin* of the universe? His point is that, even if they are the rule for the whole of nature, thought and intelligence may be *emergent* properties, not originating or original ones. 'I cannot see', Philo says, 'why the operations of a world, constituted, arranged, adjusted, can with any propriety be extended to a world, which is in its embryo-state, and is advancing towards that constitution and arrangement' (DNR: 50).

It is a good question, emphasizing again that Cleanthes seems to be presuming much more than his actual evidence entitles him to conclude. Philo drives home his point about the gross disproportion between the evidence available to Cleanthes, on the one hand, and the conclusion he draws from it, on the other, as follows: 'A very small part of this great system, during a very short time, is very imperfectly discovered to us: And do we thence pronounce decisively concerning the origin of the whole?' (DNR: 51). Again, we see the first three criteria in evidence.

Philo summarizes the foregoing points in the following questions: 'is a part of nature a rule for another part very wide of the former? Is it a rule for the whole?' (DNR: 51). The moral of the story, the upshot of his criticisms, is scepticism: 'Could you . . . blame me', he asks, 'if I had answered at first, *that I did not know*, and was sensible that this subject lay vastly beyond the reach of my faculties?' (DNR: 51)

9.   But, not content to let it rest there, Philo moves to a new, and potentially fatal, criticism, based now on the fourth criterion of analogical arguments. He puts the challenge as follows:

> When two *species* of objects have always been observed to be conjoined together, I can *infer*, by custom, the existence of one whenever I *see* the existence of the other: And this I call an argument from experience. But how this argument can have place, where the objects, as in the present case, are single, individual, without parallel, or specific resemblance, may be difficult to explain.
>
> (DNR: 51)

Very simply, the universe, by definition, is one of a kind, literally unique. It is the one and only sum total of all that is real. As such, there cannot possibly be another like it, with which to compare it, with which to make an analogy. Thus, no analogy involving the universe as such can be made, even in principle. Thus Cleanthes is deluding himself when he thinks that he is deriving a warranted conclusion about the universe as a whole from an analogy between it and some aspect of the universe.

There can be no such analogy, thus no such conclusion. To think otherwise is a prime example of the earlier-mentioned absence of discernment among the vulgar, hasty to tie up all loose ends (DNR: 49).

10. Philo's next criticism also has the potential not just to weaken Cleanthes' claimed analogy between things within the universe and the universe as a whole but to de-legitimize it entirely, thereby bankrupting Cleanthes' argument. That argument is *a posteriori* or empirical, as we saw. Its roots, then, can be nowhere but in experience. It relies on two analogical claims, one of which is between various aspects of the universe and the universe itself in its totality, while the other, not now at issue, is between means–end order in natural and artificial things. But, being empirical, for the argument to work, 'it were requisite, that we had experience of the origin of worlds' (DNR: 51–2). And surely, Philo stresses, nobody will tell him 'with a serious countenance . . . that we have experience of [such an origin]' (DNR: 51). Thus, Cleanthes' argument cannot even get started, and we are left once again with only the haste and intellectual sloppiness of the vulgar.

Cleanthes' rebuttal

If left to stand, points 9 and 10 could be fatal to Cleanthes' case. His immediate response is brief and incomplete, cut off by Philo who uses Cleanthes' counterpoint, or what he anticipates to be Cleanthes' counterpoint, to further press his own attack. Cleanthes' first point is essentially *ad hominem*, that is, he attacks Philo himself at least as much as Philo's criticisms. He accuses Philo of trickery, of abusing terms in order to subvert philosophical reasoning (DNR: 52). But the real substance of Cleanthes' response is his second point, the one that Philo cuts across. It is Cleanthes' suggestion that his design argument is, in significant respects, closely akin to the now well-established argument for 'the Copernican system' (DNR: 52).

This is Cleanthes' second appeal to a likeness to the Copernican theory, the first having come up in Part I (DNR: 38). Now Philo cuts him off before he can develop his case, but we can be fairly sure what

Cleanthes has in mind. Let us, then, construct his Copernican defence for ourselves.

Roughly, the Copernican theory is that, contrary to how it looks, the sun does not rotate around the earth, and the earth is not the centre, stationary or otherwise, of the (known) universe. To be sure, we, here on the earth, *do* seem to see the sun in motion around the earth (at least part of it), for we seem to see the sun rise in the east and set in the west. And, pre-Copernicus, we surmise that it travels around the portion of the earth's circumference that is hidden from our view. But, as Hume and we well know, contrary to how it seems, the earth is itself twice rotating, daily on its axis and yearly in orbit of the sun. To us, however, sentient beings of such and such a kind on the surface of the earth, it just does not look or feel like that. Or, more accurately, it does not look or feel the way that, pre-Copernicus, we might imagine such a combination of perpetual motions would look or feel. For, with pre-Copernican expectations, we would expect our being on a spinning rock hurtling through space to look and feel like being on a Ferris wheel, dizzying and sickening, under constant wind pressure. But, that expectation notwithstanding, *this* is just what such a combination of constant rotations feels like to beings like us on a planet like this, that is, not at all like being on a Ferris wheel. So, as Cleanthes says in Part I, the earth's being in two kinds of constant motion is 'most contrary to our natural conceptions, to appearances, and to our very senses' (DNR: 40). Our everyday experience being what it is, is not the fact that we are on such a permanent journey through space the 'most surprising paradox'? (DNR: 40).

In the eighteenth century it was not possible to observe the earth from afar. But it was possible to observe the moon, as well as some of the planets in our solar system, and, by analogy, to project findings about them on to our understanding of the earth. Thus, Cleanthes' point that, '[t]o prove *by experience* the origin of the universe from mind is not more contrary to common speech than to prove the motion of the earth *from the same principle*' (DNR: 52, my emphasis).

In sum, then, Cleanthes' rebuttal is that the Copernican theory is a good example of a theory, once considered outlandish, but now solidly established as true. We do not observe the earth's orbit of the sun, but, by analogy to things we do observe, the moon and other planets, we are justified to infer that the earth behaves in similar fashion. That is to say, we *do* have an experiential basis for our conclusions about the earth, albeit proxy experience. And likewise with the universe as a whole. It may be worth noting that this rebuttal, like the argument in whose defence it is deployed, relies on an analogy, this one between Cleanthes' and Copernicus's respective arguments.

Philo's turning of the Copernican tables

However, far from its being a defence of Cleanthes, Philo sees the Copernican theory as a particularly apt illustration of his (Philo's) own points, thus, in effect, as a further condemnation of Cleanthes' case for design. And in this he is right.

The earth is not unique in the relevant sense. Of course, it is unique in a way. For instance, it is the only planet on which we, human beings, exist. But, in its very nature as a planet, it is not unique. In that respect, it resembles Mars, Jupiter, even a non-planet like the moon, in significant and relevant respects. Now, Philo asks, what is the *universe*, that is, the entire cosmos, analogous to? (DNR: 52). Not a planet, surely. For a planet is not the one and only total of all reality. Nothing else but the universe is that. So the Copernican counterpoint does not even begin to give Cleanthes what he needs, namely, warrant to claim a significant likeness between the universe as a whole and a particular part or feature of the universe. And that is a serious setback for Cleanthes' case.

Nor is it the only one. For, in likening his natural-religion project to the arguments for the Copernican theory, Cleanthes unintentionally concedes to Philo a damaging point, namely, that analogies only hold between things in virtue of their being instances of types (or 'species') of things. For the whole force of the Copernican analogies between the earth and other orbiting bodies is that they are all examples of large masses in orbit. It is that fact, and that fact alone, which permits using them as proxies for the earth, in the first place. Observations of the moon or of Mars can serve as proxy for the (at the time) unavailable observation of the earth, because, and only because, all are large masses rotating through space. All one-of-a-kind features are scrupulously discarded.

Part II ends with Philo, yet again, pressing his point that Cleanthes' entire argument is hasty and ill-conceived. He emphasizes that the analogies between the earth and the moon and the earth and other planets were all, at the time, carefully and painstakingly made, with measurements to support every step: 'In [the] cautious proceeding of the astronomers, you may read your own condemnation, Cleanthes' (DNR: 53). And not just that. Any careful, that is, not hasty, attempt to analogize the Copernican theory to Cleanthes' argument for design in nature shows clearly that the prudent lesson to learn here is the sceptical one, namely, that 'the subject in which you [Cleanthes] are engaged exceeds all human reason and enquiry' (DNR: 53).

A design objection to Cleanthes' design argument

Philo does not make the following objection, but it comes up fairly naturally from Cleanthes' likening of the universe to artefacts such as houses, machines, furniture, and so on. So let us mention it very briefly. It is that in all those cases, there is something that those artefacts are for; a house is for dwelling in, this machine is for baling and binding hay, that piece of furniture is for sitting on, and the like. But what is the universe for? What is its purpose? It does not seem to have one. It is even an odd question, although arising naturally from Cleanthes' analogy. That is, it is odd to suppose that there could be a purpose for the totality of all reality.

Suppose we suggest a purpose on Cleanthes' behalf, namely, that the purpose of the universe is to be a proving ground for the human race. But that seems to be making ourselves exceedingly, and arguably excessively, important. Certainly it looks that way without evidence to justify ascribing such importance to ourselves in the total scheme of things. After all, is it at all plausible or reasonable to suppose that the totality of *all* reality, past, present, and future, exists so that we, latecomers to this minor planet, could be tested on our worthiness to be rewarded after death? And that is even to ignore our warrant to suppose that, for individual human persons, there *is* an after death. Philo's previously-quoted words seem apt once again: 'The narrow views of a peasant, who makes his domestic oeconomy the rule for the government of kingdoms, is in comparison a pardonable sophism.'

Philo's first suggestion of materialism

Briefly, before moving on from Part II, let us go back to pick up something – Philo's suggestion of materialism – that, had we discussed it
in place, might have deflected us from the line of criticism that Philo
was then developing. The suggestion, made twice in Part II (DNR: 48
and 50), will become quite prominent in Parts VI, VII, and VIII.

First, as we saw earlier in this chapter, there is Philo's essentially sceptical suggestion that, for all we know, matter may contain
within itself 'the source or spring of order originally' (DNR: 48).
Then, second, while criticizing Cleanthes' insistence that thought or
intelligence is the ultimate source and principle of all occurrences in
the natural world, Philo asks: 'What peculiar privilege has *this little
agitation of the brain which we call thought*, that we must thus make
it the model of the whole universe? (DNR: 50, my emphasis). The
suggestion is clear, and clearly materialistic. It is that, perhaps,
thought, like everything else in existence, is no more than purely physical processes; that thought and mind are sequences of brain activity,
which is to say, sequences of electrical impulses. The contrast is to
dualism, which, earlier, we saw may be implicit in Cleanthes' position (as Philo re-stated it), and which would regard thought and mind
as intrinsically non-physical.

Chapter 5

Cleanthes' second design argument

The 'irregular' argument

(*Dialogues*, Part III)

Introduction

Part III opens with Cleanthes re-grouped and counter-attacking. He sets out two thought-experiments, whose purpose is to show the intuitive power of the design hypothesis, thus also to show that Philo's objections are just quibbles, 'abstruse cavils' as he calls them (DNR: 54). Cleanthes follows up his thought-experiments with a new form of design argument, which he calls an 'irregular' form (DNR: 57). This second version of the argument is meant to show that the idea of design in nature is 'incontestable' (DNR: 57), and Cleanthes' argument raises the question whether certain basic religious beliefs are instinctual, thus incapable of being disbelieved by us. If they are, then we are religious in our very nature, and will remain so regardless of the fate of arguments for and against religious belief. If basic religious beliefs are natural or instinctual in this way, it does not follow that they are true, of course; that is a separate matter. But it would mean that, like our belief in the existence of a world outside our own immediate consciousness, nature has not left this to our choice.

Cleanthes' reformulated position is meant to silence Philo, and, in its wake, he is silent. It is Demea who responds, essentially reiterating his distinction between the allegedly known existence and the allegedly unknowable nature of the deity. Cleanthes does not answer him now, but he will strongly attack him at the start of Part IV. Part III ends with the case for design in nature seemingly recovered from Philo's attacks in Part II.

The 'irregular' design argument

Cleanthes' new strategy

Following his now more-or-less routine point that Philo's objections are worthless, and that it is only Philo's cleverness in presenting them that makes them appear plausible at all (DNR: 54), Cleanthes again takes up the Copernican point. But he does so now in a way that changes the focus and direction of his argument quite significantly. He casts Philo in with various reactionary critics of the Copernican theory who, 'blinded by old systems, and supported by some sensible appearances' (DNR: 54), denied the compelling conclusion of the new theory. No less compelling, he goes on, is the analogy between means–end order in man-made things and in nature. In his estimation, the resemblance between them is 'self-evident and undeniable' (DNR: 54).

Cleanthes now changes tack in arguing for that resemblance. Although he is no less convinced of the merit of his argument in Part II than before Philo's criticism, he thinks that Philo, whom he continues to take for a thoroughgoing Pyrrhonistic sceptic, will never grant that merit. He thinks that Philo will always be content to point out the possibility that Cleanthes is wrong, regardless of how remote a possibility it may be. So, now thinking it futile to appeal to Philo's reasonableness, Cleanthes proposes instead to tune him in to certain basic feelings and dispositions that he himself, just like Cleanthes and the rest of us, has.

Two thought-experiments

Convinced that Pyrrhonistic scepticism laces Philo into a kind of intellectual straitjacket, Cleanthes challenges him to respond honestly to two thought-experiments. His doing so illustrates his conviction that Philo's 'objections . . . are no better than the abstruse cavils of those philosophers, who denied motion' (DNR: 54), and so they 'ought to be refuted in the same manner, by *illustrations, examples, and instances, rather than by serious argument* and philosophy' (DNR: 54, emphasis added). Implicit in this change of approach there is a concession, namely, Cleanthes' agreement that no extreme sceptic will be converted from his scepticism by sheer force of argument. Hence Cleanthes' change of tack from intellect to feeling, as the focus in his new approach to winning agreement to the proposition that there is design, thus mind, at work in the natural world.

The voice in the clouds

Suppose we heard an articulate voice in the clouds, 'much louder and more melodious than any which human art could ever reach' (DNR: 54). Suppose the voice were heard simultaneously all over the world, and understood in their own language by all who heard it. Furthermore, suppose the message conveyed were 'altogether worthy of a benevolent Being, superior to mankind' (DNR: 54). Supposing these things, what would we think? At a minimum, would we not immediately regard what we had heard as, first, a *voice*, and second, an *intelligent* voice? That is, would we not unhesitatingly accept that what we heard was a voice expressing the thoughts of an intelligent being?

But couldn't we be wrong? The Pyrrhonist can be expected to object in just that way. For instance, might not the 'voice' really be a piece of technological wizardry, not a real voice at all? Or perhaps what we heard as a voice was really only 'some accidental whistling of the winds' (DNR: 55). The first of these would have been an unthinkable objection in the eighteenth century, but not today. Both represent, at the very least, theoretical or logical possibilities; there is no formal contradiction in thinking or saying either one. So let us grant, as we must, the possibility that we are wrong in our interpretation of what we heard in Cleanthes' thought-experiment.

Granting that, what point is Cleanthes trying to make? It is a two-part point. In the first place, it is that, while there is room, *after the fact*, for doubt, in the initial situation we would have no doubt.

After the fact, there is room for doubt, not just doubt that we heard a voice at all, but doubt about the interpretation that, initially, we either put on what we heard or were inclined to put on what we heard. To Cleanthes, such 'on second thoughts' doubts reflect the spirit of Philo's sceptical questions about the core analogy in the design argument. For instance, in the spirit of Philo's objections in Part II, is not the voice louder than any voice we have heard (present-day amplification equipment is not to the point)? Is it not more melodious? Is it not understood across all language differences? Is it not heard simultaneously around the world, thus far beyond the range of any (unaided) human voice? And so on. These are genuine disanalogies between the hypothesized voice in the clouds and a normal human voice, and so might call into question our initial appraisal of the source of what we heard, namely, that the source was an intelligent being.

Yet, these disanalogies notwithstanding, and allowing the possibility that we could be wrong, the essence of Cleanthes' point is that, when we *first* hear the sounds from the clouds, we immediately take them to issue from an intelligent voice. And, likewise, when we notice means–end order virtually everywhere in (biological) nature, at all levels of (biological) nature, are we not immediately struck with the idea that this cannot be just happenstance? Does it not immediately strike us that here are plain manifestations of purpose and intention?

Cleanthes' suggestion is that, before we could even begin to think about what has occurred, we would have already heard the sounds as a voice. His point is that so doing is just natural, instinctual. His point, furthermore, is that, subsequently-raised doubts and objections and disanalogies aside, we would respond in exactly the same way the next time too. In effect, then, if I may put words in his mouth, he is asking Philo, 'don't you just deeply feel that there is purpose and intention manifest in the vast intricacies of our orderly world?'

'Natural volumes'

Cleanthes' second thought-experiment is the so-called 'natural volumes' or 'natural books' example (DNR: 55–6). I shall not discuss Hume's own version of this, however, as I think it is needlessly far-fetched, and too counter-intuitive to be persuasive. Instead I offer what I think may be a less incredible, thus (if I am right) more powerful, variation, which retains the spirit and thrust of the original.

But first, a very brief sketch of Hume's own version. It has Cleanthes speculating about books not being man-made things at all, but arising instead, like plants or animals, from natural reproductive processes. We are not meant to think that this happens (or has happened) in fact, of course, or that it is even remotely likely. The point Cleanthes is trying to get at has the form of the question; what would we think, if . . .? What would we think, *if* books were produced and reproduced by gestation?

At any rate, not pursuing Cleanthes' own version, here is a variation on his point that is meant to avoid the oddity of supposing that an obvious artefact, a book, could be a biological entity instead.

Suppose that in the leaves of all leafy plants and vegetables there are characters inscribed, and that these characters are indistinguishable in shape from the letters of our alphabet. It does not matter to the thought-experiment which language we mean, so there is no need to specify. Any will do. These characters have been discovered in such plants through the whole of recorded history, and fossil findings show us that prehistoric leafy plants had the inscriptions too. Furthermore, the characters are found to be arranged so as always to convey meaning to us; the arrangements of characters in the leaves are the same in kind as the arrangements of letters, words, and spaces in books and newspapers. What would we make of this? Would we think that it was no more significant than the meaning we attach at present to the patterns of thorns in rose bushes, or to blades of grass in our back gardens, which is to say, none? In the circumstances, surely not. Surely we would not think this phenomenon was just a curious coincidence thrown up by nature. Instead, would it not be completely natural to suppose that there was meaning here, that the arrangement of the characters in the plant leaves was a clear manifestation of intention, purpose, and intelligence? I think it is virtually certain that we would see the phenomenon that way, or, at the very least, that we would be *inclined* to see it that way.

The point of this thought-experiment is that, to Cleanthes, the means–end order we find in nature is no less wondrous than the letters in the leaves of plants, if there were such letters. But the extent and complexity of means–end order in nature greatly surpasses the extent and complexity of order in artefacts, including speech and writing; 'the anatomy of an animal affords many stronger instances of design than the perusal of Livy or Tacitus' (DNR: 56). Yet, perhaps because means–end order is everywhere in (biological) nature, we tend to take it for granted, thus failing to be struck by its remarkability. Think of the saying, 'familiarity breeds contempt', or at least, disregard. The 'natural volumes' example, or my foregoing variation on it, is intended to jolt us out of that jadedness of outlook to, first, a vivid appreciation of the literal marvellousness of the natural order, and second, an acknowledgement that thinking all such marvels could be just the result of chance operations in brute nature is simply too incredible to take seriously.

Bringing it to a point, Cleanthes issues the following challenge: 'assert either that a rational volume [in our case, the marked plants] is no proof of a rational cause, or admit of a similar cause to all the works of nature' (DNR: 56). To him, the issue, at bottom, is as direct and simple as that.

Cleanthes' two thought-experiments are specific and concrete. Instead of a detailed, abstract argument, they are aimed directly at getting Philo (and us) to nod in immediate, pre-reflective agreement, thereby puncturing what Cleanthes sees as the artificiality of sceptical counter-arguments. Cleanthes' aim is to attune us to our unmediated, natural, felt reaction to such experiences, and then to enlist that feeling in service of natural religion.

Who is the more reasonable sceptic, Cleanthes or Philo?

Developing his view of the Pyrrhonistic sceptic's arguments as through and through artificial, resting only on a bare logical possibility of error in the reasoning of non-sceptics, Cleanthes contrasts what he calls the 'reasonable' sceptic with the Pyrrhonistic, saying of the former that his aim is only 'to reject abstruse, remote and refined arguments; to adhere to common sense and *the plain instincts of nature*; and to assent, wherever any reasons strike him with so full a force, that he *cannot*, without the greatest violence, prevent it' (DNR: 56, emphasis added).

And, lest the relevance be missed, Cleanthes drives his point home with the following words: 'Now the arguments for natural religion are plainly of this kind; and nothing but the most perverse, obstinate meta-physics can reject them' (DNR: 56). In his eyes, then, the conflict is between honestly acknowledging what we plainly *feel* to be the case, that the world's order reflects intelligence, and stubbornly, for vested interests, resisting the power of that obvious interpretation with far-fetched counter-instances that we have to contort our imaginations in order to produce.

Cleanthes himself embraces 'reasonable scepticism' (DNR: 56), while seeing Philo as an unmitigated Pyrrhonist. By Cleanthes' lights, the reasonable sceptic proportions his assent to the evidence, thus does not attempt to subvert the power of the overwhelmingly obvious. This is interesting, for Philo sees himself as being a reasonable, and not an extreme, sceptic too. That being so, these two creations of Hume's, Philo and Cleanthes, battle for the soul of scepticism itself, and, in particular, for its proper place in regard to religious belief. It is a battle overlapping the earlier-mentioned contest between them to be the truer evidentialist, inasmuch as Cleanthes' 'reasonable sceptic' and a committed evidentialist amount to one and the same.

The 'irregular' argument

The ground thus prepared, Cleanthes presents his second design argu-ment. Not unexpectedly in the circumstances, it is rooted in a concrete instance of the kind of order that Cleanthes is convinced cannot be explained in naturalistic terms:

> consider, anatomize the eye: Survey its structure and contriv-ance; and tell me, from your own *feeling*, if the idea of a contriver does not *immediately flow in upon you with a force like that of sensation*. The most obvious conclusion surely is in favour of design; and it requires time, reflection and study, to summon up those frivolous, though abstruse, objections, which can support infidelity ... To what degree, therefore, of blind dogmatism must one have attained, to reject such *natural* and such convincing arguments?
>
> (DNR: 56, emphasis added)

83

He thinks this argument's power is 'irresistible' (DNR: 57). And he is confident there are others like it. In the end, his point is that it takes no effort to see that he is right; the feeling of design in the physical world is 'natural' (DNR: 56). It is *disagreement* that requires an effort.

The basic point in the new argument is that human beings have a natural propensity or disposition to see design in the physical universe, and that this propensity or tendency is triggered by certain experiences of order. J.C.A. Gaskin's term for this propensity is 'feeling of design' (Gaskin 1988: 127).

The two terms, 'propensity' and 'feeling of design', are not synonyms, but they are sufficiently close in meaning to permit our not pressing matters to a decision between them. For what is important here is what they have in common, namely, that both capture the *involuntariness* of a feeling that sometimes comes over us when we have certain experiences of order in nature. As Cleanthes puts it, the sense that there is design in nature immediately flows in upon us, unbidden, with a force akin, although not identical, to that of sensation. That is, it is not an interpretation that, with contemplation and reflection, we select from among competing interpretations. On the contrary, his point is that we are essentially passive in respect to this feeling of designedness, this disposition to see nature as intended to be the ways it is. And this passivity is the new point to which Cleanthes is here drawing attention and giving emphasis.

What is irregular about the 'irregular' argument?

Why does Hume refer to this argument as irregular? Nelson Pike suggests that the argument's irregularity is its reliance on examples, together with its principal emphasis on feeling, and not primarily on reason, in response to those examples (Pike 1970: 232). In a letter to his friend, Sir Gilbert Elliot, asking for assistance in strengthening the arguments he was giving to Cleanthes, Hume says: 'I cou'd wish that Cleanthes' Argument could be so analys'd, as to be render'd quite formal and regular'(LCD: 26). Apparently, though, Elliot was not much help, and the argument was never made formal and regular, that is, it was not freed from its reliance on feeling or from making its case through illustration, thus remaining irregular. In the absence of definitive, or even more, evidence, this suggestion of Pike's seems as plausible as any. That being said, though, 'irregular' is maybe not a good description, and Hume's intention in using the word remains somewhat unclear.

The argument in the 'irregular' argument

The argument in the irregular argument is this. Upon hearing the sounds coming from the sky, our immediate reaction is that they are words, that there is a voice with a mind behind it. When in normal circumstances we hear a voice behind us in a room, or on the street, immediately our tendency is to suppose that there is a mind behind it, that a person is speaking. Hearing those sounds in those circumstances immediately triggers that response. This is implicit in our hearing the sounds as a *voice* in the first place. Cleanthes' point here, then, is that our hearing articulate speech in everyday circumstances stands to our disposition to suppose such speech manifests mind, as our hearing articulate speech in the clouds would stand to our disposition to suppose *that* speech is a manifestation of mind too. This is the first stage in a two-stage argument.

The second stage is this. To anatomize the eye is immediately to have the idea of design come over us. Putting the two stages together, we get the following:

1. Our experience of the means–end order in the eye is to our sense (feeling, propensity) of design, as our hearing the voice in the clouds is to our sense of its being a manifestation of mind.
2. Our hearing the voice in the clouds is to our sense of its being a manifestation of mind, as our hearing a voice in ordinary, everyday circumstances is to our sense that there is mind manifest in it.

For ease of reference, let the step from seeing the complex order in an eye to interpreting that order as design be A; let the step from hearing the voice in the clouds to supposing it is a manifestation of mind be B; and let the step from hearing an ordinary voice to supposing *it* is a manifestation of mind be C. What is now easy to see is Cleanthes' two-stage analogical argument to take us from A to C, that is, to bring us to the conclusion that our experience of means–end order in the eye stands to our sense of design in nature, as our hearing an ordinary voice stands to our sense that there is a mind manifest in it. So, the argument goes, just as we do not hesitate over the latter step – from ordinary voice to mind – neither ought we to hesitate over the former – from eye to design. The evidence for the eye-to-design step is as good as, and of a kind with, the evidence for the commonplace step from ordinary voice to mind. Somewhat formalized, the mechanism of this two-stage argument is this; by virtue of the ratio of A to B and of B to C, we get A to C.

In the irregular design argument, we are presented with two things. The first is an emphasis on our propensity, in certain circumstances, to see design in nature. The second is an analogical argument about ratios or proportionalities. This raises the question of the relationship between those two things, the propensity and the argument. The relationship seems to be as follows.

In everyday circumstances, speech triggers our propensity to suppose there are other minds, and, at the same time, speech is evidence that there are other minds. Similarly, certain experiences of order, in an eye for instance, trigger our propensity to suppose there is design in nature. So, by analogy, those experiences of order are also *evidence* of design. In neither case is the evidence conclusive, or claimed to be. The pivot of the argument is the analogy that is claimed, and the strength of the argument traces to the strength of that analogy.

Are basic religious beliefs natural beliefs?

Is this feeling of design, this propensity to see design in the physical universe, a natural belief in design, in the official sense of the term 'natural belief'? That is the sense of the terms, 'natural belief' and 'instinctual belief', when they are used to represent Hume's mitigated scepticism, which is his antidote to Pyrrhonistic scepticism. And does Hume think that this feeling of design is a natural belief, in that sense? The second question is an important one to answer in any account of Hume's thinking on religion, and it raises a contentious issue among commentators on his work.

Let us take up the question by first defining 'natural belief', then by seeing the case for a 'yes' answer to either or both questions, and ending with the case for 'no'. My own view is that the right answer to both questions is 'no'.

The marks of a natural or instinctual belief

Let us follow J.C.A. Gaskin's identification (Gaskin, 1988, 117–19) of 'instinctual' or 'natural' belief, for Hume, as the combination of the four following points, each of which is a necessary condition of a belief's being a natural belief. The four together amount to the sufficient condition of a belief's being a natural belief:

1. Natural beliefs are ordinary beliefs of common life.
2. They are not believed (or disbelieved) on the strength of evidence, or derived from reasoning.
3. They are universal beliefs among mankind.
4. Without them, we could not function adequately in the world at all.

Our natural beliefs are effective against the *convincingness* of sceptical arguments, that is, they prevent those arguments and doubts taking root in our consciousness, and overturning our belief in the existence of the physical world, causal connections, and so on. But their doing this is no evidence of their *truth,* thus not of the falsity of Pyrrhonism. Parenthetically, although it would take us significantly off our present course to follow it, it is important to note both that the subject of natural belief is one of the most controversial topics in Hume's philosophy and that my interpretation of it would be contested in various ways by various authoritative Hume scholars.

The case for 'yes'

There is evidence, both direct and circumstantial, to think that Hume regards certain fundamental religious beliefs are natural or instinctual. Let us start with the direct evidence.

In the *Natural History of Religion*, Hume says this: '[t]he whole frame of nature bespeaks an intelligent author; and no rational enquirer can, after serious reflection, suspend his *belief* a moment with regard to the primary principles of genuine Theism and Religion' (NHR: 134, emphasis added). A little later on in the same book he adds that, '[t]he *belief* of invisible, intelligent power has been *very generally diffused over the human race, in all places and in all ages*' (NHR: 134, emphasis added). These two remarks seem to show us Hume saying that the first and third criteria of natural belief are met by certain fundamental religious beliefs, that is to say, the quoted lines seem to show him saying that such beliefs are both ordinary beliefs of common life and universal beliefs of mankind, respectively. That is the extent of the direct evidence. The rest of the case for a 'yes' answer is circumstantial.

Earlier we saw several texts in which Cleanthes maintains that we have a natural propensity or disposition to see design in the physical universe. This is our *feeling* of design in nature. It is a feeling that comes to us unbidden, like sensation. It is involuntary, and we are passive in our reception of it. Thus, is it not a product of reason or reflection. And late in the *Dialogues*, Philo will agree with Cleanthes on this: 'In many views of the universe, and of its parts, particularly the latter, the beauty and fitness of final causes *strike us with such irresistible force*, that *all objections appear (what I believe they really are) mere cavils and sophisms*' (DNR: 104, emphasis added). This is virtually an echo of Cleanthes' introduction of the irregular argument in Part III. A little further on in the book, in Part XII, Philo puts the concession this way: 'A *purpose*, an *intention*, a *design* strikes everywhere the most careless, the most stupid thinker; and *no man can be so hardened in absurd systems, as at all times to reject it*' (DNR: 116, emphasis added). And two pages after that, Philo does not object to Cleanthes' claim that: 'The comparison of the universe to a machine of human contrivance is so obvious and natural, and is justified by so many instances of order and design in nature, that *it must immediately strike unprejudiced apprehensions, and procure universal approbation*' (DNR: 118, emphasis added).

Let us pick up three of the emphasized lines in these quotations from late in the *Dialogues*. They are: 'all objections appear (what I believe they really are) mere cavils and sophisms' (Philo); 'no man can be so hardened in absurd systems, as at all times to reject [design]'

(Philo); and 'it must immediately . . . procure universal approbation' (Cleanthes). The first and second of these, separately and together, say that there can be no reasonable disagreement with the idea of design in nature. The third statement says that there would be immediate universal approval of the idea of design in nature; thus, surely, universal agreement on it. But if there is universal agreement on something, then, surely, there is universal belief in it. If I approve of something, agree that it is indeed the case, then, surely, I believe that it is the case. Here again, then, as with the direct evidence, we have evidence that the first and third criteria are met.

Furthermore, in the first of the three passages just quoted, we see Philo agreeing that, '[a] purpose, an intention, a design strikes everywhere the most careless, the most stupid thinker'. The words to note are 'strikes everywhere the most careless . . . thinker'. That is, the idea of purpose and design in nature strikes us, it comes to us; we do not think it up as part of a theory. It just simply comes to us, unbidden. In this line we have evidence that the second criterion is met, as Philo is the principal voice of the author himself. That second criterion, let us recall, is that natural beliefs are not based in evidence or achieved through any process of reasoning.

True, we do not have evidence that the fourth criterion is met. That is, we do not have evidence that we simply could not function at all in the world without religious belief. But we do have evidence, direct and circumstantial, for the other three criteria. Thus, while the case for a 'yes' answer may not be conclusive, such that it could not be rationally denied by anybody with adequate knowledge of Hume, that case seems strong none the less.

It is strong enough to convince some influential Hume scholars. Ronald J. Butler puts the case for 'yes' as follows:

> Despite all the opportunities he has, Philo at no stage explicitly rejects the hypothesis of design; and indeed his insistence that in nature matter and form are inseparable fortifies his appeal to design as a natural belief not needing the support of additional arguments . . . Philo can consistently muster all the rational arguments against design at his command and still maintain that *our own nature* prevents us from wholly disbelieving the fact of

design. By the tenth dialogue all three [principal characters] have affirmed or re-affirmed that there is natural belief in design.

(Butler 1960: 87)

And, in his commentary on the *Dialogues*, Nelson Pike may be inclining towards the view that, for Hume, belief in a deity as designer of means–end order in nature may be a natural belief, in the relevant sense of the term (Pike 1970: 225–35).

As we turn now to the case for 'no', let us note that Hume does indeed accept that we have a strong natural disposition to believe that there is not just order but design in nature. It is a disposition (or, in Gaskin's word, 'feeling') that, once we have it, we cannot seem to shake off, and even powerful counter-arguments to the design hypothesis do not seem capable of purging us of it. With that not in dispute, the question before us is whether this natural *disposition*, this tendency in our nature, is itself a natural or instinctual *belief*, or, at least, the source of such a belief? To answer 'yes' to this question is to endorse the view that, for Hume, certain bedrock religious beliefs are indeed natural or instinctual beliefs. And to answer 'no' is to deny that Hume thinks any religious beliefs are natural beliefs.

The case for 'no'

The case for 'no' is simply that no religious belief meets all four criteria. Let us look at them one by one.

The ordinariness criterion of natural beliefs

The first criterion is that a natural belief is an ordinary belief of common life. Now, on the one hand, it seems plainly true that many people's belief in God is well integrated into their day-to-day activities; their faith is a normal thing for them, without thereby denying the extraordinariness or momentousness of its content, if true. But on the other hand, it does not seem that religious belief is always an ordinary belief. Mystics, for instance, do not seem to hold their religious beliefs in an ordinary way, and perhaps neither do certain sequestered orders of monks and nuns. But the concept of ordinary seems to permit relativization, such that a given sequestered nun would hold her religious beliefs in a way ordinary for nuns of that persuasion. At any rate, we cannot justifiably say that religious belief fails the test of ordinariness, in one obvious sense of the term.

The 'no reasoning' criterion of natural beliefs

The second criterion is that a natural belief is (and must be) arrived at without reasoning and not be dependent on evidence. I think it is very widely true of religious beliefs, basic religious beliefs especially, that people do not acquire them through reasoning. But it does not have to be true. Furthermore, I think it is also very widely true of basic religious beliefs that they are not abandoned because of arguments brought against them. But again this does not have to be true. Both ways, it only happens to be true. Bertrand Russell, whose work, in spirit and content, is very close to Hume's in certain respects, illustrates both points. In the first volume of his *Autobiography*, Russell tells an amusing story about his coming (for a short time as a young man) to be convinced by a particular argument for the existence of God, thus, on that basis, to accept the existence of God, while later in life he speculated on what he might say to God, if he met God, about his subsequent (and thenceforth lifelong) lack of belief in God. He would tell God, he told us, that there was not enough evidence. The former story illustrates a person's coming to religious belief by way of reasoning, while the latter illustrates a person's withholding (or withdrawing) belief because of insufficiency of reason. Hume himself, in his own life, illustrates a version of the second point. In Chapter 1, we saw the large role that his reading of the empiricist philosophers Locke and Clarke played in his abandonment of faith, while a student at the University of Edinburgh.

Natural beliefs do not wax and wane with the evidence for or against them. But both the Russell and Hume stories just told suggest this is sometimes false of religious beliefs.

The universality criterion of natural beliefs

The third criterion of a belief's being a natural belief is that it is universal. It is believed by human persons at all times and places, and it is so held because we cannot not believe it. Let us agree that the point is not meant to include infants or the seriously mentally incompetent. Yet, even with those classes of persons set aside, it is clear that religious beliefs, and the design belief in particular, fail this test. Surely most of us could give examples of people, intelligent, rational people, who hold no religious beliefs at all. And Hume himself, in the 'Introduction' to *The Natural History of Religion*, says this:

> The belief of invisible, intelligent power has been very generally diffused over the human race, in all places and in all ages; but it has neither perhaps been so universal as to admit of no exception, nor has it been, in any degree, uniform in the ideas, which it has suggested. Some nations have been discovered, who entertained no sentiments of Religion, if travellers and historians may be credited; and no two nations, and scarce any two men, have ever agreed precisely in the same sentiments. It would appear, therefore, that this preconception springs *not from an original instinct* or primary impression of nature ... since every instinct of this kind has been found absolutely universal in all nations and ages ... The first religious principles must be secondary.
>
> (NHR: 134, emphasis added)

And, in these observations, surely Hume is right.

The unavoidability criterion of natural beliefs

The fourth criterion is that of unavoidability. A belief is a natural belief, if human beings simply could not function in the world without it. Now this and the third criterion shade into one another, for the point of it is not just that certain people could not function without a particular belief. It is that *none* of us could function without it.

It must be granted, surely, that there are people who could not cope with their lives at all without the comfort or inspiration of religion. But that neither indicates nor supports a universal version of the point. For it is obvious that some others among us *do* function without religious belief, and function very well. Thus, religious beliefs fail the fourth test of naturalness.

All in all, it seems quite plain that religious beliefs do not meet the third or fourth criteria. Thus, as each criterion is necessary, religious beliefs are not natural beliefs, in the relevant sense of the term. Nor, for just the same reasons, does Hume think that they are natural beliefs.

The influential Hume scholar, Donald Livingston, in his latest book, describes Hume's thinking on the status of religious belief this way: 'we may think of belief in divinity not as a natural belief on the order of belief in self, world, and society but as a *virtually* natural belief deeply embedded in participation in common life but more variable and more vulnerable to reflection' (Livingston 1998: 65, emphasis added).

Natural beliefs are vulnerable, to use Livingston's term, to philosophical reasoning and speculation only in a special context, the rarified setting of the theoretician's study, but not outside (THN: 269). Common life is impossible without them. Not so religious belief, though, for, notwithstanding Hume's own hesitation on this point in Part XII, 'the atheist, who, I assert, is only nominally so, and can never possibly be in earnest' (DNR: 120), there are atheists. But even if there were not, there certainly are agnostics, persons who neither believe nor disbelieve in a deity, and agnosticism is neither a crazy nor foolish position. And that is enough to place religious belief in a different category to belief in the existence of the physical world, the self, and causal connections. For, in practice, insofar as those beliefs are concerned, there is no room for agnosticism. But Livingston is right that, for Hume, and perhaps in fact too, religious beliefs, for many who have them, go deep, perhaps deeper than most (or perhaps all) of their other non-natural beliefs. For Hume seems to be right to say, near the end of Part XII, 'astonishment indeed will naturally arise from the greatness of the object' (DNR: 129), that is, from the orderliness of the universe at all levels.

Chapter 6

'A mind like
the human'

(*Dialogues*, Parts IV and V)

Introduction

Cleanthes' design hypothesis comes under serious
criticism in Parts IV and V, first from Demea, then
from Philo. The principal target of their criticisms is
Cleanthes' likening of the deity to the mind of a human
being, a similarity he thinks is warranted by his analogy
between order in man-made and in natural things. It is
his prime instance of the principle, 'like effects prove
like causes' (DNR: 67), to which he and Philo are both
committed.

Both Philo and Demea think this alleged likeness
commits the design theorist to an unwelcome anthropomorphism. In addition, Philo thinks polytheism fits
Cleanthes' data better than theism. Briefly, anthropomorphism is the practice or policy of using terms
appropriate to human nature to describe divine nature,
while polytheism is the theory that there are multiple
gods, not, as theists maintain, just one.

Philo's next criticism is a 'regress' argument
to show that the logic of Cleanthes' own reasoning

compels him to seek out the source of the divine mind's orderliness, that to terminate his inquiry at the hypothesis of a divine mind is arbitrary. Philo enjoys the irony in this criticism, for, having himself been charged earlier with intellectual inconsistency and perhaps dishonesty, he is now in a position to reverse the charges, and accuse Cleanthes of arbitrarily and self-servingly terminating his own inquiry. Philo's next criticism turns on his introduction of a purely naturalistic hypothesis to explain order in the world. He argues that this candidate-explanation fares at least as well as Cleanthes' supernaturalistic one. Briefly, a naturalistic explanation shuns supernaturalism; it is a this-worldly explanation through and through. If Philo's naturalistic hypothesis is plausible, then there is reason to think that Cleanthes' theistic, supernaturalistic, conclusion is excessive and unwarranted.

Cleanthes' response to Philo's criticisms is two-fold. He accuses Philo of a scepticism so extreme that it would make explanation of anything at all impossible, thus suggesting that the cost of Philo's attack is far beyond what any reasonable person would pay. This first line of response continues a theme we discussed in Chapter 3, namely, which of Philo and Cleanthes is the truer evidentialist, thus the more reasonable and prudent in argument? Cleanthes' second line of response to Philo is his insistence that none of Philo's criticisms gets 'rid of the hypothesis of design in the universe' (DNR: 71). Unexpectedly, Philo had volunteered a concession on that very point a moment earlier, and he will do so again in Parts X and XII.

Cleanthes insists that failure to eliminate the design hypothesis means victory for him, inasmuch as, he maintains, it is 'a sufficient foundation for religion' (DNR: 71) and fully justifies his claim to 'have found a Deity' (DNR: 65). In effect, then, he takes Philo to have conceded him his entire case. Naturally, Philo himself has a different interpretation. We will take up the issue in Chapter 10, where we will discuss Part XII of the *Dialogues*, for by then we will have all the pieces of the puzzle in hand.

Philo broadens the focus of his sceptical outlook in Parts IV and V. Now, in addition to emphasizing our inability to know what is the case, he includes as well our inability to know what is *not* the case. This is potentially very damaging to Cleanthes' position, for it opens the door to various possibilities that are deeply at odds with theism and that, for all we know, may be true. Furthermore, some of these possibilities appear to fit better with Cleanthes' basic analogy than his own theistic hypothesis. And that gives us additional reason to think that Cleanthes' persistence in that hypothesis, on the basis of that analogy, may be unwarranted.

Mysticism, anthropomorphism, scepticism
(*Dialogues*, Part IV)

Cleanthes' and Demea's continuing disagreement

Mysticism

Part III ended with Cleanthes and Demea in disagreement. Part IV opens on that same note. Furthermore, as he was for much of Part III, Philo is silent here at the beginning of Part IV.

As Cleanthes sees it, Demea's Distinction leads to scepticism or atheism, with the difference between the two not mattering much in actual practice. He describes Demea's insistence on the unknowability of the divine nature as 'mysticism' (DNR: 60), a position he views as robbing religion of all content. As he puts it, 'if our ideas, so far as they go, be not just and adequate, and correspondent to [the deity's] real nature, I know not what there is in this subject worth insisting on. Is the name, without any meaning, of such mighty importance?' (DNR: 60).

Demea's first point in response is that the supposedly 'calm and philosophical Cleanthes ... would attempt to refute his antagonists, by affixing a nick-name to them' (DNR: 60), thereby opening himself up to pejorative name-calling in reply, 'anthropomorphite', for instance. Oddly enough, while right in general, Demea is wrong in this particular case. We have seen Cleanthes, much more than either Philo or Demea, respond to his rivals' points in *ad hominem*, that is, personal, sometimes abusive, fashion; but here, in response to Demea's Distinction, 'mysticism' does not seem either excessive or unwarranted. In particular, it does not have the personal connotations of 'caviller', 'quibbler', 'blind dogmatis[t]', and other terms we have seen (and will continue to see) him use of his opponents. Furthermore, although Cleanthes intends the word 'mysticism' to be dismissive, it is an appropriate term in the circumstances, and one that some thinkers who emphasize the limits of reason themselves employ. Two examples of this that come to mind are the medieval German mystic, Meister Eckhart (*c.* 1260–1327) and Ludwig Wittgenstein, the latter towards the end of his 1921 book, *Tractatus Logico-Philosophicus*.

The 'bundle' theory of mind

Verbal tone aside, anthropomorphism is now out in the open, where it will remain. Demea insists that Cleanthes' basic analogy issues in a conception of the deity as '[a] composition of various faculties, sentiments, ideas' (DNR: 61). That, Demea points out to him, is what 'you assert, when you represent the Deity as similar to a human mind and understanding' (DNR: 60–1). And surely he is right. But what is the problem with that? Two things, essentially.

The first problem is that it ties Cleanthes' concept of the divine nature to Hume's own, very controversial, and to some religious people scandalous, concept of the self, the so-called 'bundle' theory. In Hume's own words from his *Treatise of Human Nature*, insofar as a strictly observational approach can tell, the self appears to be nothing but a 'bundle or collection of different perceptions' (THN: 252), although, in his Appendix to the *Treatise*, Hume goes on to confess complete bafflement about the true nature of the self (THN: 633). At any rate, if Demea is right about where Cleanthes' analogy leads, then Cleanthes has to give up the traditional theistic notion of the divine nature as essentially simple, that is, uncompounded or non-composite. But, in the tradition, divine simplicity, so understood, is the basis for thinking that the deity could neither de-compose nor change, and so, as Demea sees it, Cleanthes would have to give up those essential traits of divinity too (DNR: 61). On a side note, arguably the fact that Hume has Demea here knocking Cleanthes' position off balance, by associating it with his (Hume's) own controversial thinking on the nature of the self, is an indication of a wry and playful mischievousness on the part of the author.

The second problem is that the 'bundle' theory is in outright opposition to all substance theories of the self, thus to all 'soul' theories. And to give up a soul theory of the self, even if not to embrace a 'bundle' theory instead, would represent a profound departure from the theistic tradition.

Cleanthes both agrees and does not agree. He agrees, if simplicity and immutability are deemed absolute. For then, he argues, we can have no understanding whatsoever of anything that might be called the divine mind. And that, he goes on, would amount in practice to atheism (DNR: 61). He makes the point forcefully in the following lines:

> For though it be allowed, that the Deity possesses attributes, of which we have no comprehension; yet ought we never to ascribe to him any attributes, which are absolutely incompatible with that intelligent nature, essential to him. A mind, whose acts and sentiments and ideas are not distinct and successive; one, that is wholly simple, and totally immutable; is a mind which has no thought, no reason, no will, no sentiment, no love, no hatred; or in a word, is no mind at all.

> (DNR: 61)

Silence

Perhaps the most important point to come out of this skirmish is what Cleanthes and Demea have in common, notwithstanding their disagreement. It is that, in the last analysis, neither one can say anything uniquely informative about the deity. Their respective positions, very different on the surface, alike converge on silence, insofar as saying something distinctive about the divine nature is concerned. On the one hand, Demea's Distinction, strictly construed, leads to silence on the central tenets of religious belief. But, on Hume's evidentialist principles, that cannot be a profound silence, rather the prudent silence appropriate to words that have no meaning. Then, on the other hand, there is Cleanthes' experimentalism, which ties meaning and knowledge to experience, and, by so doing, anthropomorphically reduces the concept of divine nature to that of human nature. That being so, the effect of both is the same, namely, silence, insofar as saying anything unique about the deity is concerned. The one, Demea's mysticism, leads to silence, plain and simple, while the other, Cleanthes' (alleged) anthropomorphism, strips talk of the deity of unique content, thus, by another route, converging on silence about divinity also. From different directions, then, both Cleanthes and Demea (unwittingly) reveal to us the factual emptiness of their respective descriptions of the deity, if and when pushed to any level beyond the merely human. It is a powerful point, inasmuch as Demea and Cleanthes between them represent the two main options available to theism to talk about the deity.

Philo's pretence

Two pages into Part IV, Philo breaks the silence he has maintained since Cleanthes' 'irregular' design argument. Addressing himself to Cleanthes, he points out that most traditional theists adhere to a concept of divine nature closer (indeed much closer) to Demea's than to Cleanthes'. Very briefly, that traditional concept is of an all-knowing, all-good, all-powerful deity. Philo is right in the main, but Demea's concept is not universal among theistic philosophers. For instance, Thomas Aquinas inclined to a much more modest view of what human beings could justifiably say of the nature of the deity. At any rate, back to Philo, who challenges Cleanthes with the question whether he really thinks that he alone is right (DNR: 61–2). Does he really think that those traditional theists who maintain, for instance, that the deity is perfectly simple, that is, not composed of parts, are, in the end, akin to atheists? (DNR: 61).

At one level, Philo is speaking in defence of Demea and the part of the tradition that Demea represents. But Philo himself, like Cleanthes, is at heart as well as in practice an experimentalist. So, he cannot really be objecting to Cleanthes' insistence that we seek out the actual empirical content of such terms as 'divine simplicity', and adhere strictly to it. So, what is he doing? Essentially this: he is making sure that the undermining effect of Cleanthes' thinking on orthodox theism is not missed. For instance, still disguising his real intent, he goes on to ask: if Cleanthes is right, what would become of the argument for the existence of a deity 'derived from the universal consent of mankind?' (DNR: 62). The point he wishes to have noted, but without himself being responsible for making, is that if the common conception of the deity is not anchored in experience, and is thereby cut off from any literal meaning, then the argument from common consent will be worthless. This is not the first time that Philo is not what he seems, nor is it the last. The argument from universal consent is not further discussed in the *Dialogues*. Hume's response to it is in his *Natural History of Religion*, where he maintains that the preponderance of historical and anthropological evidence shows that the first religions were not theistic at all, but polytheistic, and that they have a naturalistic origin, namely human beings' normal fears and hopes in the face of an unknowable future.

Philo's regress objection, and the suggestion of a naturalistic explanation of order

The regress objection

The principal 'inconvenience' of anthropomorphism that Philo aims to show is that it undermines Cleanthes' analogy between divine and human natures (DNR: 62). But, Philo goes on, even if Cleanthes' analogy between 'a plan . . . in the divine mind' and 'the plan of a house . . . an architect forms in his head' (DNR: 62) were to hold, we would still have to go on to inquire into 'the cause of this cause, which you have assigned as satisfactory and conclusive' (DNR: 62). Specifically, what is the cause of the order, the plan for instance, in the divine mind itself? As he pungently states the point, 'a mental world or universe of ideas requires a cause as much as does a material world or universe of objects; and if similar in its arrangement must require a similar cause' (DNR: 62). As we find it in a footnote at the end of this page in the *Dialogues*, the footnoted text being Hume's original draft of the point, this only stands to 'reason' (DNR: 62, n.4).

Philo's attack here is two-pronged. First, there is Cleanthes' vulnerability to anthropomorphism, which threatens to rob theistic belief of religiously significant content. And second, there is the apparently self-serving arbitrariness of stopping the inquiry at the concept of a divine mind.

Sharpening the second prong, Philo puts this question: 'How therefore shall we satisfy ourselves concerning the cause of that Being whom you suppose the Author of nature?' (DNR: 63). The clear suggestion, although not stated explicitly, is that we cannot possibly satisfy that curiosity, that any such line of inquiry would be, in principle, open-ended. That being so, Cleanthes' options, both unappealing, seem to be these: to push on hopelessly in an infinite regress, whose result is no explanation at all of order in the universe; or to stop arbitrarily, which, when the self-serving disguise is peeled away, comes to the same thing.

A naturalistic suggestion

The ground thus prepared, Philo opens up an alternative possibility: 'But if we stop and go no farther; why go so far? Why not stop at the material world?' (DNR: 63). Perhaps it contains 'the principle of its order within itself' (DNR: 64).

Anticipating the objection that this is a preposterous suggestion, that it is taking the very thing so obviously in need of explanation – order throughout the natural world – to be the explanation of itself, Philo counters as follows; that if, '[t]o say, that the different ideas, which compose the reason of the supreme Being, fall into order, of themselves, and by their own nature' has a precise meaning, then, 'why [is it] not as good sense to say, that the parts of the material world fall into order, of themselves, and by their own nature?' (DNR: 64). 'Can the one opinion be intelligible, while the other is not so?' (DNR: 64). The hint of materialism in this suggestion will become much more than just a hint later on, as we will see in the next chapter. Here, though, it is not yet even a hint in its own right, just relative to what Philo is taking to be Cleanthes' assumption that no explanation need be sought for the organizing principles of order among the ideas in the divine plan, or mind.

It is true, Philo agrees, that we have experience of ideas in our own minds becoming organized, or occurring to us already organized, 'without any known cause' (DNR: 64). Sometimes, I deliberately piece my ideas together, as, for instance, in trying to compose this paragraph. But other times, indeed more often than not, it is as though I find my ideas already organized, at least partially so. That is, I seem to have ideas connected together without my ever having first of all set out to connect them. That seems to be a widespread fact of our experience. And, as such, it seems to be a point in favour of what Cleanthes may be taking for granted about the ordering of ideas in the divine mind. But, while that much is indeed true, this is true too, namely, that 'we have a much larger experience of matter, which does the same; as in all instances of generation and vegetation' (DNR: 64).

We do not know the principle of order in the former case (mind), and neither do we in the latter (matter, generation and vegetation in particular). In both cases, we discover order; but its causes remain unknown. Here too then, on the *known* causes or principles of order, the material world seems to be at least on equal footing with the world of thoughts and ideas. Furthermore, Philo goes on, we have experience of disorder in both thoughts and matter, madness and rotting, respectively. All in all, then, mind seems no better off, and offers us no better model of intelligibility, than where we started, namely, with order in physical nature. It would be only a prejudice to go on supposing that order in the former is more essential, deeper, less in need of explanation, than order in the latter. For the upshot in both spheres is the same, namely, that the ultimate principles of order in both 'far exceed the narrow bounds of human understanding' (DNR: 64). Thus, in the end, we are forced back into scepticism.

Of course we may, with fancy talk, *pretend* to understand and even to explain the basis of order in matter. But, in the final analysis, that will amount to no more than 'the disguise of ignorance' (DNR: 64), which, while it may have 'greater conformity to vulgar prejudices' (65), is still 'really [saying] the same thing with the sceptics' (DNR: 64). Note that Philo is making a point here that is virtually tantamount to one at which, a moment ago, he pretended to be scandalized, when it was made by Cleanthes; namely, that a concept of divinity detached from experience, the wellspring of literal meaningfulness, will be meaningless.

In response, Cleanthes raises two points. The first of them confronts Philo with a deep and vexing question, namely, whether his position collapses into a hopeless scepticism according to which no explanation of anything at all would be possible. Cleanthes' second point is that Philo, focusing on the philosophical give and take in the argument, the points and the counterpoints, has lost sight of the biggest and most obvious point of all in the context of their argument. Let us take Cleanthes' two response points separately, starting with the second.

Cleanthes' second response: that Philo fails to see the wood for the trees

Suppose Philo is right. Suppose we really are no better off understanding or explaining order in mind (including a conjectured divine mind) than in matter. Suppose that, ultimately, all our efforts in this area do indeed tumble back into scepticism. Cleanthes does not accept any of these suppositions, of course, but let that pass. Supposing Philo is right about these things, so what? That is, so what, insofar as the fundamental purpose of Cleanthes' whole enterprise right from the start is concerned? For the purpose of that venture into natural religion was to establish the existence of a deity. And, he now insists, even if his argument is indeed vulnerable to the stream of follow-up questions coming from Philo, has he (Cleanthes) still not done what he set out to? Has he not shown that the 'order and arrangement of nature, the curious adjustment of final causes, the plain use and intention of every part and organ', all 'in the clearest language', 'bespeak . . . an intelligent cause or Author'? (DNR: 65). So, if Philo asks, 'what is the cause of this cause?', Cleanthes' answer is 'I know not; I care not; that concerns not me. I have found a Deity; and here I stop my enquiry' (DNR: 65).

Philosophers may press on with more questions, seeking more answers. Perhaps they are wiser than Cleanthes. But he, by getting so far, has achieved what he set out to. He, by getting so far, has achieved the goal that is of *religious* significance, even if it be admitted to lack ultimate theoretical or philosophical significance. That being so, there is no arbitrariness in his stopping here. There is nothing ad hoc or underhand about it. Perhaps the road on which Cleanthes started goes on farther, but he bought a ticket to go only this far. He set out to find a deity, and, he claims, he has done so. No further inquiries matter, so far as he, in his natural religion, is concerned.

Is he right? Do his arguments, in fact, get him to his original destination? There is still much evidence to be heard on that question, and so Cleanthes is being at least premature in claiming success. But, supposing that his arguments *do* warrant his inference to a divine author of nature, then I think we must agree that he would be justified in breaking off his journey here.

Cleanthes' first response: that Philo is a hopeless sceptic with regard to explanation

Cleanthes' first response to Philo is the charge that he (Philo) had finally short-circuited his own position, that his scepticism is now exposed in its full absurdity. Cleanthes' point is that the 'regress' objection leads Philo, unwittingly, to a position where he has to deny that there can be any explanation of anything at all. And that, Cleanthes is convinced, would be conclusive proof both that Philo is a Pyrrhonistic sceptic after all and that his sceptical opposition to the design hypothesis is inherently absurd (DNR: 65). As Cleanthes says: 'You seem not sensible, how easy it is to answer [your objection]. Even in common life, if I assign a cause for any event; is it any objection, Philo, that I cannot assign the cause of that cause, and answer every new question, which may incessantly be started? And what philosophers could possibly submit to so rigid a rule?' (DNR: 65).

The point is simple but powerful. If I cannot be said to have identified a cause unless and until I have successfully traced back the full causal sequence that has led to the occurrence now under explanation, then nothing is ever explained. For instance, if, in order to explain the noise in my son's room a short while ago, I have to give not just the cause of the noise – a picture's falling – but also the cause of the picture's fall – the blind's pushing against it – and then, as well, the cause of the blind's movement – the strong gust of wind through the open window – and then the cause of the gust, and then the cause of that, and so on and on, then there is no explanation at all of the noise in my son's room. (Note: this is not saying that there is no *cause* of the noise, just no explanation.) For, if the first explanation awaits the last, when there neither is, nor can be, a last, then there is no first either. Under those conditions, not only is no explanation actual, none is possible, for the chain of causal questions is endless. But that, Cleanthes is here maintaining, is precisely where Philo's line of sceptical questioning about the cause of the deity leads. And where is that? To total, unmitigated, scepticism about explanations.

In essence, then, Cleanthes' argument is that, distinctions between mitigated and extreme scepticism and protests of attachment only to the former notwithstanding, Philo has shown himself to be a total sceptic after all, and not just 'when we carry our speculations into the two eternities' (DNR: 36), as he put it in Part I. Maybe total scepticism at large is not his official position, but it is his position in fact. Perhaps he has so shown himself unwittingly, perhaps even without his own prior realization that he really is a sceptic of the Pyrrhonistic sort, and without fully understanding the logic of his own position, but he shows himself in that line of questioning to be a total sceptic none the less.

The line of questioning on which Cleanthes bases his charge is central to Philo's, which is to say Hume's, thinking on the design hypothesis. Accordingly, Cleanthes' response is a powerful challenge with serious implications. For, if the scepticism reflected in that thinking is discredited, then, proportionately, Hume's criticism of the design hypothesis will be discredited. In addition, within the wider context of Hume's philosophy as a whole, powerful reason will have been given to see him as an extreme sceptic after all.

In general, Cleanthes' core point is a good one. We are entitled to reject any hypothesis that leads, by strict logic, to an absurd outcome. This is the basis of the proof-method that logicians call *reductio ad absurdum*, the 'I reduce (such-and-such) to logical incoherence' method. The question before us now is whether Philo has indeed trapped himself in just such a *reductio*.

Philo's response

There are two parts to Philo's response.

Explanations and general laws

The first part is that, for instance, workaday scientists in the course of their research routinely explain particular occurrences by reference to general laws, even though, in the last analysis, they may have no good explanation of those laws themselves. The law of gravity goes a long way towards explaining the fall of the picture in my son's room, but what causes gravity itself? In terms of what is to be explained? And then what causes that cause? And so on as before. That is, Philo denies he is maintaining, even covertly, that there is no explanation of anything here and now until there is explanation of everything that happened in its causal history. He would agree that gravity is a good explanation of the picture's fall, even though we may be unable to account for gravity itself, or for the cause of gravity.

But here the unexplained residue in a given scientific explanation is a general law or laws of nature. What is the situation when that residue is not a general law but some particular thing? On this, Philo maintains it is not good scientific practice to explain a particular occurrence by reference to some other particular, which itself remains unexplained; that, in those circumstances, the follow-up question is legitimate and must be answered, before an explanation of the initial occurrence can be said to be final. Of course, in actual practice, we often *do* explain particular occurrences in terms of particular causes; for instance, the impact on the picture of this blind in motion caused the picture to fall. But Philo's point is that, in the sciences, the final goal and terminus is explanation in terms of basic laws of nature. Any explanation short of that is interim.

In opposition to Philo (thus to Hume) on this point, Nelson Pike, in his edition of the *Dialogues*, notes that, for instance, we explain the movements of the tides by reference to phases of the moon and, he goes on, this 'would be a fully acceptable explanation of the tides, even if we had no accompanying explanation of the existence or nature of the moon' (Pike 1970: 162).

But, even granting that, could there be an *ultimate* explanation in terms of a particular thing? For a fully acceptable explanation, to use Pike's term, could, in a given case, fall far short of ultimacy. This is an important question in the philosophy of religion, for, in the last analysis, theistic explanation is explanation in terms of a particular, personal being, the deity, offered as the ultimate explanation of the existence of the universe. And so is deistic explanation. Thus, if, in virtue of the kind of explanation that it is, such explanation is illegitimate as an ultimate explanation, then both theism and deism may be disqualified as candidate ultimate explanations, without any need to look into the merits of their particular arguments.

I do not know of a good argument to establish that ultimate explanation cannot be explanation in terms of a particular thing, personal or non-personal. So I am agnostic on the point, and thus also on Philo's first response to Cleanthes' charge that he is a Pyrrhonistic sceptic about explanation.

Supernaturalistic and naturalistic explanations relativized

Philo's second point in response to Cleanthes' charge of Pyrrhonism about explanation is essentially a comparative one. In his words,

> if [order] requires a cause in both [supernaturalistic and naturalistic systems], what do we gain by your system, in tracing the universe of objects into a similar universe of ideas? The first step, which we make, leads us on forever. It were, therefore, wise in us, to limit all our enquiries to the present world, without looking farther. No satisfaction can ever be attained by these speculations, which so far exceed the narrow bounds of human understanding.
>
> (DNR: 64)

The point that Philo is making here is not that Cleanthes' design explanation fails to explain, because it leaves questions about itself unanswered. Instead, it is that Cleanthes' design explanation fails to explain *any better* than a naturalistic explanation, which holds that the ultimate principle of order is indigenous in nature. Again, 'if [order] requires a cause in both [matter and mind], what do we gain by your system, in tracing the universe of objects into a similar universe of ideas?' And, in the same vein:

> in like manner, when it is asked, what cause produces order in the ideas of the supreme Being, can any other reason be assigned by you, anthropomorphites, than that it is a rational faculty, and that such is the nature of the Deity? But why a similar answer will not be equally satisfactory in accounting for the order of the

world, without having recourse to any such intelligent Creator as you insist on, may be difficult to determine.

(DNR: 65)

Philo's point is that both supernaturalistic and naturalistic explanations are on the same footing. Each of them invites the very same sequence of follow-up questions, and they are equal in their respective inabilities to answer satisfactorily. Consequently, it is fair to say that the theistic, supernaturalistic explanation in terms of design is no better than its naturalistic rival at avoiding the regression trap. In the last analysis, '[c]an the one opinion be intelligible, while the other is not so?' (DNR: 64).

But Cleanthes cannot rest content with the score tied, so to speak, between these two explanations. For, right from its first introduction in Part II, his design argument was offered as a better explanation of order in nature than any of its rivals. That being so, faring no worse, but also no better, than naturalistic explanations means that the design argument has so far failed to do what it set itself to do. Although his first response to Cleanthes' charge may be inconclusive, Philo's second response shows him to have the better of the exchange.

Like effects, like causes (*Dialogues*, Part V)

At the start of Part V, promising to show Cleanthes 'still more inconveniences . . . in [his] anthropomorphism' (DNR: 67), Philo focuses on a fundamental idea in the design argument, namely, '[l]ike effects prove like causes' (DNR: 67). Indeed, to both Philo and Cleanthes, '[t]his *is* the experimental argument' (DNR: 67, emphasis added). And, as Philo now reminds Cleanthes, 'you say too, [it] is the sole [religious] argument' (DNR: 67). His point is that, in the last analysis, Cleanthes' case will stand or fall by this principle. That fall, though, if it were to come, could be incremental and cumulative, but no less conclusive on that account. As Philo puts it, in a foretaste for Cleanthes of what is to come, '[e]very departure on either side diminishes the probability, and renders the experiment less conclusive' (DNR: 67).

Trying to erode Cleanthes' analogy

Philo starts a list of such departures. He is careful to say that it is not traditional theism, 'the true system of theism', that is embarrassed by these, but Cleanthes' 'hypothesis of experimental theism' (DNR: 67). Philo does not specify the differences that matter between the two systems, and in fact he is (again) being disingenuous. For, by Cleanthes' so-called 'experimental theism' is meant, in effect, the design hypothesis. But that, in one form or another, is the principal natural religionist argument for traditional theism. Philo's distinction here, then, between 'the true system of theism' and Cleanthes' 'experimental theism', is a further instance of Hume taking care to guard himself against accusations of impiety, or of being an intellectual enemy of theism.

The first item on Philo's list of departures from the like effects/like causes principle is 'all the new discoveries in astronomy' (DNR: 67). He maintains that these instances of 'the immense grandeur and magnificence of the works of nature' (DNR: 67) make it all the more unlikely that their cause resembles the cause of artefacts. The second item on his list is from the opposite end of the spectrum, microscopic now, not macroscopic. It is the 'discoveries by microscopes, as they open a new universe in miniature' (DNR: 68). And then, third, there are the new discoveries in the other sciences, for instance, anatomy, chemistry, botany (DNR: 68).

Cleanthes interrupts. All that Philo is doing, albeit unwittingly, he maintains, is to give 'new instances of art and contrivance', thus corroboration of his, Cleanthes', fundamental point, which is that there is clear and unmistakable evidence of design at work in physical nature (DNR: 68). So far as Cleanthes is concerned, all Philo has just done is identify various dimensions of physical nature where the extent of orderliness is amazing, and to which only a supernaturalistic explanation can do justice.

'A mind like the human'

The next exchange between Cleanthes and Philo is especially revealing. Essentially, it shows us that, in an important way, their respective understandings of what is at issue between them are at cross-purposes. The exchange plays out as follows.

Immediately after Cleanthes' interruption that those various sciences in which new discoveries are being made give further corroboration to his basic idea of design in physical nature, Philo emphasizes that any mind that might be inferred from that evidence would be 'a mind like the human' (DNR: 68). Cleanthes agrees, saying that he knows of no other kind of mind. Philo, more emphatic still, goes on, 'the liker the better' (DNR: 68). To which Cleanthes, with no hesitation, agrees.

In this exchange we see Philo getting ready to spring a trap that (he thinks) will clearly show 'the inconveniences of [Cleanthes'] anthropomorphism' and which, furthermore, he expects to take him to an even bigger point, namely, that Cleanthes' stated conclusion, even if granted, would be virtually empty. But, in the same exchange, we see Cleanthes thinking that his case is being handed to him on a plate. And, funnily enough, each, by his own lights, is right. Hence my point above that Cleanthes' and Philo's understandings of their respective places in the discussion are at cross purposes with one another.

Take Cleanthes first. When he introduced his design argument in Part II, he announced his intent to establish that 'the Author of nature is somewhat similar to the mind of man' (DNR: 45). 'Somewhat' is a vague term, deliberately so. And, for that matter, so is 'similar'. These are terms whose scope and content remain to be filled in. For Cleanthes, the principal thing to establish is that there is a personal being behind the natural world, having some kind of similarity to the mind of man. The details are secondary in importance. And so now, here in Part V, he sees Philo granting him what he has sought from the start, namely, some similarity. And Cleanthes is willing to take yes for an answer, so to speak.

Now to Philo. As he sees it, the expression, 'somewhat similar', could mean virtually anything. So, as he sees it, for Cleanthes to win a concession on that would just about amount to nothing, or at least to very little above nothing. And this is an important thing to keep in mind at three upcoming, controversial, places in the *Dialogues*. The first of them is the second-to-last paragraph here in Part V (DNR: 71). The others are the final paragraph in Part X (DNR: 104) and throughout

Part XII. In each of these places, against the run of play in the argument, Philo concedes Cleanthes' analogy, thereby raising a serious question about Philo's, thus Hume's, aims and achievements in the *Dialogues*. But in Philo's contribution to the present exchange, Hume is giving us, in advance, an important clue to make sense of those puzzling 'concession' passages to come. The likeness is to a mystery writer who, without announcement or fanfare, equips us early on in a book to untangle a later puzzle.

Philo's anthropomorphic trap: strict proportionality between causes and effects

Cleanthes agrees that he knows of no mind other than one like the human. Let us put aside as inconsequential any dissenting thoughts we might have about monkey minds, bat minds, or salamander minds, for instance, as they too, given the complete lack of specificity about what is meant by similarity to a human mind, are 'like the human', in one way or other. Philo pounces, triumphantly, on Cleanthes' agreement. His point is that Cleanthes, by agreeing, 'must renounce all claim to infinity in any of the attributes of the Deity' (DNR: 68). For Cleanthes bound his argument to a criterion of proportionality of causes to effects, but no human effect traces to an infinite cause. Furthermore, on the same principle of proportionality, Cleanthes must give up any idea of perfection in the deity, thus perfect knowledge or perfect wisdom (DNR: 68–9). In addition, in a hint of the problem of evil that he will so damagingly press in Parts X and XI, Philo suggests that the fact of 'many inexplicable difficulties in the works of nature' (DNR: 69) is a fact that tells against any religiously significant conception of a supernatural author of nature (DNR: 69). There is a hint here too of scepticism regarding our ability to conduct any meaningful discussion about the value or disvalue of the universe overall, thus a hint of scepticism about the whole enterprise of natural religion itself.

But, even though, in reality, we are in no position to estimate the overall value or disvalue of the universe, suppose, for the sake of argument, we agree that it is indeed perfect. What follows? That the cause of this perfection is its maker? But, on the proportioning analogy of divine to human manufacture, we are entitled to no such conclusion. For is it not a commonplace of our experience that, for instance, exquisite pieces of work are often imitations, or at least not complete originals? Their makers have often copied (or been influenced by) some previous pieces of work, which themselves may have been copies (and had influences) too, with the result that, gradually, over time and by repeated trial and error, the present exquisite object is produced. If we are serious about the analogy between artefacts and the universe, do we not have to take this commonplace of improvement in design and manufacture over time into account? But doing so robs Cleanthes of his inference to an exalted, one-of-a-kind, supernatural designer and creator of the universe. As Philo summarizes the point: 'Many worlds might have been botched and bungled, throughout an eternity, ere this system was struck out . . . a slow, but continued improvement carried on during infinite ages in the art of world-making' (DNR: 69).

Philo does not say that he believes this. He does not have to. Nor would doing so fit with his scepticism. His point is that, for all we know, something like this might well be true. It might well be more likely to be true than Cleanthes' hypothesis. But who can tell? Attempting to do so would intolerably strain the evidence, thus, to withhold a verdict is the prudent thing: 'In such subjects, who can determine, where the truth; nay, who can conjecture where the probability, lies . . .?' (DNR: 69). Scepticism, then, is the sensible position.

Turning back to Cleanthes' analogy, Philo maintains that it tilts against 'the unity of the Deity' (DNR: 69). This is not a reversion to the 'bundle' theory of mind, introduced by Demea in Part IV. Unity here does not mean the individuality of a complex or composite thing. What Philo is getting at is that, in our experience of the design and manufacture of things, houses, ships, cities, commonwealths, and so on, there is almost always cooperation among a large number of people, some creative, some merely labourers. None of these individuals, usually, is indispensable or supreme; collaboration and cooperation compensate for the relative modesty of the talents of each participant in the project. And in large and complex creative projects, is this not the lesson of experience? On Cleanthes' analogy, then, ought he not infer the existence of a *team* of deities? In effect, Philo is here maintaining that, if Cleanthes insists on inferring a supernatural source of the universe, then the logic of his position points to a polytheistic conclusion, not a monotheistic one (DNR: 69–70). Once again, like effects, like causes.

An Ockhamist defence of Cleanthes

In defence of Cleanthes' single-deity hypothesis, perhaps it could be argued that Philo's polytheistic alternative offends the principle of economy in reasoning often known as Ockham's Razor. This principle, named for the medieval English theologian and philosopher, William of Ockham (*c.* 1285–1349), is that entities are not to be multiplied beyond necessity. In essence, Ockham's Razor is a recommendation that we ought always to seek to explain the most in terms of the fewest possible principles. But Philo brushes this aside as a feeble defence of Cleanthes' hypothesis: 'this principle applies not to the present case' (DNR: 70). Why not? The answer is, better fit with our experience.

Philo explains his answer as follows. If we knew (or had good reason to believe) in advance that there was a single deity, then his (Philo's) point about polytheism would indeed be in breach of Ockham's Razor. But we don't. And given that we don't, given that we are starting from the fact of a vastly complicated universe and, by reference to explanations of order in very complex artefacts, imprudently speculating about a supernatural explanation of order in it, then a team of deities makes more sense than a single, supreme deity.

In a variation on an example he uses in his *Enquiry concerning Human Understanding* (EHU: 14G/136), Hume gives Philo the following illustration of the point. Suppose we are shown a balance scale, with only one of its scales visible. On the scale there is a weight, a huge pile of gravel, say. But the scale is balanced, thus we know that 'concealed from sight...[there is] some counterpoising weight equal to [the pile of gravel]' (DNR: 70). But we do not know if that counterpoising weight is a single thing, or several things, or a pile of many things. Now consider that the weight on the visible scale is enormous; it is a *huge* pile of gravel. Seeing the scale in balance, we know that the counterpoising weight on the scale that is hidden from view is equally enormous. But now, which is the more plausible inference; that the hidden, counterpoising weight is one single thing, or several things, or a pile of many things (say, another huge pile of gravel)? Surely, clearly, in the circumstances, the last of these is the most plausible inference. If we independently knew that there existed, and was available to this building contractor, a single piece of 'Big Bang matter', or 'Black Hole matter', that is, stuff of extraordinary density, mass, and weight, then, perhaps, we could have some justification in thinking that the hidden, counterpoising weight was a single thing, not a pile of many things. Or if we knew that, earlier, there had been several very large and very heavy boulders nearby that could fit on one side of the scale, then we might favour the second option. Otherwise not. In the circumstances, when all we know is that there is a huge pile of gravel on this visible side of this balanced scale, the inference to a counterpoising weight due to a combination of many things, another huge pile of gravel, say, is the most plausible inference. Thus, there is no offence against Ockhamism here. And that there is not is significant, for Hume is a good Ockhamist.

Scepticism redux

But here again it is really the sceptical conclusion that Philo favours. The real question, the one that ought to guide us here, he thinks, is this: 'By what phenomena in nature can we pretend to decide the controversy?' (DNR: 70). In theory, we could eventually examine the hidden scale, thus settling that question. But insofar as the ultimate source of order in the physical universe is concerned, there seems to be no such possibility even in theory.

'Why not become a perfect anthropomorphite?'

Further pressing the 'inconveniences of . . . anthropomorphism', Philo thinks that Cleanthes ought not just to accept a polytheistic conclusion to his analogical argument, but to go further and accept also that the gods mate and procreate in a fashion more-or-less akin to humans. And why stop there? '[W]hy not become a perfect anthropomorphite?' (DNR: 70). Why not attribute bodies, thus eyes, noses, mouths, ears, and so on to the gods? Why not embrace a full-blooded paganism, in other words?

Philo knows how offensive to Cleanthes (and to the other theist, Demea), how belittling and ridiculing, all of this is. Thus Hume, whose voice Philo is, intends this to be offensive to the Christian theism represented by Cleanthes (as well as to that represented by Demea). The author's mask is here virtually transparent.

Philo's concession of design

Yet, with all that said, and notwithstanding the power of his objections and criticisms, Philo volunteers this concession: 'a man, who follows your hypothesis, is able, perhaps, to assert, or conjecture, that the universe, sometime, arose from something like design' (DNR: 71). In the circumstances, this is unexpected, to say the least, and seems gratuitous. He goes on immediately to add this important qualification: 'But beyond that position he cannot ascertain one single circumstance, and is left afterwards to fix every point of his theology, by the utmost licence of fancy and hypothesis' (DNR: 71).

In or out of context, it is a weak concession. Out of context, in quotation, say, it is weak, hedged with qualification. But in context, which is how Hume intends us to take it, it is weaker still. As a concession made after the damage that Philo has been doing to the design hypothesis, it is especially feeble, perhaps a sop to a position believed to have been stripped of content. None the less, it is a concession. Furthermore, it is made again, and in stronger terms, in Parts X and XII.

Cleanthes, as we saw, thinks that the mere fact of similarity, however undeveloped, between the causes of order in man-made things and in things found in nature is sufficient for religion. His point is that any such similarity has to be between mind and mind, inasmuch as order in man-made things traces to mind. And what is similar to a mind but another mind? Recall his words from Part IV: 'I have found a Deity; and here I stop my enquiry' (DNR: 65). In Part XII, Philo will suggest something, not itself a mind, that is similar to a mind. And he is right; minds are not similar only to minds, just as tennis racquets are not similar only to tennis racquets, or to racquets, for that matter.

Philo's weakening of his already-weak concession

Not content to leave it there, unwilling to end on this note of concession, feeble and emasculated though it is, Philo returns to some possibilities that, for all we know, could well be true on Cleanthes' analogy. Each is a possibility fitting that analogy at least as well as Cleanthes' single-deity hypothesis. Arguably, each fits the analogy even better than that hypothesis. The possibilities are these:

> This world, for aught [we know], is very faulty and imperfect, compared to a superior standard; and was only the first rude essay of some infant Deity, who afterwards abandoned it, ashamed of his lame performance; it is the work only of some dependent, inferior Deity; and is the object of derision to his superiors; it is the production of old age and dotage in some superannuated Deity; and ever since his death, has run on . . . the first impulse and active force, which it received from him.
>
> (DNR: 71)

As before, Hume knows what he is doing. As before, the offence and insult to Christian theism is intended. He has Philo notice Demea's 'horror' at these suppositions. And he endeavours to preserve his own capacity to deny (if need be) that these views are his own by having Philo insist that he is just being a good logician, just drawing out implications of Cleanthes' 'experimental theism' (DNR: 67), in supposed contradistinction to the more traditional theism favoured by Demea and supposedly by Philo himself.

Cleanthes' 'sufficient foundation for religion'

Cleanthes has the last word, but it is of doubtful weight. Professing not to be horrified at all, maintaining that these for-all-we-know hypotheses of Philo's reflect only his heated imagination, not the logic of Cleanthes' analogy, Cleanthes asserts what, for him, is the central point. It is that Philo 'never get[s] rid of the hypothesis of design in the universe; but [is] obliged, at every turn, to have recourse to it' (DNR: 71). The sheer fact of Philo's concession, in complete separation from its faintness both in and out of context, is enough for

Cleanthes. He concludes: '[t]o this concession I adhere steadily; and this I regard as a sufficient foundation for religion' (DNR: 71). Cleanthes' final words in Part V, then, echo his final words in Part IV (DNR: 65).

Whose burden of proof?

In this victory-claim of Cleanthes' we may notice an interesting shift, or at least an attempted shift. It is of the burden of proof from the natural religionist to the critic of that position. For Cleanthes here seems to be implicitly suggesting that if his hypothesis of design is not defeated, then it is triumphant. That by not losing in the strong sense of being conclusively shown to be false, his hypothesis is successful. But that is not the way he started out. In Part II, when he first introduced his design argument, his tone was robust, and his expectation was to establish convincingly the positive thesis that there exists an author of nature somewhat similar to the mind of man. But now, with no announcement, he seems to be assuming that it is Philo's burden of proof to conclusively refute the design theory.

In mitigation, perhaps Cleanthes thinks this because he believes that all of Philo's objections and criticisms trace to an extreme and absurd scepticism. That being so, he may then be thinking that, as the discussion has actually developed, and as (from his perspective) no non-extreme and non-absurd arguments have been brought against his theory, the burden of proof rightly rests on the critic. Let us suppose that this *is* Cleanthes' thinking. Furthermore, supposing that, let us grant him the point, for the sake of the argument. But he is still not entitled to think that, if it is not conclusively refuted, his position wins. The reason is that not all of Philo's objections issue from his scepticism. For instance, the objections to the anthropomorphic tendencies in Cleanthes' argument are not based in scepticism. Nor is the naturalistic alternative. And these are among the most potent of criticisms of Cleanthes' theory.

Chapter 7

Naturalism and scepticism

(*Dialogues*, Parts VI, VII, and VIII)

Introduction

Between Cleanthes' first argument for natural design in Part II and the start of Part VI, the uncontested assumption in the *Dialogues* is that order in nature needs explaining, with the design hypothesis being the only substantive candidate-explanation. But that changes in Part VI. For this reason, Part VI represents a significant turning point in the *Dialogues*.

  Does natural order – both the means–end order in organisms and the patterns of regularity that are in evidence throughout the whole of nature, both biological and non-biological – really need explanation? Perhaps the term 'orderly universe' adds nothing to the term 'universe', appearances notwithstanding. Perhaps order (of either or both kinds) is an essential, intrinsic feature of *any* universe, and of any occurrence. Perhaps, that is, order (means–end order or mere regularity) is not an additional fact, over and above the existence of material things and processes. This is the basic idea, suggested but undeveloped in Part IV (DNR: 63–4),

that comes up for exploration and criticism in Parts VI, VII, and VIII. This thoroughgoing naturalistic hypothesis is now put into competition with Cleanthes' supernaturalism. At first look, it may seem to be very implausible, outrageous even, but, by the end of Part VIII, arguably Philo will have gone a long way towards making it a plausible and serious rival to the design hypothesis.

In this rival naturalism, we meet embryonic forms of three ideas that, subsequently in the history of science, were revolutionary. They are: the idea of living matter, which is the core concept in biology; the idea of evolution by way of unguided adaptiveness of organisms to environments; and the idea that stable structures could emerge from collisions of atoms, that is, through random, blind forces of attraction and repulsion. As noted earlier, both the science of biology and Darwin's theory of evolution by way of natural selection were still over a century in the future when Hume was writing his *Dialogues*.

By the close of Part VIII, the supposition that natural order needs explaining in terms of something more fundamental than itself, an idea that seemed obvious and compelling in Parts II and III, is an option, not a necessity. By the end of Part VIII, there has occurred a remarkable shift in focus, such that the idea of natural order as a basic fact, needing no ulterior explanation in terms of something deeper or more ultimate, is an idea to be taken seriously.

But, in the last analysis, who can establish which, of these two fundamentally incompatible positions, naturalism and supernaturalism, is the more basic? Given no satisfactory proof either way, Philo sees sceptical non-commitment as the prudent and reasonable course.

The hypothesis of living matter and an inherent principle of order (*Dialogues*, Part VI)

'A new species of anthropomorphism'

Although Part V closed on Cleanthes' insistence that the hypothesis of design in nature stood unrefuted as a sufficient basis for religious belief, Part VI opens with his fellow theist, Demea, completely unpersuaded by Cleanthes' point, and, paying no heed to Philo's concession, summarizing the damage done by Philo's criticisms. It is, by any reasonable measure, a damning survey:

> It must be a slight fabric, indeed . . . which can be erected on so tottering a foundation. While we are uncertain, whether there is one Deity or many; whether the Deity or Deities, to whom we owe our existence, be perfect or imperfect, subordinate or supreme, dead or alive; what trust or confidence can we repose in them? What devotion or worship address to them? What veneration or obedience pay them? To all the purposes of life, the theory of religion becomes altogether useless: And even with regard to speculative consequences, its uncertainty . . . must render it totally precarious and unsatisfactory.
>
> (DNR: 72)

In short, Demea is asking, incredulously, how Cleanthes could possibly be serious in thinking that what now remains of his design theory is 'a sufficient foundation for religion' (DNR: 71), in any meaningful sense of the word 'religion'. And, as we will see in Part XII, Demea's bleak assessment at this point in the conversation will still be good at the end, when, after his departure, Cleanthes and Philo take stock.

But Philo is far from finished. There is more in his opposition to the design hypothesis than the largely negative enterprise of exposing shortcomings in it. There is a positive side too, '[a]nother hypothesis', that, he thinks, will 'render [the design theory] still more unsatisfactory' (DNR: 72). He stresses that this new hypothesis fits well with Cleanthes' experimentalist maxim, 'like effects arise from like causes', which, Philo reminds us, Cleanthes 'supposes the foundation of all religion' (DNR: 72). The new principle that Philo has in mind is 'that where several known circumstances are *observed* to be similar, the unknown will also be *found* similar' (DNR: 72).

Mimicking Cleanthes in Part II, Philo suggests we 'survey the universe' (DNR: 72). Doing so without pre-disposition to any particular interpretation, any theistic or quasi-theistic interpretation, in particular, do we not find, Philo asks, that 'so far as [the universe] falls under our knowledge, it bears a great resemblance to an animal or organized body, and seems actuated with a like principle of life and motion'? (DNR: 72). That is, when we look without prejudice, do we

not find that the universe resembles a living thing, an organism ('organized body', (DNR: 72)) of some sort? There is continuous change in
nature, but not disorder, or much disorder. Damage is repaired. For
instance, new growth occurs after a forest fire, wounds heal, waste
fertilizes, and so on and on. And, as far as our observation goes, these
things just happen of their own accord, naturally, without outside
prompting or manipulation. Where, in our experience, is it obvious that
such things happen? In living organisms, of course. Thus, perhaps the
right analogue to change in nature is change in organisms. That is the
gist of Philo's new hypothesis.

Forsaking any claim to novelty in this idea, Philo reminds
Cleanthes that similar views were held in antiquity, perhaps by
Plato in some of his late dialogues and, later still, by some of the
Stoics, although he names none. In so raising this ancient hypothesis, Philo is careful to note that it was various '*theists* of antiquity'
(my emphasis) who subscribed to it, his point being that this conjecture
is not alien or hostile to religion. But, while true enough up to a
point, this is another of those remarks of Philo's that we must take
with a pinch of salt. For, while not incompatible with religion, in the
sense that there is no formal contradiction between it and religious
belief of the sort favoured by Cleanthes, this old/new hypothesis
yet further erodes Cleanthes' kind of supernaturalistic religion.
How? By effectively undermining the mind–body dualism that Philo,
rightly, sees reflected in Cleanthes' version of theism. After all,
Cleanthes' deity is a mind that is outside physical nature, yet, somehow, creates and then interacts with it. But, in Philo's words, 'nothing
[is] more repugnant to common experience ... than mind without
body; a mere spiritual substance ... of which [the ancients] had not
observed one single instance throughout all nature' (DNR: 73). In
short, Cleanthes' dualism of mind and body is not warranted by actual
experience.

As described here by Philo, this hypothesis of old, applied to the
deity or deities, is a form of pantheism, a theory associated in modern
times with the Dutch philosopher Baruch Spinoza (1632–77). Briefly,
pantheism is a theory maintaining that body and mind are co-extensive
in the deity, in effect, that the universe and the deity are one and the
same. It is the idea that the self-same universe may alternately be

described in physical terms or in terms of intelligence, but that this dualism of descriptions reflects no dualism in reality, no dualism of things, in other words. For instance, a human person may be described in purely physical terms or in terms of mind and intelligence, without, on this theory, any suggestion that mind is a separate thing or substance from the body, a separate thing from a properly functioning brain, in particular. A variation on this pantheistic conception of the universe and the deity will come up in Part VIII.

Philo's main point here is that this 'new species of anthropomorphism' (DNR: 73), the notion of the universe as organism, not as artefact, has the better fit with experience, thus the stronger claim on Cleanthes (DNR: 73–4). We may think of this theory's undermining of the notion of spiritual substance in a more positive light as well, that is, as offering us a plausible way of supposing an original principle of order to be in matter itself, namely, matter understood as living matter (DNR: 73). And that is the new direction now being taken in the conversation.

Cleanthes' concession and criticism

Cleanthes responds that he had never thought of this idea before, and so he needs time to reflect on it. But he does agree that, at face value, the theory is 'a pretty natural one' (DNR: 74). Prompted to give his first thoughts on the matter, Cleanthes suggests that, while there are some resemblances between the universe and an animal body, there are deep differences too. For instance, '[n]o organs of sense; no seat of thought or reason; no one precise origin of motion and action' (DNR: 74). But the inference he draws from these disanalogies is not the dismissal of Philo's conjecture, but its modification. He thinks the evidence suggests a closer likeness to a vegetable than an animal, a lower level of organism, that is. And an effect of this modification would be a weakening of the pantheistic notion of 'the soul of the world' (DNR: 74), as vegetables do not have souls, in the relevant sense. That is Cleanthes' first criticism. Philo will reply to it in Part VII.

Cleanthes' concession and first criticism

Cleanthes' concession is both strategic and his first criticism of Philo's naturalistic hypothesis. The strategy is to keep at bay an analogy between the universe and animals, for that might be able to supply a viable form of the pantheistic 'soul of the world' idea. And his first criticism is that an analogy between order in the universe at large and in plants does not upset his own basic idea that the ultimate source of order is mind. What Cleanthes does not foresee, however, is that, from the analogy between the universe and plant life, Philo may be able to develop a hypothesis that *will* be a rival to Cleanthes' own. And we will see Philo attempt just that in Part VII.

But Cleanthes thinks his concession about plant life really amounts to nothing. This is not just because he thinks a source of order outside plant life would still be needed. It is also, and more so, because he thinks there is no such analogy to begin with. Let us now turn to that, his second criticism.

Cleanthes' 'eternity' criticism

Cleanthes' second criticism of Philo's conjecture takes back the foregoing concession. The criticism is that, 'your theory seems to imply the eternity of the world; and that is a principle which, I think, can be refuted by the strongest reasons and probabilities' (DNR: 74). Thus, the concession of some resemblance between order in the universe and in vegetation is quickly to be nullified in what Cleanthes thinks is a decisive refutation of Philo's conjecture that the universe more resembles an organism than an artefact.

Cleanthes does not make it clear why he thinks that Philo's hypothesis entails the eternity of the universe, but we may speculate that his thinking is more-or-less as follows. Philo's purpose in introducing the hypothesis that the universe may resemble an organism more than an artefact is to get away from Cleanthes' idea that the universe is created, that order in nature is introduced into nature by its designer or creator. Getting away from Cleanthes' idea means conjecturing that, perhaps, the principles of natural order are innate in the physical universe. If that is right, then they were not put there, but were always already present. And that may be thought to lead to the idea that the universe is eternal, that it has existed without beginning. It does not, however, lead to that idea in the sense of logically entailing it, but it may lead to it in the psychological sense that it brings the idea readily to mind.

At any rate, thinking that Philo's conjecture entails the eternity of the universe, Cleanthes thinks he can refute that conjecture by showing that the universe is not eternal. Briefly, his argument is this. First, we know that cherry trees were introduced into Europe from Asia in Roman times; we know that grape vines were not in France more than two thousand years ago; we know that farm animals, including dogs and horses, were not in America before the fifteenth century (actually, this is false, thus we do not know this, but let that pass). Second, if the universe is eternal, how likely is it that, for instance, grape vines would not have got to France until recent times, relative to the (conjectured) eternal past of the universe? Third, surely, it is not at all likely. And likewise for the other examples of things particularly well suited to their current European environments, cherry trees in Greece, Spain, and Italy, for instance. Bringing it to a point, Cleanthes maintains that these, and other considerations like them, 'seem convincing proofs of the youth, or rather infancy, of the world' (DNR: 75). Thus, he thinks he has defeated Philo's conjecture.

'[A]n eternal, inherent principle of order'

Philo's response is very interesting, both for what is said and what is unsaid. What is unsaid is anything pertaining directly to Cleanthes' examples of grapes, cherry trees or livestock. Instead of engaging in discussion of those points, none of which is especially plausible anyway, Philo brings the main underlying point clearly into the open. It is that, in our experience, all changes in nature, even cataclysmic changes, fundamental changes, are really changes 'from one state of order to another' (DNR: 76). And, in a point he knows that Cleanthes cannot deny without inconsistency with his own design argument, Philo suggests that 'what we see in the parts [of nature], we may infer in the whole [of nature]' (DNR: 76). His point is that we never find the natural world in a state totally devoid of order; that, on the contrary, we always and only find it in some already orderly state or states. Thus, insofar as actual experience is concerned, we have no experience whatever of nature without order, always the opposite. Given that, Philo goes on, 'were I obliged to defend any particular system of this nature (which I never willingly should do), I esteem none more plausible than that which ascribes an eternal, inherent principle of order to the world; though attended with great and continual revolutions and alterations' (DNR: 76).

On this hypothesis, order is not a marvel to be explained. Instead, it is a natural, inherent part of the universe all the way through. In his words, '[i]nstead of admiring the order of natural beings, we should clearly see, that it was absolutely impossible for them, in the smallest article, ever to admit of any other disposition' (DNR: 76–7). In short, the universe may be more or less orderly, but it is never absolutely without order; the concept of a universe (or of any particular natural object) completely without order is an oxymoron, an inherently self-defeating concept.

A serious, substantive rival to Cleanthes' design theory is now out in the open.

But, while introduced into discussion by Philo, Philo does not endorse or subscribe to this hypothesis. As he said in his parenthetical remark in lines quoted just above, endorsement is something 'which I never willingly should do'. Instead, he uses the hypothesis to show, first, that the design theory is not the only serious account of natural order that is available to us, and second, that, of the two substantive theories now in play, arguably the naturalistic is the more plausible and compelling.

Part VI ends on a familiar note. For, after introducing this naturalistic hypothesis of order as a deep and inseparable feature of the natural world, Philo reverts to his scepticism with the point that, insofar as deciding on the truth of any of the various rival theories is concerned, the evidence warrants no decisive verdict; they are all 'on a like footing' (DNR: 77).

Ranking four causal principles: reason, instinct, generation, vegetation (*Dialogues*, Part VII)

Consolidating the naturalistic hypothesis

Although it begins with Philo claiming to have just then had 'a new idea' (DNR: 78), nothing essentially new comes up in Part VII. Notwithstanding that, however, something very important in the development of the argument occurs there, namely, Philo's consolidation of the hypothesis that order in nature needs no prior explanation; that, without orderliness of some sort, nothing at all would or could exist.

Disregarding Cleanthes' two criticisms of his conjectured analogy between order in the universe at large and in organisms, Philo begins as follows: 'If the universe bears a greater likeness to animal bodies and to vegetables, than to the works of human art, it is more probable that its cause resembles the cause of the former than that of the latter, and its origin ought rather to be ascribed to generation or vegetation than to reason or design' (DNR: 78). Demea, still Hume's set-up man for important points, asks for elaboration. Philo obliges, giving a concise summary of both Cleanthes' line of reasoning and his own. This summary adds nothing new to either. Philo's emphasis is barbed, however, for he lays stress on Cleanthes' design argument as an inference from 'one very small part of nature', namely, reason in human beings, to the operation of reason throughout nature at large (DNR: 78).

Demea's next question is the question, surely, on the tips of all our tongues; how are we to think of the literal generation of a universe? In answering, Philo again adds nothing substantially new. His suggestion is to think of the universe as a vast and complex organism, which, over time, generates and regenerates, constantly expanding, '[vegetating] into new worlds' (DNR: 79).

Hume is marking time in these exchanges between Philo and Demea. Demea's questions, which are purely information seeking, and Philo's answers are a literary device to give this naturalistic hypothesis time to sink in.

But then Demea, now presumably grasping the meaning and, more importantly, the significance for religion, of Philo's naturalistic conjecture, incredulously and challengingly expostulates, 'what wild, arbitrary suppositions are these? What *data* have you for such extraordinary conclusions?. . . is the slight, imaginary resemblance of the world to a vegetable or an animal sufficient to establish the same inference with regard to both? Objects, which are in general so widely different; ought they to be a standard for each other?' (DNR: 79).

Philo's two layers of alternatives to design: scepticism and naturalism

This is music to Philo's ears. It is the perfect lead-in to his fundamental point, that sceptical non-commitment to any global hypothesis is the right and prudent stance to take. He does not let the opportunity pass: 'Right', he agrees at once (DNR: 79). Our experience is simply insufficient to afford us any 'probable conjecture concerning the whole of things' (DNR: 79).

But that is not all. If, as Cleanthes has all along been insisting, 'we must needs fix on some hypothesis', then we ought to adopt the hypothesis that offers both the greater and the more widespread resemblance between the objects being compared. And that, Philo leaves no doubt, is the organism hypothesis, not the design hypothesis. If we put aside any bias towards the latter based on greater familiarity with it, and examine the empirical evidence fairly and thoroughly, then, Philo thinks, we surely will favour his conjectured naturalism over Cleanthes' supernaturalism.

Demea's next question is a variation on his previous question. And, once again, Philo takes it as an opportunity to advance his case. The question is whether Philo can be more specific in describing the operation of generation as (perhaps) the most basic causal principle known to us. Philo responds that he can do at least as well in explaining generation as the source of order in nature as Cleanthes can in explaining design as the source of order (DNR: 79). In effect, Philo continues to emphasize that now, in contradistinction to earlier in the discussion, the design hypothesis can be assessed, not just in its own right, but relative to a rival hypothesis that, at a minimum, is no less plausible. And the significance of that is this: that now, a person whose bent of mind is not sceptical but is towards some cosmically explanatory hypothesis, is no longer in the position of choosing between the design hypothesis and no explanation at all. That is, such a person, not Philo himself of course, but a person disinclined to scepticism in such matters, is no longer in the position of having to downplay the obvious shortcomings of the design argument's analogy in order to avoid the worse – to such a mentality – outcome of simply having no explanation at all, no matter how flawed. For now, weighing and balancing the pros and cons of two cosmic hypotheses, one supernaturalistic, the other naturalistic, such a person is no longer choosing between something (substantive) and nothing (substantive), but between two substantive somethings. And in so choosing, it is the relative overall strength of each that matters, a verdict Philo is confident any reasonable, unbiased person will render in favour of the naturalistic generation hypothesis.

But none of this subtracts from his own favoured stance, namely, scepticism on all questions of such magnitude and so far in excess of the reach of our experience. Philo, that is, is now arguing simultaneously on two levels and to two audiences: first, against Cleanthes' design hypothesis and for a rival hypothesis, to an audience whose disposition is to endorse the stronger hypothesis overall; and second, against committing to any such hypothesis at all, in the circumstances.

There is nothing disingenuous in this. Both levels of argument are conducted in good faith. The second reflects his own true leanings. But the former is not dishonest or disingenuous. Think of it, Philo's conjectured naturalism that is, as reflecting a common tack in debate, namely, pursuing an issue *for the sake of argument*. That is, pursuing an issue to see where it would come out, when doing so requires granting either assumptions or data that the investigator, in his own right, either doubts or does not accept. And Philo here thinks he can win on both levels, that is, that, either way, the design hypothesis will be seen by reasonable, unbiased persons to come up shorter in both comparisons than the alternatives.

Addressing Demea, but with Cleanthes just as much in mind, Philo develops both themes: that Cleanthes' hypothesis cannot justifiably be reckoned superior overall to the rival naturalism that he himself has conjectured; but that both hypotheses are overall inferior to a prudent scepticism. He presents the first theme as follows. We find four causal principles 'in this little corner of the world', namely, reason, instinct, generation, and vegetation, but who can even guess how may more principles there may be throughout the cosmos as a whole? (DNR: 80). Alert to such variety and multiplicity, it is just a prejudice, 'a palpable and egregious partiality' (DNR: 80), to suppose that human reason is the key to unlock the secrets of nature throughout the whole of the universe. And anyway, we do not even understand how reason works. We do not even understand its workings any better than those of vegetation (DNR: 80).

Perhaps the order in organisms is evidence of design

Demea responds with an idea that surely would occur to any religious believer, confronted with a comprehensive naturalistic account of nature. It is, for instance, not uncommon for theists to respond this way to the Darwinian idea that it is not reason and design that is reflected in the emergence and development of life, but adaptation of organisms to their environments, resulting in the survival and propagation of the most adaptable, the so-called fittest. A fairly common theistic response to that hypothesis is that, perhaps, evolution is the mechanism through which the deity implements the divine plan. In Demea's words, 'this power [of generation and regeneration] would still be an additional argument for design in its Author' (DNR: 80).

This is the first new point to come up in Part VII, the first step to a new level in the conversation. And it is interesting that Hume gives the suggestion to Demea and not to Cleanthes, the committed design theorist. That Hume does so suggests, I think, that to think of natural selection as *itself* evidence of design, thus of intelligence behind the observable universe, is a very natural thought in the circumstances. It does not require any previous commitment to the hypothesis of design in nature. Demea goes on, '[f]or whence could arise so wonderful a faculty but from design? Or how can order spring from any thing, which perceives not that order which it bestows?' (DNR: 80–1). How could blind forces result in a universe such as ours?

It is a natural question. But Philo immediately suggests that the naturalistic hypothesis satisfies it quite well, at least compared to the alternative offered by Cleanthes. Philo invites Demea to look around him. 'A tree bestows order and organization on that tree which springs from it, without knowing the order: an animal, in the same manner, on its offspring: a bird, on its nest' (DNR: 81). All are commonplace instances of order issuing from blind occurrences. But the point, ultimately, is a relative one. Philo makes that point as follows: 'And instances of this kind are even more frequent in the world, than those of order, which arise from reason and contrivance' (DNR: 81). In terms of sheer quantity of experience, we have much more familiarity with blind order than with intended order.

But Philo is aware that this answer does not really satisfy the question that Demea is asking. Indeed, in a deep sense, Philo's response so far does not really address the question at all. For what the religious believer will urge in regard to trees, animals, birds, and so on bestowing order on their respective offspring is this: that, true enough, the trees, animals, and birds are unaware of what they are doing, but is it not reasonable to believe that, behind all those blind occurrences, there is a master intelligence and a master plan? The believer will suggest that the deity works through blind nature. And merely to emphasize that there is a vast amount of order generated by living organisms, unaware of what they are doing, does nothing at all to make the believer stop and think that, perhaps, there is no master intelligence behind the scenes, no puppeteer pulling the strings, so to speak.

Philo's response: begging the question and scepticism

Begging the question

Now that we have the religious believer's real, or deep, question out in the open, what does Philo say? This: 'To say that this order in animals and vegetables proceeds ultimately from design is begging the question; nor can that great point be ascertained otherwise than by proving *a priori*, both that order is, from its nature, inseparably attached to thought, and that it can never, of itself, or from original unknown principles, belong to matter' (DNR: 81).

There are two things here that need to be kept distinct. On one of them, Philo is right; while, on the other, the situation is more ambiguous. But, very briefly, before getting to those two things, two points of terminology: first, recall that *a priori* means from first principles alone, with no help from experience; and second, 'begging the question' is the name of the fallacy a person commits when he or she presupposes as true the very thing that is supposedly being proved. In effect, to beg the question in an argument is to argue in a circle. Now back to the two things that, in Philo's response to Demea's very natural suggestion, we must keep distinct.

The two things are these: on the one hand, *proving* that there is a master plan or mind behind the (in themselves) blind operations of plant and animal generation and regeneration, and on the other, *keeping open the possibility* that there is a master plan or mind behind blind nature. Philo's 'begging the question' response targets the first of these two things, not the second. His point is that such a plan or mind can never be established from the experiential evidence. Or, to put the same point in different language, we have no experiential evidence to defeat the rival naturalistic hypothesis that there is no plan at all behind blind natural forces. And in this Philo is right. But the second of the two things we distinguished between, the possibility of a master plan behind the seemingly blind processes by which nature reproduces itself, remains open. Philo's response does nothing to shut that down.

But Philo's response was *never intended* to block that possibility. If anything, the contrary. In other words, it is *scepticism* about ultimate explanations of natural forces that is aided here. The supernaturalistic possibility remains open. But so does the rival naturalistic one. And the point is that we have no evidence available to us to prove or disprove either one. The only way we can claim victory either way would be to beg the question against one of the two possibilities. But that would be only a sham victory, not a real one.

Scepticism

In responding to Demea's natural, and very good, question, it is his sceptical agenda that, in the last analysis, Philo advances. He has introduced a naturalistic hypothesis, specifically a biological hypothesis, as a possible explanation of order and change in nature. And he has told us that, if somehow forced (against his better judgement) to choose between the supernaturalistic and naturalistic hypotheses, he would choose the latter (DNR: 76). But the real point is that he does not choose. For he is an evidentialist in such matters. And he wants to remind Cleanthes that so is he. The evidence to warrant choosing one of the two hypotheses over the other is just not there, which is but another way of articulating the sceptic's position. As we will see him say in a slightly different context in a moment, '[t]he matter seems entirely arbitrary' (DNR: 81).

But if that is so, why does Philo say that, if forced to choose, he would choose naturalism over supernaturalism? It might be objected against him that surely a consistent scepticism would forbid even that. But the objection would fail. The reason is this: Philo thinks that there is a better balance of evidence for naturalism than for supernaturalism; but he does not think this better balance is good enough to justify believing that naturalism is true. In his words, '[j]udging by our limited and imperfect experience, generation has some privileges above reason: For we see every day the latter arise from the former, never the former from the latter' (DNR: 81). Scepticism does not mean that all substantive positions are equal, that none is more probable, on the available evidence, than another.

Back to Cleanthes' accusation in Part IV that Philo is a Pyrrhonistic sceptic about explanation

Aside from a few remarks at the very end, Cleanthes is silent in Part VII. But his presence is felt throughout. Indeed, here in Part VII, Demea has in effect been functioning as a sort of mouthpiece for a Cleanthes-like approach. And now, at this stage in his response to Demea's questions, Philo makes an explicit connection to Cleanthes. It is to insist that the line of thinking that Demea has just been venturing, namely, that surely the occurrence of natural order through generation is itself 'an additional argument for design' (DNR: 80), could never be self-consistently made by Cleanthes. Philo is here reverting to Cleanthes' accusation in Part IV that his, Philo's, criticism at that time leads to complete scepticism about explanation of anything at all (DNR: 65). Philo's criticism at that point was that it is always open to us to ask about the source of the order in the alleged author of nature itself. Recalling Cleanthes' point from that earlier place in the conversation, Philo now turns it to his own sceptical, purpose, as follows: 'We must stop somewhere, says [Cleanthes]; nor is it ever within the reach of human capacity to explain ultimate causes, or show the last connections of any objects. It is sufficient, if the steps, so far as we go, are supported by experience and observation' (DNR: 81).

Recall that, at the time, Cleanthes had been objecting, reasonably enough, to Philo that, if Philo insisted on an answer to every follow-up question that could arise in an inquiry, we would never be able to explain anything at all. Cleanthes' idea at the time was that this was clearly an absurd consequence of Philo's position, thereby evidence of absurdly extreme scepticism in that position itself. But now, here in Part VII, having reminded Cleanthes of those earlier remarks, Philo goes on:

> Now that vegetation and generation, as well as reason, are experienced to be principles of order in nature, is undeniable. If I rest my system . . . on the former, preferably to the latter, it is at my choice. The matter seems entirely arbitrary. And when Cleanthes asks me what is the cause of my great vegetative or generative faculty, I am equally entitled to ask him the cause of his great reasoning principle.

> (DNR: 81)

We are unable to give a good, that is, experience-based, conclusive, answer either way. Both mutually-exclusive hypotheses, naturalism and supernaturalism, remain open. And to see *that* is seeing the whole dispute through the sceptic's eyes.

Thus, Philo, agreeing that his conjectured naturalism cannot finally defeat Cleanthes' supernaturalism, finesses the discussion into a strong case for the position that he holds in its own right, and that is scepticism.

Scepticism and naturalism (again)

But Philo is not dispassionate in so developing his case for scepticism. He doubly jibes Cleanthes throughout. First, by insisting that the logic of Cleanthes' own earlier protest leads Cleanthes to suspension of belief here in regard to a supposed master mind behind the processes of generation and regeneration. And second, by continuing to remind Cleanthes that, scepticism aside, the balance of evidence better favours the naturalistic over the supernaturalistic hypothesis. Philo repeats the latter point as follows:

> The steps [in my naturalistic inference], I confess, are wide; yet there is some small appearance of analogy in each step ... The steps [in Cleanthes' supernaturalistic inference] are ... equally wide, and the analogy less striking ... I have at least some faint shadow of experience ... Reason, in innumerable instances, is observed to arise from the principle of generation, and never to arise from any other principle.

> (DNR: 82)

This is a powerful point on which, surely, Philo is right. We *do* have vast, repeated, experience of intelligence developing in physical organisms. And we have no experience whatsoever of intelligence apart from physical organisms. Thus, insofar as such experience goes, the naturalistic account of mind and intelligence is stronger than any supernaturalistic rival account.

Cleanthes' insistence on the futility of scepticism

Part VII ends on the topic of scepticism, but not as the best outcome of discussions about natural religion. Instead, it is the negative face of scepticism that is shown here. For the final note in Part VII is Cleanthes' response to Philo's two-level attack on the design hypothesis. While offering no counter-argument, Cleanthes maintains that

Philo has simply lost touch with reality, that his argument amounts to nothing more than an assembling of 'out-of-the-way difficulties' (DNR: 83). Without offering any specifics, Cleanthes insists that he 'clearly see[s], in general, their fallacy and error' (DNR: 83), but that they are too many and far-fetched to go into their details. In addition to the *ad hominem* flavour in those remarks, Cleanthes resorts to another argument-device that students of logic classify as a fallacy, namely, the fallacy known as *ad populum*. This is the fallacy of supposing that a particular opinion must be false just because it is widely disbelieved. Cleanthes' version is this: 'common sense and reason is entirely against you' (DNR: 83).

But this accusation rings odd. For Philo has been *arguing*, albeit indirectly, for a sceptical stance as the most prudent, while Cleanthes, who has been silent, here offers no argument or reason to reject Philo's case, other than the sheer fact that it reflects scepticism. To Cleanthes, scepticism is still a one-size-fits-all position, hopelessly at odds with reason and experience. The irony, though, is that Philo's case for scepticism regarding religion relies on reason and experience. At any rate, the last words in Part VII, spoken by Cleanthes, are these: 'such whimsies, as you have delivered, may puzzle, but never can convince us' (DNR: 83). These are telling words, for they virtually repeat Hume's own words about Pyrrhonistic scepticism in his *Enquiry concerning Human Understanding*. There, Hume had said this: 'sceptical . . . arguments . . . admit of no answer and produce no conviction. Their only effect is to cause that momentary amazement and irresolution and confusion, which is the result of scepticism' (EHU: 155, n.1)

An oddity in Cleanthes' closing remarks

There is something very odd in these remarks of Cleanthes' here at the end of Part VII. As we just saw, he responds to the sceptical tenor of Philo's case. And, to be sure, as we also saw, scepticism is indeed the outcome that Philo desires to reach. But the odd thing about Cleanthes' response is that Philo's naturalistic hypothesis poses a far more dangerous threat to Cleanthes' position than scepticism does, or ever could. And that is especially so, if Cleanthes is right to view scepticism as a one-size-fits-all, sheerly negative, position. For scepticism on the subject of natural religion infects supernaturalism and naturalism equally, and the worst result that either would face could be interpreted as a 'no decision'. But if a strong case is made out for naturalism, then, proportionately, the supernaturalistic position is weakened, and could, in theory, be shown to be false. But no success of scepticism's could ever, in the very nature of things, establish that. So it is odd that Cleanthes, in his summary response here at the close of Part VII, does not respond at all to the threat that, in principle, could have the more serious consequences for his own position. He sees, of course, that scepticism is really Philo's desired destination. But that does not change the fact that Cleanthes' theory has more to lose from an ascendant naturalism than from an ascendant scepticism.

'The old Epicurean hypothesis' (*Dialogues*, Part VIII)

Part VIII opens with Philo contesting Cleanthes' dismissal of him as just a naysayer, in Cleanthes' wholly negative sense of the word 'sceptic'. So understood, a sceptic's criticisms of the design hypothesis need not be taken seriously. Philo's response continues to be that, in the circumstances, the sceptic is being prudent, that 'in such questions as the present . . . [questions not] adapted to the narrow compass of human reason . . . a hundred contradictory views may preserve a kind of imperfect analogy; and invention has here full scope to exert itself' (DNR: 84). Philo's scepticism is the view that 'for aught [anybody] knows' (DNR: 71), virtually anything could be true of the ultimate 'springs and principles of the universe' (DNR: 49). And presently we will see Part VIII close as it opens, with Philo emphasizing the good sense of a sceptical response to intellectual ambitions such as Cleanthes'.

'The old Epicurean hypothesis'

Among the 'hundred contradictory views' that have plausibility, there is what Philo calls 'the old Epicurean hypothesis' (DNR: 84). While quickly disclaiming it as 'the most absurd system, that has yet been proposed' (DNR: 84), Philo proceeds to offer a modified version of it that must strike any unbiased reader as certainly *not* the most absurd

137

system yet proposed. By now, of course, we know that Hume, by having Philo so disclaim allegiance to the theory, is building in deniability for himself, should the need for it arise.

Finite and infinite

Let us suppose that matter is finite. This represents Hume's modification of the ancient Epicureans' argument that, in the last analysis, the universe is made up of combinations of an infinite number of atomic particles. If the supposition is granted, even if only for the sake of argument, then it follows that there is only a finite number of possible combinations of those particles. So, in an eternal universe, all possible combinations of particles will repeat an infinite number of times. Note that, in Philo's 'Epicurean' hypothesis, matter is finite, but time is infinite. That is, the universe is finite in the sense that the number of its contents is finite, but it is infinite in duration (DNR: 84). The idea is one that, in various forms, present-day physics takes seriously: one such form, for instance, is the idea of a universe that continues to expand until it reaches the possible limits of expansion, then it contracts back upon itself until the limits of contraction are reached, and then it expands again, and so on and on for ever without end.

What about the origin of motion?

Demea raises an interesting objection. It is that Philo's hypothesis 'supposes . . . that matter can acquire motion, without any voluntary agent or first mover' (DNR: 84).

This interjection is interesting in several ways. First, it continues from Part VII the practice of Demea, not Cleanthes, engaging in the give-and-take of argument over the design hypothesis; Cleanthes prefers to peremptorily dismiss Philo lock, stock, and barrel, without getting into the specifics of his arguments. And by now the irony will be lost on no one. For we see Cleanthes, who accuses Philo of sheer dogmatism in tilting towards scepticism, his accusation of 'the most perverse, obstinate metaphysics' (DNR: 56) being just one example, here refusing to engage in open debate, preferring, with few exceptions, to proclaim Philo a sceptic, thus a crank, thus not needing to be treated seriously. Who really is the dogmatist?

Demea's interjection also brings a rival ancient idea into play, namely, that the basic condition of matter is rest, thus that any deviation from rest, which is to say, motion, needs explanation. And third, Demea's objection keeps Cleanthes' designer hypothesis before us, with its suggestion than no explanation of motion could be ultimate which did not include an *intention* to introduce motion into a universe that, in its own right, is absolutely static. And if the ultimate condition of matter *is* rest, then no material explanation of motion could succeed.

Philo's immediate response to Demea recalls his point in Part VII that to think of order as an add-on to matter just begs the very question at issue, and in a manner favourable to the design hypothesis. And likewise here, in regard to motion. As Philo, with some illustrations (DNR: 84), now puts the point: 'The beginning of motion in matter itself is as conceivable *a priori* as its communication from mind and intelligence' (DNR: 85). In the absence of evidence to settle the point, or even to justify a tilt towards the design hypothesis, to assume that motion requires a non-material, non-naturalistic, explanation is just a prejudice. But not just that. Such an assumption would actually be going in the face of the evidence, albeit limited, that *is* available to us. In Philo's words: 'whatever the causes are, the fact is certain, that matter is, and always has been in continual agitation, *as far as human experience or tradition reaches*' (DNR: 85, emphasis added). 'There is not probably, at present, in the whole universe, one particle of matter at absolute rest' (DNR: 85). *That*, if anything at all substantive, is what Philo thinks the evidence warrants believing.

A kind of 'Big Bang' theory

Philo now doubles back to pick up the issue in the terms in which we met it prior to Part VIII, that is, as the issue of accounting for order in the material universe. To just what problem must a naturalistic hypothesis suggest a plausible solution? Philo deftly states the issue as follows: 'Is there a system, an order, an oeconomy of things, by which matter can preserve that perpetual agitation, which seems essential to it, and yet maintain a constancy in the forms, which it produces?' (DNR: 85). His answer: 'There certainly is such an oeconomy: For this is actually the case with the present world' (DNR: 85). The world's structure may have the 'appearance of art and contrivance' (DNR: 85), but this effect is wholly produced by 'the continual motion of matter ... in less than infinite transpositions' (DNR: 85). That is to say, stable structures are one possible outcome of a finite number of combinations of a finite number of basic particles over infinite time.

How is this combination of stability and ceaseless change to be explained? Hume offers the following conjecture, which I shall set out as a series of numbered steps: (1) suppose an initial enormous force, 'a blind, unguided force' (DNR: 86), for instance, the Big Bang of present-day physics' best theory of the cosmos; (2) this initial force throws the particles into motion, all of them in motion at once; (3) this motion is completely random; particles collide, repel each other, destroy each other, the survivors collide again, and so on; there is no pattern at all in these occurrences; (4) some of these collisions of particles result in some particles bonding together; (5) some of these bondings are destroyed, that is, ripped apart, in subsequent collisions with other particles; but at the same time, (6) others among these bondings are not torn apart, but hold; (7) some of these surviving particle-collections bond with others among the unattached particles that collide with them, as well as with other structures of bonded particles; (8) in this way, more complex bondings are formed, and some of them endure; (9) these bondings do not halt the motion of the bonded particles, the bonds are such that the particles in motion remain bonded with other particles, which, on the hypothesis, are also in constant motion; (10) over billions of years more and more such particle-structures are formed, and many of them have become complex; (11) in addition, some have become large, and some of those very large. In this step-by-step way, a world such as ours is formed. It is a world of both macroscopic and microscopic objects of many sorts. These objects are stable structures. But each one of them is made up of an enormous number of particles, each of which remains in motion, although without flying out of its bonds with other particles in motion. The world thus formed is both a stable structure in its own right and contains within itself stable objects of various shapes and sizes, each of which has its own complex structure of particles in cease-less motion.

What explains the initial bondings, that is to say, those in the period just after the Big Bang-like force creates particles in various random motions? Nothing but chance. Those initial bondings result only from random collisions among particles in random motion. It just so happens that some particles attach to others, and that those attachments or bonds are stronger than the force of other particles' collisions with them. Thus, certain bondings survive, and become more complex.

On this 'Epicurean' hypothesis, the question, Why do the parti-cles bond initially?, is on a par with the question, Why do the particles collide?, or the question, Why do they move? To all, the answer is the same; they just do. Or the question, Why is there force? There just is. Those are the basic, brute facts. And, Philo goes on;

> is it not possible that [the universe] may settle at last, so as not to lose its motion and active force (for that we have supposed inherent in it), yet so as to preserve an uniformity of appearance, amidst the continual motion and fluctuation of its parts? This we find to be the case with the universe at present. Every individual is perpetually changing, and every part of every individual, and yet the whole remains, in appearance, the same . . . may not this account for all the appearing wisdom and contrivance which is in the universe?

(DNR: 86)

Philo does not claim this hypothesis is true, and neither does he endorse it as his own position. Consistent with his scepticism, he could not do either one of these things. But he does maintain that, given the avail-able evidence, it is a 'plausible' hypothesis (87). And, he obviously thinks, a more plausible hypothesis than its theistic rival.

His thinking here, then, is this; if we insist on pushing forward our speculations on the ultimate explanation of order in nature, the naturalistic 'Epicurean' hypothesis is more plausible than Cleanthes' theistic alternative. But, to repeat, he recommends scepticism over both of them.

Hume's anticipation of a theory of evolution by natural selection

Philo immediately goes on to conjecture that the 'Epicurean' particle theory he has just sketched out may explain the existence and behaviour of organisms too, both plant and animal life-forms. This conjecture amounts to an anticipation, in broad outline, of an evolution-by-natural-selection theory such as Darwin's in the nineteenth century. The objective of this additional conjecture remains the same as Philo's original conjecture about non-living things. That objective is to undercut the theistic supposition that order in nature, whether in living or non-living things, is a wonder and a marvel demanding special explanation.

Applying his 'Epicurean' hypothesis to organisms, Philo maintains: 'It is in vain, therefore, to insist upon the uses in the parts of animals or vegetables, and their curious adjustment to each other. I would fain know how an animal could subsist, unless its parts were so aligned?' (DNR: 87). We may take this on two levels at once: first, as a point about the internal structure of an animal or vegetable body; and second, as a point about an animal or vegetable body's self-adaptation to its environment. Generalizing, Philo then asks: 'And if [this] were not so, could the world subsist? Must it not dissolve as well as the animal, and pass through new positions and situations; till in a great, but finite succession, it fall at last into the present or some such order?' (DNR: 87).

At both the level of individual organisms and of the universe as a whole, Philo's hypothesis is that structures, organic structures, say, that happen to have formed strong bonds among their component particles, and whose parts function in a way that is conducive to the organism's successful adaptation to its environment, survive. Those that do not form such bonds do not survive. That is the core idea in natural-selection theories.

Cleanthes' objection and victory claim, and scepticism again

Breaking his silence, Cleanthes responds condescendingly. Noting that Philo had introduced his naturalistic hypothesis by saying that it had just then occurred to him, Cleanthes tells Philo he can fully believe that it was a spur-of-the-moment hypothesis, that it is half-baked at best. There are, Cleanthes assures him, 'insuperable objections' to it (DNR: 87). However, no list of such deadly objections is forthcoming. Instead, Cleanthes offers this one objection: that Philo's account of the emergence and preservation of order through the unguided actions of blind forces could never explain 'whence arise the many conveniences and advantages which men and all animals possess' (DNR: 87). Why, for instance, do we have two eyes? So useful, but how improbable if there is no benevolent guidance at work behind the scenes in nature, if it is just unscripted occurrences all the way down. And why would domestic farm animals have come to be, if all there is is blind nature? Cleanthes brings it to this point, namely, that 'any *one* of [these] is a sufficient proof of design, and of a benevolent design, which gave rise to the order and arrangement of the universe' (DNR: 87, emphasis added).

This is the first time that Cleanthes attributes benevolence (or any moral attribute) to the deity. Up to now, his inference has been only to a designer possessing intelligence and intentionality of a certain human-like kind. It is also notable that Cleanthes' objection makes clear that, in his conception of the universe, the universe exists for the benefit of human beings (and maybe other animate life-forms too).

Turning now to the substance of Cleanthes' objection, it seems clear that it carries little weight. If our species had not evolved on this planet, then others would, or might, whether other variations on primate life or life-forms of a quite different sort. And a Cleanthes-like objection could be made against any attribute in their make-up too; why *this* feature?, or that? And so on for any feature at all. Why do we have skin, for instance? At one level, it is a silly question. Our having skin is not an additional fact about our make up. Without some skin-like coating, no primate life could exist at all. And so on for many features of any life-form we care to imagine. The basic point is that, given the occurrence of *some* situations – for instance, the emergence of certain stable, enduring, forms of life, whether plant or animal – there have to be certain features without which those life-forms simply could not exist at all. And if those necessary features were not in place, then *others* would obtain, *other* life-forms, for instance. And then the same question could be asked about those; why do *these* features of those life-forms exist? And so on, without end, for any situation that nature throws up. As Philo said, 'I would fain know how an animal could subsist, unless its parts were so aligned?' (DNR: 87).

At bottom, Cleanthes' objection seems to reduce to the question: why is there anything rather than just nothing at all? And, even assuming that this is an intelligible question, it gets us absolutely nowhere. For a thinker like Philo has only to point out that the question, Why something rather than just nothing at all?, takes in the supposed Author of nature too. And, for reasons that will become very clear in Part IX, Cleanthes cannot block that inevitable widening of that question by suggesting that the Author of nature *had* to exist, or that the existence of the Author of nature is a self-explaining fact, unlike all other facts. In short, far from Cleanthes' objection's not being 'insuperable', it has scarcely any weight or force at all.

In responding, Philo ignores the substance of Cleanthes' objection, and instead goes straight to the point he has been consistent all along in wanting to establish, namely, that scepticism is the warranted and sensible position to adopt in such matters. In his words, a 'total suspense of judgment is here our only reasonable resource' (DNR: 88–9).

Philo makes that point this way. In the first place, he does not dispute Cleanthes' claim that his hypothesis is 'incomplete and imperfect' (DNR: 88). He agrees, even emphasizes, that it is. After all, in the circumstances, what else could ever reasonably be expected? (DNR: 88). But what of Cleanthes' own hypothesis? How does that fare? Much worse, in Philo's estimation. Repeating earlier criticisms of Cleanthes' hypothesis, Philo again gives us good reason to agree with him that the theistic hypothesis of design fares less well than his own naturalistic, natural-selection hypothesis, which, in its turn, makes a less compelling claim on our minds than the sceptic's advice to suspend all final verdicts on such ultimate questions.

Those repeated criticisms are these: (1) Experience shows us that 'ideas are copied from real objects, and are ectypal, not archetypal' (DNR: 88). That is to say, in the final analysis, ideas are copies (ectypes) of things and situations, not the prototypes (archetypes) of things and situations. (This is Philo's variation on his point in Part VII that experience shows us reason emerging from generation, not vice versa: the empirical data suggest matter before mind, not mind before matter.) (2) Where thought or reason *does* influence matter, it is never found to be pure, detached, mental substance, existing separately in its own right, that does the influencing. Rather, mind affecting matter is always found in situations 'where ... matter is so conjoined with it, as to have an equal reciprocal influence upon it' (DNR: 88). (This is a variation on two points that Philo made earlier: first, that Cleanthes' theory presupposes some literal form of mind–body dualism, whereas, second, all the experiential evidence points to mind only in conjunction with matter, and maybe even to the mind itself being material. On the second of these two points, recall Philo's controversial line in Part II, 'this little agitation of the brain which we call thought' (DNR: 50) and his discussion of pantheism in Part VI (DNR: 73)). (3) *All* theories and conjectures on such questions as those which preoccupy natural religion are vulnerable to embarrassing criticisms that expose their significant gaps, and this is no less true, arguably more so, of 'all religious systems' than of naturalistic ones, for 'all religious systems ... are subject to great and insuperable difficulties' (DNR: 88, note his adoption of Cleanthes' word, 'insuperable'). (4) The outcome is stalemate, thus 'a complete triumph for the sceptic; who tells [us], that no system ought ever to be embraced with regard to such subjects' (DNR: 88).

At the close of Part VIII, Cleanthes' design hypothesis, notwithstanding the relative ease with which, in certain circumstances, it occurs to us, seems doubly at a disadvantage. In the first place, upon examination, it does not seem to be more plausible than the rival naturalistic hypothesis developed by Philo, whereas we were led to think by Cleanthes that it would be clearly recognized as superior to any rivals. Recall his promise in Part I that we would find 'the religious hypothesis ... [to be] founded on the simplest and *most obvious* arguments' (DNR: 40, my emphasis). Then, second, we have seen good reason to think that any substantive hypothesis, whether naturalistic or supernaturalistic, concerning 'the creation and formation of the universe; the existence and properties of spirits' (DNR: 36–7), and such like, may simply be beyond the powers of our understanding. Either way, then, we seem to have good reason not to accept the design hypothesis.

Chapter 8

Further weakening
of natural religion

(*Dialogues*, Part IX)

Introduction

The philosophical case for the existence of a deity is further weakened in Part IX. This occurs in two ways. First, Demea presents an argument for the existence of God that withers under devastating criticism from Cleanthes; and second, Philo offers a new suggestion to increase the plausibility of the naturalistic hypothesis that he sketched out in Parts VI, VII, and VIII. Demea's argument is a version of what is often called 'the cosmological argument', essentially an argument to prove that the cosmos or physical universe itself had a cause. If it did, then, being itself outside the physical universe, that cause would be something non-physical.

Part IX differs from the other eleven parts of Hume's *Dialogues* in two ways. First, unlike the *Dialogues* overall, it is largely about logical necessity, and the principal argument discussed in it is deductive, not inductive. Essentially, a deductive argument aims to prove that, once its premises are granted, its conclusion

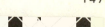

necessarily follows; that is to say, that its conclusion *has* to follow, there being (allegedly) no other possibility open. By contrast, an inductive argument aims to prove that, once its premises are granted, its conclusion probably follows. Cleanthes' design argument in Part II, for instance, is an inductive argument. The second difference between Part IX and the rest of the book is that, except transitionally at the beginning, the subject of scepticism does not come up in it at all.

Demea's case for a necessary first cause

Part IX opens with Demea accepting Philo's sceptical criticisms of Cleanthes' arguments. But, on the issue of the deity's existence itself, he does not think that scepticism is warranted. And neither does he think that scepticism undercuts all proofs of the existence of a deity. For Demea is convinced that, if we replace Cleanthes' inductive argument with the right sort of deductive argument, then the existence of the deity can indeed be proven. Thus, granting Philo's criticisms of Cleanthes, Demea thinks the lesson to be learned is that we had 'better adhere to that simple and sublime argument *a priori*, which, by offering to us infallible demonstration, cuts off at once all doubt and difficulty' (DNR: 90).

The terms 'demonstration' and 'a priori'

Before going further, let us be clear about the meaning of 'demonstration'. The word has a quasi-technical meaning in philosophy that is a bit at odds with how we use the word in everyday contexts. As philosophers use it, to demonstrate something means to prove it. Even more than that, it means to prove it in the strictest possible sense. A successful demonstration, then, in the relevant sense, leaves no doubt behind, no possible doubt at all; a successful demonstration necessitates its conclusion. To demonstrate that something is true, then, is to prove it deductively. Outside the world of philosophy, by contrast, to demonstrate something often means pointing it out or giving it a trial run, a salesperson demonstrating a vacuum cleaner to a potential customer, for instance.

Demea describes his argument as *a priori*. Recall from the first chapter that the domain of the *a priori* is that of the purely conceptual, approximating pretty much to the domains of formal logic and mathematics. The term of contrast, as we know, is *a posteriori*. As used by Hume and many others before and since, the domain of the *a posteriori* is that of things that, at least in principle, could be experienced by us through our senses. Even the best *a posteriori* proofs would not eliminate all possible doubt; all reasonable doubt, perhaps, but not all possible doubt. For instance, it might be said that O.J. Simpson's guilt in the murders of his ex-wife and her friend is beyond all reasonable doubt; but it is not beyond all possible doubt. There is no formal contradiction in saying that he is not guilty, thus, saying he is not guilty does not have to be false. It happens to be false, surely, but it does not have to be false.

By offering an *a priori* demonstration, Demea intends three things. The first is that, unlike Cleanthes' *a posteriori* argument, his will not rely on experience. Instead, it will use only propositions which, he thinks, have to be true, for instance, that nothing exists without a cause, together with logical relations among such propositions. Second, his argument will be deductive, not, like Cleanthes' arguments, inductive. Third, and in consequence of the first two points together, he intends (and expects) his argument to place the existence of the deity beyond all possible doubt.

Is Demea inconsistent?

Can Demea really mean what he is saying here? Can he really be proposing an argument to prove the existence of the deity? Recall that, in both Parts I and II, Demea emphasized the narrow limits of human reason, and that, at the beginning of Part II, he strongly disapproved of Cleanthes' proposal to (inductively) prove the existence of a deity (DNR: 43). Back then, Demea insisted that the existence of the deity was simply 'unquestionable and self-evident', as Philo described his thinking at the time (DNR: 44). Against this background, how can he himself now be setting out to prove the existence of God? What sense can it possibly make to undertake to prove something he regards as self-evident? Has he forgotten his earlier position? Has he changed his mind? Is he simply being inconsistent?

Perhaps he is being inconsistent. I do not think we can eliminate the possibility. But neither is inconsistency the only reasonable interpretation. My own idea is that Demea is not inconsistent, and briefly I will suggest why.

What does it mean that something is self-evident? Self-evident to whom? And in what circumstances? Does Demea mean that the existence of the deity is self-evident to infants or the mentally incompetent? I do not think he means this at all. Does he mean that it is obvious to mentally competent adults at every moment in their waking lives? I do not think he means that either. What then? I think he means that the existence of the deity is self-evident and obvious to any mentally competent adult who thinks about it. But there is thinking about it and thinking about it. So we need a further clarification. What Demea means, I am suggesting, is that anybody who thinks about it *in the right sort of way* will recognize the obviousness and self-evidence of the deity's existence. What way is the right sort? To Demea, the right sort of way is *a priori* and deductive, that is, reasoning deductively from necessarily true first principles. It is not empirical. It does not involve building up a case from aspects of our experience of the world. For such experience, given its limits, must proportionately limit any conclusion based on it, which is his reason to reject Cleanthes' approach.

Let us now examine what Demea believes is the right way of coming to see that the deity exists.

Demea's argument

His argument, Demea assures us, is 'the common one' (DNR: 90). And if my suggestion just above is right, it would have to be. For if his argument is to provide a setting in which we come to see the self-evidence of divine existence, then it cannot be a remote, or difficult, or unusual argument.

The steps in his argument are these:

1. 'Whatever exists must have a cause or reason of its existence; it being absolutely impossible for any thing to produce itself, or be the cause of its own existence' (DNR: 90); let us refer to this as the first principle of causation,

so,

2. if we ask for the cause of some thing or event, whatever that thing or event might be, we will be led to some prior thing or event, and if, in turn, we ask for the cause of that, then we will be led to some yet prior thing or event, and so on and on, either to infinity or, until 'at last [we] have recourse to some ultimate cause, that is *necessarily* existent' (DNR: 90); and there is no third alternative,

but,

3. the first of these alternative outcomes, the eternal-universe option, can be proved to be absurd; for, while it would give a cause of the existence of each individual item in the infinite series, it would leave the series as a whole, which of course is a thing too, without any cause; so, that first alternative can be dismissed as violating the first principle of causation (DNR: 90),

so,

4. only the second alternative remains, namely, there has to be some ultimate cause that necessarily exists (DNR: 91),

but,

5. that ultimate cause would have to be 'a necessarily existent Being, who carries the reason of his existence in himself; and who cannot be supposed not to exist without an express contradiction' (DNR: 91),

consequently,

6. '[t]here is . . . such a Being, that is, there is a Deity' (DNR: 91).

Essentially, the gist of the argument is that, as everything has a cause other than itself, the universe as a whole, which is also a thing, must have a cause other than itself too. But this reasoning will only provide *an intellectually satisfactory* account of the cause of the universe, which the first principle of causation seems to require, if that cause does not itself have a prior cause. That is, the cause of the universe must be the ultimate or first cause. Reason demands it, otherwise we will be facing into the first alternative. But, Demea believes, Step 3 in his argument shows that alternative to be absurd. Thus, the ultimate cause must both be the cause of itself and must exist necessarily, that is, it could not not exist.

This is the context of thinking about the deity in which, according to Demea, it will be obvious and self-evident to us that God exists.

Is Demea's conclusion self-evident?

Neither self-evidence nor obviousness is necessarily the same as simplicity. Sometimes obvious or self-evident things are simple, but they do not have to be. Now it seems pretty clear that Demea's argument is not simple. Neither is it uncontroversial. It raises obvious questions; for instance, how do we justify the idea that the first cause of the universe does not itself need a prior cause? Or the idea that the universe itself, even if it is eternal, does? There may be good answers to these questions; we do not want to pre-judge. But that such questions come up right away is enough to convince us that any obviousness or self-evidence that Demea's argument might establish will be obviousness or self-evidence only for those who carefully follow the argument. In other words, paradoxically, the obviousness or self-evidence, if any, that the premises in Demea's argument bring us to seeing in its conclusion is not transparent.

Cleanthes' first response to Demea's argument makes just that point. He begins his criticism by calling the argument 'metaphysical' (DNR: 91). By this, he means that the argument is abstract, divorced from both life and religion, of 'little consequence to the cause of true piety and religion' (DNR: 91). A few pages later, Philo will say the same thing: 'the argument *a priori* has seldom been found very convincing, except to people of a metaphysical head, who have accustomed themselves to abstract reasoning' (DNR: 93). If both Cleanthes and Philo are right about this, Demea's argument will fail to bring people at large to see that the existence of the deity is obvious or self-evident. For, to be that, it must reflect a 'common' line of thinking, in one common meaning of the word 'common'.

Our suspicion has to be that Demea's argument does not demonstrate God's existence in the sense of placing it beyond all doubt for all and sundry. But does it even succeed in demonstrating its conclusion for the intellectual elite who may follow it all the way through? That is a question directed to the substance, not the degree of difficulty, of the argument, so let us take it up by way of examination of Cleanthes' counter-argument.

Cleanthes' criticisms

Cleanthes makes four fundamental criticisms.

'Nothing is demonstrable, unless the contrary implies a contradiction'

First, Cleanthes maintains that,

> there is an evident absurdity in pretending to demonstrate a matter of fact, or to prove it by any arguments *a priori*. Nothing is demonstrable, unless the contrary implies a contradiction. Nothing, that is distinctly conceivable, implies a contradiction. Whatever we conceive as existent, we can also conceive as non-existent. There is no Being, therefore, whose non-existence implies a contradiction. Consequently there is no Being, whose existence is demonstrable.
>
> (DNR: 91; see EHU: 25, 163–4 for the
> same argument in Hume's own voice)

This argument is presented as an 'entirely decisive' rebuttal (DNR: 91). In it, Cleanthes speaks for Hume himself. His point is driven entirely by Hume's fundamental distinction between *a priori* and *a posteriori* truths.

For present purposes, two dimensions of the distinction (Hume's Fork) are notable: first, nothing can be demonstrated, that is, proven in the strictest sense, unless its opposite, its contrary, implies a contradiction; thus, second, the actual existence or the actual occurrence of something can never be demonstrated. What does this mean? And is it true?

What does it mean to say that 'nothing is demonstrable, unless the contrary implies a contradiction'? For instance, could it be demonstrated, in the technical sense of the term we have committed to use, that there are now two books on my desk? Let us see. In trying, perhaps we will get a clear grasp of what Hume (thus Cleanthes, here in criticism of Demea's deductive argument) means. Here, then, for experimental purposes, is an attempt to demonstrate that there are now two books on my desk.

Right now there are seven books on my desk. Therefore, there are now two books on my desk. Is this not a strict proof, a demonstration, of the proposition that now there are two books on my desk? That is, granting the truth of the premise, there are now seven books on my desk (and there are), and given the respective meanings of 'seven' and 'two', does not the conclusion, there are now two books on my desk, have to be true? Yes, it does. So, is not Hume (and also Cleanthes) wrong to insist that the actual existence or occurrence of something can never be demonstrated? No. Why not? Because there is no contradiction in denying the conclusion of my argument, the proposition, 'there are now two books on my desk', although there is a contradiction in denying the proposition, 'there are two books on my desk whenever there are seven books on my desk'.

Hume's point is that a demonstrable proposition is one that can be deduced from propositions that are necessarily true, that is, from propositions that could not possibly be false. An example of such a proposition would be, 'twice two are four', or 'a bachelor is an unmarried man', or 'there are two books on my desk whenever there are seven books on my desk'. A successful demonstrative *argument*, then, is a valid deduction from necessarily true premises, that is, it is an argument whose conclusion really does follow from premises that could not possibly be false. Thus the conclusion in such an argument will be a necessary truth too. On these understandings, it is clear that the proposition, 'there are now two books on my desk' has not been demonstrated, in the strict sense of that term. That is, it has not been proved to be true of necessity. For, even though it does really follow from its premise, that premise, right now there are seven books on my desk, is itself not necessarily true.

The point holds at large. Any proposition that can be denied without self-contradiction is not *necessarily* true, even if it happens to be true as a matter of fact. When any such proposition is true, it just happens to be true, but it did not have to be. For instance, after I clean my desk, the proposition, 'there are now two books on my desk', will (perhaps) be false.

But propositions like that, 'there are now two books on my desk', propositions that just happen to be true (or false), are the only kinds of propositions giving us concrete information about what exists or occurs in the real world. Propositions that are necessarily true, 'there are two books on my desk whenever there are seven books on my desk', have the virtue of necessary truth, but the price they pay for it is that they can never give us concrete information about what exists or occurs in actual fact. For instance, from knowing that there are two books on my desk whenever there are seven books on my desk, I do not know that there are, in actual fact, any books in existence, or desks either, or how many, or where they might be found, and so on. To know any of those things, I have to consult the world, not just the meaning of the words 'book' and 'desk'. To see that this is right, consider the true statement, 'there are two plymys on my oghamam, whenever there are seven plymys on my oghamam'. Does it follow that plymys exist? Or oghamams? (Let me save you a visit to your dictionary. To the best of my knowledge, the words, if they are words, 'plymy' and 'oghamam' have no meaning. I just made them up.)

Cleanthes is essentially presenting Demea with the following dilemma. On the one hand, if his (Demea's) argument is a genuine and successful demonstration, then its conclusion, while necessarily true, will be unable to give us concrete information about what exists or occurs in actual fact. But, on the other hand, if Demea's argument *does*, in its conclusion, give us concrete information about something that exists in actual fact, then that information is not infallible; it is not immune to error or doubt. And the dilemma is that Demea cannot have it both ways. It is one or the other, never both together. Either his argument has the logical virtue of demonstration, at the cost of confining the argument to the realm of the purely conceptual and abstract; or it has the empirical, experiential virtue of real existence, but at the cost of always being open to error and doubt.

This first criticism is summed up in Cleanthes' point that, '[t]he words, *necessary existence*, have no meaning' (DNR: 92).

Perhaps, if anything exists necessarily, the physical universe does

Suppose Cleanthes is wrong. Suppose, for the sake of argument, that there is something whose existence is necessary, something that could not possibly not exist. Why could that thing not be the material universe itself? Why the deity, and only the deity? We do not know the ultimate nature of matter. So, 'for aught we can determine, it may contain some qualities, which, were they known, would make its non-existence appear as great a contradiction as that twice two is five' (DNR: 92). Obviously, given his banishment of necessity from juris-diction over existence, Cleanthes does not think that the universe does in fact exist necessarily. Instead, his point is the relative one that, if the idea of necessary existence were meaningful, then, for all we know, the universe would have as good a claim to it as the deity.

Perhaps the universe is eternal

Furthermore, switching now from the concept 'necessity' to the concept 'eternity', if the universe is indeed eternal, then 'it seems absurd to inquire for a general cause or first Author' (DNR: 92), that is, a cause predating an eternal universe. Cleanthes' point here is meant to establish that, in another way too, if there does in fact exist some-thing not subject to the first principle of causation, then, for all the evidence that Demea has offered, that thing could as well be the universe itself as the deity. Parenthetically, we know from Part VI that Cleanthes himself denies the eternity of the universe (DNR: 74). It is worth observing that this criticism, like its immediate predecessor, relies on a favourite argument-device of *Philo*'s, namely, the sceptical suggestion that, for all we know, such-and-such might very well be the case. It is curious to find it used here by Cleanthes, considering his unreceptivity to it when applied to his own argument.

Very briefly, a side-note. Some adherents to the cosmological argument would reject Cleanthes' supposition that to ascribe a cause to an eternal universe would be absurd. Such thinkers differentiate between the two following kinds of causes: causes that have temporal priority over their effects, and causes that have logical priority over their effects. An example of the former would be my *first* letting go of this book, then its falling to the floor. An example of the latter would be the relationship that the rules of tennis have to the playing of tennis. The rules do not necessarily pre*date* the playing of the game, but no game with a racquet and a ball is tennis unless the rules of that game are in force (at least to a sufficient degree).

The fallacy of composition

Cleanthes now takes up Demea's point that, over and above the cause or explanation of each individual item in the universe, the universe itself needs a cause or explanation:

> But the whole, you say, wants a cause. I answer, that the uniting of these parts into a whole, like the uniting of several distinct counties into one kingdom, or several distinct members into one body, is performed merely by an arbitrary act of the mind, and has no influence on the nature of things. Did I show you the particular causes of each individual in a collection of twenty particles of matter, I should think it very unreasonable, should you afterwards ask me, what was the cause of the whole twenty. This is sufficiently explained in explaining the cause of the parts.
>
> (DNR: 92)

Suppose I am given an explanation of why each of five persons, to all appearances unassociated with one another, are standing at a street corner. This one is waiting for a bus; that one is admiring the building across the way; the third is taking a break from jogging; the fourth is pausing before going into a shop to buy a watch on display in the shop window; while the fifth is awaiting favourable opportunity to snatch the purse of the fourth. Those explanations in hand, suppose I still go on to ask why the *group* is there at the corner. It would be a natural reaction to think that I am confused. It would be natural to think I am asking for a cause that does not exist, there being no cause of the five's being there, over and above the individual causes bringing each person singly to that place now. My follow-up question seems to be based on a misunderstanding of the fact that this group of five is only an arbitrary group, having no group cause. To use an expression introduced by the English philosopher, Gilbert Ryle (1900–76), my follow-up question seems to reflect a 'category mistake'. For there is a *group* here only in the sense that I choose to classify those persons as now constituting one. But the five persons involved are not there as a group; they are not there *together*. And Cleanthes' objection is that the same is (or at least may be) true of the universe, understood as a succession (infinite and eternal, or not) of individual occurrences. That is, the universe is not (or at least may not be) itself another thing requiring or having a cause over and above the cause of each of the occurrences comprising it.

Bertrand Russell gives a very good example of the same thing. It is that to suppose the universe must have a cause, because each item in the universe has a cause, is like supposing that the human race must have a mother because each individual person has a mother. In sum, Cleanthes' point is that to suppose, just because each item in a group or series has a certain property, p, that the group or series itself must also have p, commits the fallacy that logicians call composition.

Rebuttals

To the fallacy-of-composition objection

Demea says nothing in his own behalf. Nor does any other character in the *Dialogues* come to his defence. But let us break ranks with the majority here. Let us see if something can be done to shore up his position.

Let us take the last criticism first; the suggestion that Demea has fallen prey to the fallacy of composition. Clearly, that objection's power depends on the tightness of fit of the analogy at its core. That is to say, if there is a strong resemblance between the universe and the five persons on the street corner, or the human race in Russell's version, then the objection is indeed decisive. For clearly, in those cases, a fallacy is committed in projecting onto the group the relevant characteristic of the individual things comprising it.

But there are examples and then there are examples. And here is another. Suppose I have an explanation of the existence of the case, the glass, the microchip, the hour-, minute-, and second-hands, the strap, and so on for all the parts of my watch, do I thereby have an explanation of the existence of the watch itself? Or may I still legitimately ask about the source or cause of *its* existence, even when armed with an account of the existence of each of its parts? For instance, what if you gave me all of the separate components in a shoebox? Then they would not constitute a watch. Yet, in both cases, all the parts assembled as a watch, and all the separate parts in a shoebox, I have a full and complete, indeed one and the same, explanation of each component. It seems clear that, in both cases, I can inquire about the *watch*'s existence, over and above inquiring about the cause or source of its components. That is, in the former case, I can inquire about the cause of the parts' existing interactively, interconnectedly.

Now which has the closer resemblance to the relationship between the things that comprise the universe, on the one hand, and, on the other, the universe as a whole? Is it the relationship between the individual people on the street corner and those people grouped together? Or is it the relationship between the components in the box and the watch? And, more to the point, how do we tell?

To the last question, the answer is that we cannot tell in a definitive way; we have no clear guideline. We do not know which of the two has the closer resemblance.

The result is that Cleanthes' 'composition' objection is not decisive. It does not refute the cosmological argument. But let us not draw the wrong conclusion from this. For the damage done to the argument by the objection is significant none the less. The objection denies success to the argument; it blocks Demea's argument's access to its conclusion. The reason it does so is that there is no definitive reason to think that the proper analogy is to the box full of watch parts, not the group at the street corner. And without that, there is no way that the cosmological argument's insistence on an answer to its central question, namely, 'What is the cause or explanation of the universe as a whole, over and above the cause or explanation of each item comprising it?,' can be justified.

But the upshot here is not stalemate, with the cosmological argument faring no worse than the 'composition' objection. For the cosmological argument, having been offered to us as a deductive argument, must establish the impossibility of the proposed alternatives, if it is to succeed in establishing that its own conclusion *has* to be true, that is, if it is to succeed in giving the promised 'infallible demonstration' (DNR: 90). But the impossibility of Hume's or Russell's alternatives has not been established. Thus, Demea's argument, understood as a deductive argument, fails.

To the existence-is-not-demonstrable objection

Let us now see about defending Demea against Cleanthes' first criticism; that nothing can be demonstrated to exist, and that the idea of necessary existence is, strictly speaking, meaningless. As we saw, that criticism turns on Cleanthes' (and Hume's) distinction between the supposedly mutually exclusive spheres of the *a priori* and the *a posteriori*, respectively. So, in defence of Demea against this criticism, let us go to its source, that *a priori* versus *a posteriori* distinction itself.

The heart of the distinction may be found in the following line from the *Enquiry concerning Human Understanding*, 'matters of fact . . . are not ascertained . . . by the mere operation of thought' (EHU: 25). As an example of what Hume means by the term 'matter of fact', think of what it means to say, 'there are two books on my desk', and of what would make that statement true and of what would make it false. For Hume, the domain of the *a posteriori* is populated entirely by empirical facts like the fact of two books on my desk, not conceptual facts like 7 plus 5 equals 12.

Now what about Hume's point that 'matters of [empirical] fact . . . are not ascertained . . . by the mere operation of thought' itself? This quoted statement looks like it is stating a fact. But is that an empirical fact or a purely conceptual fact? That is, is the quoted statement itself *a posteriori* or *a priori*? And how do we tell?

If it is *a priori*, then, by Hume's own lights, it cannot tell us anything about what is so in the actual world of our experience. But if it is *a posteriori*, then, it is always subject to falsification, and we could not conclude with certainty that any given case was not an exception to it. Thus, if the quoted statement is *a posteriori*, then Demea could legitimately maintain that his argument's existential or factual conclusion, there exists a being who caused the universe itself, is (or at least may be) an exception to the rule.

The question then is whether this strategy of attacking Hume's Fork successfully defends Demea's argument against the criticism that no argument can *demonstrate* existence. The answer is yes and no.

Yes, it is enough to save the cosmological argument from the refutation that Hume, as Cleanthes, thinks he inflicts upon it. But no, inasmuch as it does not give the cosmological argument enough to prove its conclusion, or even to advance its conclusion. And remember that the point of the cosmological argument is not merely to keep open the *possibility* that there is a necessarily existent cause of the universe. Its point is to prove that there *must* be such a cause. Not being refuted does not do that. Thus, not being refuted does not mean that the argument succeeds. It means only that the argument does not *have* to fail. But that is far less than Demea wanted, and thought he had achieved. It is also far less than he needs, if he is either to demonstrate the existence of the deity or lead us to seeing that the deity's existence is obvious and self-evident.

To the two for-all-we-know objections

For all we know, if something exists necessarily or eternally, it could be the universe. To rebut Cleanthes' second and third objections, it is not necessary to prove that something does exist either necessarily or eternally. What must be proven is that the universe could not possibly be such a thing. That is, the for-all-we-know hypotheses must be shown to be impossible. But I do not know of an argument capable of that.

Philo's naturalistic hypothesis again

So far in Part IX, Philo has been silent. But, given his strict empiricism, we may feel sure that, while we have only a hint to go on directly, he agrees with Cleanthes' reasons to reject Demea's argument. That hint is his comment, 'the reasonings, which you have urged, Cleanthes, may well excuse me . . . from starting any farther difficulties' (DNR: 93). But Philo tells us that Demea's argument, and in particular its emphasis upon the concept of necessity, has suggested 'another topic' to him. This turns out to be an addition to the naturalistic hypothesis he sketched out in Parts VI, VII, and VIII.

Laws of nature

Thus prompted by Demea's argument, Philo suggests that, perhaps, order and regularity in the physical universe reflect a kind of necessity. The necessity he is thinking of would result, perhaps, from the nature of physical things and physical processes themselves. In effect, Philo's suggestion is that maybe the basic laws of physics reflect the ways things have to be, given certain initial conditions, for instance, the 'blind, unguided force' of Part VIII (DNR: 86) or the 'Big Bang' of present-day cosmology. Or, to take a different example, given the atmosphere that exists at the surface of the earth, and given the chemical constitution of water, water *has* to boil at 100 degrees Celsius (212 degrees Fahrenheit) and *has* to freeze at 0 Celsius (32 Fahrenheit), respectively. Arguably, the earth's atmosphere could have been different, and arguably water could have had a different molecular structure (but would it then be water?). But, given that both the atmosphere and the chemical nature of water are what they are, then water *has* to boil at 100 degrees Celsius. This is not logical, but physical (chemical) necessity.

Philo's point is this: if such necessity obtains throughout the whole of the universe, then, order and regularity are not wondrous or additional facts needing to be explained over and above any explanation we might have of the existence of matter in the first place. In Philo's words, 'may it not happen, that, could we penetrate into the intimate nature of bodies, we should clearly see why it was absolutely impossible [that things and events in nature] . . . could ever admit of any other disposition?' (DNR: 93). This suggestion is a variation on two things: Philo's earlier suggestion in Part IV that, perhaps, nature 'contain[s] the principle of its order within itself' (DNR: 64); and Cleanthes' second objection here in Part IX, namely, that, for all we know, the physical universe itself exists necessarily (DNR: 92).

Chapter 9

The problem of evil

(*Dialogues*, Parts X and XI)

Introduction

There is cruelty in abundance in the world. There is also malice, lying, cheating, and theft. There is bad Samaritanship, murder, and torture. There are diseases, birth defects, harmful genetic mutations aplenty. There is cancer and Alzheimer's disease, polio and smallpox, natural disasters galore. All this being so, how can theists possibly 'assert the moral attributes of the Deity . . . to be of the same nature with these virtues in human creatures?' (DNR: 100). This question, put to Cleanthes by Philo, takes us to theism's most vexing, and potentially fatal, problem; its problem of evil.

As we find it in Parts X and XI of the *Dialogues*, the problem of evil is really two problems. In the words of J.C.A. Gaskin, these are the consistency problem and the inference problem (1988: 53, 58). Very recently, he has restated the distinction in this way:

> The consistency problem is the difficulty (perhaps impossibility) of reconciling, or seeing as consistent, the facts of evil in the world and belief in a God who is limitlessly powerful and

163

perfectly good. The inference problem is the difficulty (perhaps impossibility) of inferring from the given facts of the world any particular moral qualities in whatever is argued to be its designing agent. The inference problem is thus the problem for natural religion. The consistency problem is primarily a problem for the already committed religious believer.

(Private correspondence, November 2000)

Hume does not press the consistency problem hard, but he maintains that the inference problem is too much for natural religion. Natural religion's fate, he maintains, is to '[n]ever find any reason for . . . [its] . . . conclusion' (DNR: 106).

This emphasis on the inference problem preserves the overall continuity in the *Dialogues*' subject-matter, namely, the fortunes of natural religion. Furthermore, discussion of the problem of evil restores to prominence the central and most fundamental theme in Hume's examination of natural religion, namely, scepticism, a topic temporarily sidelined in Part IX.

In brief summary, Hume's main conclusions, insofar as evil is concerned, are these: it is logically possible for the known facts of evil and the concept of a supremely good, powerful, and wise deity to co-exist; there is no purely formal or logical contradiction between them; but the known facts of evil convincingly defeat natural religion; even more than that, though, the known facts of evil give us good reason to think that there is no deity, among whose attributes are moral attributes, including caring about us; this last point is Philo's (Hume's) moral atheism, another term of Gaskin's.

Hume's discussion of the problem of evil in the *Dialogues* is a watershed in the philosophy of religion. It is the *locus classicus* of the topic, from which virtually all subsequent discussions have emerged and to which, as often as not, they refer.

Theism's problem of evil (*Dialogues*, Part X)

Demea speaking, and not speaking, for Hume

Part X opens with Demea insisting that, in a sense, 'each man feels . . . the truth of religion within his own breast' (DNR: 95). The point is reminiscent of Cleanthes' 'irregular' argument in Part III, although the feelings that are now emphasized, terror, unworthiness, misery, are quite different to that cited by Cleanthes, namely, wonder at the world's manifest orderliness. With one qualification, Demea is here speaking for Hume himself, thus making each of the principal characters in the book the spokesman, at least once, for the author.

I say that Demea speaks for Hume here because, in these opening remarks, he echoes the fundamental idea in *The Natural History of Religion*, Hume's anthropology of religious belief. Demea's claim is that:

> from a consciousness of his imbecility and misery, rather than from any reasoning, [each man] is led to seek protection from that Being, on whom he and all nature is dependent . . . Wretched creatures that we are! What resource for us amidst the innumerable ills of life, did not religion suggest some methods of atonement, and appease those terrors, with which we are incessantly agitated and tormented?

(DNR: 95)

In these lines we hear something close to Hume's own voice in *The Natural History*: 'men are much oftener thrown on their knees by the melancholy than by the agreeable passions' (NHR: 143), and '[t]he primary religion of mankind arises chiefly from an anxious fear of future events' (NHR: 176).

In another sense, though, Demea, here at the start of Part X, does *not* speak for Hume, although Philo, in agreeing with him, does. What I mean is this. Demea's point is that our fear and dread in face of the unknown brings us to a recognition of 'the truth of religion' (DNR: 95). But, as an expression of Hume's own views, that is potentially misleading, for it might suggest that a person comes to see that there really is a deity such as standard theism (or a close approximation to it) describes. And that is far from being Hume's own position.

Philo, agreeing with Demea, is more circumspect: 'I am indeed persuaded . . . that the best and indeed only method of bringing every one to a due sense of religion is by just representations of the misery and wickedness of men' (DNR: 95). Philo's 'due sense of religion' is more cautious, less committal, than Demea's 'truth of religion'. For all that Philo is agreeing to is that, in dread of an unknown future, and beset with pain and misery and unhappiness, it is *unsurprising* that human beings invoke religion for comfort and hope. Philo's point is that we, in noting this turning to religion in such circumstances, will come to see religion for what it is, a comfort and a refuge, thereby getting a 'due sense' of it. That is, Philo, reflecting the views of Hume himself, accepts the natural emergence of religious belief in certain kinds of common circumstances; but this is far from committing oneself to the truth of religion.

From religious motivation to indictment: Philo's transformation of the question

Demea and Philo agree that, with the exception of the German philosopher, Gottfried Wilhelm Leibniz (1646–1716), everybody recognizes that the human condition is essentially miserable, beset by pain and suffering, both physical and mental. Furthermore, they agree that religion is rooted in that misery (DNR: 95–6). As Demea summarizes the state of nature:

> [t]he whole earth . . . is cursed and polluted. A perpetual war is kindled amongst all living creatures. Necessity, hunger, want, stimulate the strong and courageous: Fear, anxiety, terror, agitate the weak and infirm. The first entrance into life gives anguish to the new-born infant and to its wretched parent: Weakness, impotence, distress, attend each stage of that life: And it is at last finished in agony and horror.
>
> (DNR: 96)

To this Philo adds the psychological terrors that afflict the human mind:

> it is here chiefly . . . that the uniform and equal maxims of nature are most apparent. Man, it is true, can, by combination, surmount all his *real* enemies . . . But does he not immediately raise up to himself *imaginary* enemies . . . who haunt him with superstitious terrors, and blast every enjoyment of life?. . . [T]his very society, by which we surmount those wild beasts, our natural enemies; what new enemies does it not raise to us?. . . Man is the greatest

enemy of man. Oppression, injustice, contempt, contumely, violence, sedition, war, calumny, treachery, fraud; by these they mutually torment each other.

(DNR: 97)

Demea, reluctant at first, goes along with this litany of 'disorders of the mind' (DNR: 98).

Demea then speculates about a person, a visitor from another planet, say, coming to the Earth for the first time. 'Were a stranger to drop, on a sudden, into this world', Demea is sure that such a visitor would be struck by the horrors he or she would everywhere find (DNR: 98). He offers this as a thought-experiment to provide an unbiased perspective on the true state of the world. But Cleanthes demurs, especially insofar as psychological torment is concerned: 'I can observe something like what you mention in some others . . . But I confess, I feel little or nothing of it in myself; and hope that it is not so common as you represent it' (DNR: 99). But his demurral is less than outright disagreement, although that, or something very close to it, will shortly come. The interesting thing about Cleanthes at this point is that he offers no evidence to warrant his disagreement, other than the quoted autobiographical remark about his own mental state.

Philo uses the opportunity presented by Demea's emphasis upon the evils in the world, and especially by his thought-experiment about a stranger dropping unannounced into our midst, to transform both the basic issue and the conversation in a fundamental way. In his hands, the miseries of human life and the evils in the natural world are re-cast as the basis of a condemnation and repudiation of the entire religious outlook, something never intended, or anticipated, by Demea, in *his* bleak assessment of the human condition. Nor, astonishingly, will Demea recognize the nature and extent to which Philo is at cross-purposes with his own, pietistic, emphasis on evil until the very end of Part XI (DNR: 114).

The shift that Philo brings about is, first of all, from a factual to a philosophical question. Demea sees pain and suffering as, in fact, often a spur to religion, and we saw Philo agree up to a point. But pain and suffering, especially pain and suffering that seem pointless, also trigger the question whether a religious outlook makes the best, or even good, sense of the world. That is, reflection on the evils in the world gives rise to the *problem* of evil, essentially a problem of justifying either the adoption or retention of a religious outlook, in light of the facts of horrendous evil. Second, and closely tied in with the first point, Philo's shift reflects a change in motivation. Demea's litany of evils and horrors is intended to win converts to the religious outlook. But Philo is bent on *indicting* it on those very same grounds.

In using the raw materials of Demea's bleak description of the condition of mankind and the world at large to transform the issue, in effect, to generate theism's problem of evil, Philo springs a trap on Demea, and exposes the fundamental difference in their respective outlooks. That difference belies the frequent convergence in their views up to this point in the conversation. But, in all of this, Demea is a convenience, not a target. For, as it has been throughout, the real target is Cleanthes' experimental theism. Thus it is that, ignoring Demea, Philo issues this challenge:

> is it possible, Cleanthes, . . . that after all these reflections, and infinitely more, which might be suggested, you can still persevere in your anthropomorphism, and assert the moral attributes of the Deity, his justice, benevolence, mercy, and rectitude, to be of the same nature with these virtues in human creatures? His power we allow infinite: Whatever he wills is executed: But neither man nor any other animal are happy: Therefore he does not will their happiness: His wisdom is infinite: He is never mistaken in choosing the means to any end: But the course of nature tends not to human or animal felicity: Therefore it is not established for that purpose. Through the whole compass of human knowledge, there are no inferences more certain and infallible than these. In what respect, then, do his benevolence and mercy resemble the benevolence and mercy of men?
>
> (DNR: 100)

And he concludes with a series of questions, often quoted to summarize the consistency problem: 'Epicurus's old questions are still unanswered. Is he willing to prevent evil, but not able? then is he impotent. Is he able, but not willing? then is he malevolent. Is he both able and willing? whence then is evil?' (DNR: 100).

A brief clarification may be useful before we go on to take the measure of Philo's challenge. The wording in the answers to the first two questions, namely, 'then is he impotent', 'then is he malevolent', may be misleading. It may seem that, in some sense, these are further questions. They are not. Hume means us to read the lines as follows: then he is impotent; and, then he is malevolent.

In the wake of Philo's just-quoted speeches, theism's problem of sustaining itself in the face of the world's manifest, abundant, seemingly pointless evils is clearly out in the open. Now, following those speeches, the idea with which Part X began, and with which Philo agrees, the idea that evil is often a motivating factor in people's either turning to religion in the first place or in their continuing to hold on to it, is now no longer the issue. Evil now, and henceforth in the *Dialogues*, is the problem of evil, and as such a potentially mortal threat to theism and to natural religion. Essentially, the transition is from a psychological and anthropological interpretation of evil to a philosophical interpretation of it, with a matching transformation of what is at stake.

The challenge to Cleanthes

From the start, Cleanthes' concept of deity has been modelled on human nature. Given the facts of evil now included in the total evidence available to us, Philo is demanding a justification for that modelling. He now goes on to include another point within the scope of his demand. It is a point that further erodes the analogy at the heart of Cleanthes' argument.

Cleanthes has argued that order in nature is strong evidence of purpose in nature. Suppose he is right. Given the facts of seemingly pointless evil, what might that purpose be? Philo's suggestion is that, at the very most, the driving force (purpose?) reflected in nature is survival, mere survival, not individual happiness: 'what ... is the object of that curious artifice and machinery ... displayed in all animals? The *preservation alone* of individuals and propagation of the species ... without any care or concern for ... happiness' (DNR: 100, my emphasis). And what religious significance would, or could, this have? For instance, how would it differ from the account of the basic forces in nature that we find in Darwin's theory of evolution by natural selection?

Philo's attack is on three levels. In the first place, he is attacking Cleanthes' alleged anthropomorphism, his likening of divine attributes to human. But second, and implicit in that, is Philo's suggestion that no meaningful or religiously significant conception of a deity or of a divine purpose survives the problem of evil. After all, if we cannot attach their usual meanings to terms like 'good' and 'benevolent' and 'just', when using them of the deity, then what, if anything, does it mean to say the deity is good or benevolent or just, or that there is purpose in nature? And the third level of attack is that which is reflected in those questions allegedly posed by the ancient Greek philosopher, Epicurus (341–270 BC). The third level, then, is the consistency problem.

Cleanthes' acceptance of the challenge, and his over-reaction

Cleanthes does not duck the challenge: 'If you can make out the present point, and prove mankind to be unhappy or corrupted, there is an end at once of all religion. For to what purpose establish the natural attributes of the Deity, while the moral are still doubtful and uncertain?' (DNR: 101). In essence, what religious significance would deism have? The answer: not much.

Cleanthes is right, surely, to accept the challenge. A thoughtful believer cannot be indifferent to the vast amounts of evil in the world. Yet, while the abundance of seemingly pointless evil is a serious difficulty for faith, Cleanthes' response seems too strong. What does he mean when he says 'there is an end at once of all religion', if Philo is right about human life being often painful and miserable?

Broadly speaking, there are two possibilities. Perhaps he means that Philo's facts of evil are formally inconsistent with the existence of a deity, that a statement of their joint existence is necessarily false. Or perhaps he means that if Philo is right, then the concept of a good, loving, benevolent deity no longer makes religious sense. But what is religious sense? In the context of Cleanthes' (and Philo's) strict evidentialism, making religious sense would be tantamount to a favourable balance of the total evidence. Thus the second interpretation of what Cleanthes means is that, if Philo is right, the balance of total evidence would shift decisively against the religious hypothesis (and outlook).

I think we can be confident that Cleanthes does not mean the first of these possibilities. That would be fundamentally out of step with his thinking throughout. The plausible interpretation, then, is the second, even though his statement of the point is a bit excessive. Shortly, we will see Cleanthes make a second overstatement.

Demea's hereafter solution and Cleanthes' rebuttal

Cleanthes has accepted Philo's challenge, in the sense just described. But he does not immediately get to try to meet it. For, at this point, Demea interjects a proposal of his own. It is a suggestion reflecting a common theistic response to the problem of evil, namely, that the solution will come in an afterlife. But this proposal is devastatingly criticized by Cleanthes, who, ironically, now seems to have forgotten his previous scolding of Philo for negativity and destructiveness when criticizing the design hypothesis.

Demea's proposed solution

Demea rejects Cleanthes' dire assessment of the religious significance of Philo's being right about human misery. His view is that if evil is a problem for the believer at all, surely it is not a very serious one; surely the solution is rather obvious. His proposed (obvious) solution is that, '[t]his world is but a point in comparison of the universe: This life but a moment in comparison of eternity. The present evil phenomena, therefore, are rectified in other regions, and in some future period of existence ... [when] the eyes of men ... [are] opened to larger views of things ...'(DNR: 101).

Cleanthes' rebuttal

But Cleanthes will have none of this. Nor can he, given the strictly experiential basis on which he has built his case for the existence of a deity: 'These arbitrary suppositions can never be admitted, contrary to matter of fact, visible and uncontroverted' (DNR: 101). He accepts that to answer Philo's evil-based challenge to natural religion, that is to solve the inference problem, requires him (Cleanthes) to argue from experience of what *is*, not to speculate about what might possibly be. (The latter would be appropriate, though, in response to the consistency problem, as we will see in a moment.) But Cleanthes goes too far in his understanding of what a response to either form of the problem of evil would require: 'The only method of supporting divine benevolence ... is to deny absolutely the misery and wickedness of man' (DNR: 102). This is Cleanthes' second overstatement.

Demea's suggestion is that the problem of evil will be solved in a hereafter. Then and there, his thinking is, a balance of good and evil will be struck; the wicked will be punished and the good rewarded. That is a possibility; there is no contradiction in asserting it. But Cleanthes is unimpressed by the mere possibility of such future occurrences. From the start, his project has been to make out a strong case for the conclusion that a deity exists. Thus, to say now that it is *possible* that a deity exists, or that it is *possible* that any deity that does exist is good, is no evidence whatsoever *that* a deity (of any kind) exists in the first place. As Cleanthes puts the point, '[t]o establish one hypothesis from another is building entirely in the air; and the utmost we ever attain, by these conjectures and fictions, is to ascertain the bare possibility of our opinion; but never can we, upon such terms, establish its reality' (DNR: 102). And Cleanthes is right.

But at the same time, Cleanthes, focused entirely upon the inference problem, misses the significance, for the consistency problem, of what Demea is saying. Insofar as that problem is concerned, it *is* enough 'to ascertain the bare possibility of our opinion', for the consistency problem is to establish that, given certain facts of evil, the existence of a deity having certain moral attributes is not logically impossible. This point will come up again, and more fully, when we discuss Philo's (that is, Hume's own) thinking on the consistency problem.

Two further things are worth noting about Cleanthes' rebuttal. The first is that, in its reliance upon a strict *a priori*/*a posteriori* distinction, Cleanthes' criticism of Demea here is reminiscent of his criticism in Part IX of Demea's first-cause argument. The second is that this (present) response to Demea in Part X will come back to haunt Cleanthes' own proposed solution to the problem of evil in Part XI, as we will shortly see.

Philo, speaking for Hume, on the consistency and inference problems

Philo responds to Cleanthes' rebuttal of Demea's proposed solution. In doing so, he picks up both threads in the discussion, the inference thread and the consistency thread. The former, briefly in the picture now (DNR: 102–3), will dominate much of the discussion in Part XI.

The inference problem

We saw Cleanthes' overstated response that the 'only method of supporting divine benevolence . . . is to deny absolutely the misery and wickedness of man'. But right away he moderates the point, emphasizing that, in his experience, '[h]ealth is more common than sickness: Pleasure than pain: Happiness than misery. And for one vexation which we meet with, we attain . . . a hundred enjoyments' (DNR: 102). At face value, this is a sensible point in the context of Cleanthes' effort, since Part II, to make out a good case for an 'Author of nature . . . somewhat similar to the mind of man' (DNR: 45). Let us, then, not hold Cleanthes to his overstatement, but focus instead upon the moderated version of his point.

But Philo is unimpressed. Even supposing Cleanthes is right about the relative quantities of pain and pleasure, happiness and unhappiness, and Philo is not admitting that Cleanthes *is* right, the real issue is not amounts of pain and suffering, but the intensity of it. Even if there is less pain than pleasure in the universe, yet surely it is a commonplace of our experience that 'it is infinitely more violent and durable' (DNR: 102). And Philo has many graphic examples to illustrate his point (DNR: 102).

Philo then goes on to suggest that Cleanthes' insistence on pleasures outnumbering pains leads to scepticism. His point is that we could never hope to corroborate Cleanthes' claim; 'it [is not] possible for you to compute, estimate, and compare all the pains and all the pleasures in the lives of all men and of all animals' (DNR: 103). Thus, Philo reasons, Cleanthes is unwittingly committing himself to 'a total scepticism' (DNR: 102).

But, in defence of Cleanthes against this charge of scepticism, it may be said that Cleanthes does not need it to be true as a matter of fact that pleasures outnumber pains. It would be enough for that to be true, insofar as our experience goes. But, while this might acquit Cleanthes on the charge of scepticism, it would not advance his position overall. That is because Philo seems to be right about the relative intensities of pains and pleasures, and that is powerful counter-evidence to Cleanthes' inference to a deity with moral attributes.

Let us turn now to Philo's thinking on the consistency problem. To do so, we turn away, for a moment, from the inference problem.

The consistency problem

Suppose that pleasure and happiness both outnumber and have greater intensity and duration than pain and misery. Philo can still justifiably maintain, against Cleanthes, that 'you have yet done nothing: For this is not, by any means, what we expect from infinite power, infinite wisdom, and infinite goodness. Why is there any misery at all in the world?' (DNR: 103). Philo proceeds to give a powerful and succinct statement of the consistency problem of supposing that evil and the God of standard theism could possibly coexist.

It is the God of standard theism that is at issue here, as Philo emphasizes infinite power, wisdom and goodness. Theism's logical problem of squaring evil with God is essentially this: 'Why is there any misery at all in the world? Not from chance surely. From some cause then. Is it from the intention of the Deity? But he is perfectly benevolent. Is it contrary to his intention? But he is almighty' (DNR: 103).

Philo offers theism two responses to the consistency problem, each addressed to a different issue.

The first is a sceptical one. In Philo's words, '[n]othing can shake the solidity of this reasoning . . . except we assert, that these subjects exceed all human capacity . . . a topic, which I have all along insisted on' (DNR: 103). But this kind of response only makes sense if the believer's problem is to actually come up with the manner in which

God and evil are squared with one another, assuming for the moment that they *are* squared. That is, a sceptical solution would work only if the believer's task is to specify what, in fact, *is* the consistency-making point.

But it is doubtful that this, in fact, is the believer's task. Instead, insofar as the consistency problem is concerned, it is to show that the deity and the facts of evil in the world are not logically inconsistent. How does that differ from the task discussed in the previous paragraph? It differs in the following important way. Logical inconsistency between two things means that those two things could never possibly co-exist. The existence of the one would make the existence of the other absolutely impossible. Or, to put the point in terms of statements; if two statements are logically inconsistent with one another, then the truth of one makes the truth of the other absolutely impossible. By impossibility here is meant impossibility in all circumstances; impossibility in all possible worlds, as the point is sometimes put. Anyhow, with logical impossibility being what it is, the task of defending two things or two statements against a charge of logical inconsistency becomes the task of showing that it is not impossible for both to exist (or both to be true) at the same time. That is to say, it is the task of showing the *possibility* of both existing together. And that is different from the task described in the previous paragraph, and to which a sceptical response would be appropriate, namely, the task of showing how, in actual reality, two things co-exist.

Think of the difference like this. In the first task, the objective is to show what, in actual fact, is the deity's reason to permit evil. But in the second task, the objective is to show only a possible way in which evil could exist in a world of divine origin. It is the difference between establishing what is the case (supposing the world does indeed have a divine origin), on the one hand, and, on the other, what could possibly be the case. And clearly the latter is the lesser of the two tasks.

Philo's concession of logical consistency

Philo gives us an indication that he too sees this difference in tasks, when he goes on to make a concession that he is not forced to make. His concession is this: 'I will allow, that pain or misery in man is *compatible* with infinite power and goodness in the Deity' (DNR: 103). Here he is emphasizing the logical consistency of the deity and the facts of evil, that is, that there is a *possible* world in which they both exist. There is no suggestion in this concession of logical possibility that he has any conception of what would be, in actual fact, the reason for evil in a world of divine origin.

The concession that Philo is making here is not to be confused with the one we saw him make towards the end of Part V, and which he will repeat both at the end of Part X and in Part XII. *That* concession was of some notion of design in the physical universe, whereas the concession now in question regarding the problem of evil is a concession that the concept of a god with moral attributes and the concept of a world with seemingly pointless evil in it are not logically inconsistent with one another.

Three questions

Three questions come up here. First, why does Philo make this concession? Second, as he drops the logical problem of evil so readily and without pressure to do so, why did he raise it in the first place? And third, are seemingly pointless evils and the God of standard theism mutually consistent in the logical sense of the word?

Why does Philo concede logical consistency?

Essentially, the answer is that the mere logic of theism and evil does not especially interest him. Philo's (Hume's) primary interest in the philosophy of religion is in experimental or empirical theism on its own terms. He is interested primarily in examining the degree to which experience supports religious belief. Of course, if a formal contradiction could be established between some fact of evil and any of the core theistic propositions, then that would be an end at once of experimental theism. And of standard theism too. But to *seek* that end in that way would be fundamentally out of step with the practice followed earlier in the *Dialogues*, namely, that of carefully assessing the experimentalist case put forth on theism's behalf. And that practice is continued in Parts X and XI, where Hume incorporates the problem of evil into that continuing investigation as a further, and crucial, dimension of the total evidence bearing on the issue under investigation.

Why does Philo raise the question of logical consistency in the first place?

The answer may be that, although he does not pursue the topic in detail, Hume none the less wishes to show the power of the logical question. That is, if God, as described in standard theism, exists, how could evil possibly be so abundant in the world? To raise the question sows a doubt that such a deity exists at all. For, while it may turn out that theism is able to show God's existence is not impossible on the facts of inscrutable evil cited, yet being able to do that does not even begin to be (or to give) a reason to believe that God actually exists. To raise the logical problem, and then to drop it as he does, enables Hume to put before us the thinness of theism's victory in surviving the logical argument, assuming for the sake of the point that it does indeed survive it.

Are God and evil logically consistent or inconsistent with one another?

But what about the logical problem in its own right? Is there a formal contradiction between the facts of evil cited and an infinite deity analogized to human nature, or not? The answer is no; Hume is right about that. Furthermore, we know enough from post-Humean philosophy of religion to be fairly confident in putting forth that position, and leaving it unargued.

Back to the inference problem, and preparation for things to come

Philo's concession on the logical issue leaves the problem of evil that really interests him alone in the spotlight. That is the inference problem. His challenge to Cleanthes, now taking into account the total evidence, and not just the various facts of order in the universe, is direct and plain: 'You must prove these pure, unmixed, and uncontrollable attributes [for instance, infinite power, infinite goodness, infinite wisdom] from the present mixed and confused phenomena and from these alone' (DNR: 103). And to leave no doubt on the point, Philo emphasizes to Cleanthes that the difficulty in his task is now much greater than before, when only facts of order were being considered. But even then, Philo was convinced that the evidence did not warrant Cleanthes' inference, as he now reminds him: 'Were the phenomena ever so pure and unmixed, yet being finite, they would be insufficient for that purpose' (DNR: 103). But the relevant facts are not all of a kind, thus how much greater the difficulty: 'How much more, where they are so jarring and discordant?' (DNR: 103).

Natural religion has now been brought to the point where it is no longer permitted to choose among the facts of our experience, emphasizing those that favour it. Its task is to prove the existence of the deity from the world as we find it, evils included. Thus the ground is prepared for Cleanthes' final draft of the experimental or experiential theism that he has been developing since Part II. He will present that final version at the start of Part XI.

But Part X readies the ground for discussions yet to come in other important ways too. As we saw, Philo emphasizes the 'mixed and confused phenomena' that experience gives us. In Part XI he will suggest that taking those data seriously fits well with the idea that the universe is utterly and completely indifferent to us, that its arrangement is neither benevolent nor malevolent. Then there are Philo's closing remarks in Part X.

Philo's concession of design (again)

'Formerly, when we argued concerning the natural attributes of intelligence and design, I needed all my sceptical and metaphysical subtilty to elude your grasp . . . the beauty and fitness of final causes strike us with such irresistible force, that all objections appear (what I believe they really are) mere cavils and sophisms' (DNR: 103–4). This is the second time Philo has conceded to Cleanthes that, on the data of order alone, an inference to an author of nature somewhat similar to the mind of man is warranted.

Can he really mean it? What has happened between his earlier, surely devastating criticisms, and now to prompt or warrant his volunteering this concession? And what does the concession amount to?

For the most part, we have to wait for Part XII to have the right perspective to answer these questions. Certainly, though, with no new evidence to account for it, it is as surprising to find Philo volunteering this concession here as it was when he first did so in Part V. But while indeed offering this concession, he does so in a way that, both here and later in Part XII, further reduces and denudes Cleanthes' position. For the key lines are those framing the concession just quoted, inasmuch as they strip the concession of all religious value. The framing lines are these. First, '[h]ere, Cleanthes, I find myself at ease in my argument. Here I triumph' (DNR: 103). By 'here', Philo means on the evidence of the 'mixed and confused phenomena', that is, on the *total* evidence. And second, 'there is no view of human life, or of the condition of mankind, from which, without the greatest violence, we can infer the moral attributes, or learn that infinite benevolence, conjoined with infinite power and infinite wisdom, which we must discover by the eyes of faith alone' (DNR: 104). In short, Philo is here announcing that the best that reason can do for faith is some version of deism. In particular, there is no justification to attribute moral properties to any such source. So, if reason supports faith, it is not in the parts of faith that really matter, those pertaining to the notion of a transcendent personal being who cares about us. This will come up again in Part XII.

Cleanthes' response to the inference problem: limited theism (*Dialogues*, Part XI)

Limited theism

Part XI begins with Cleanthes responding to Philo's challenge. The total evidence is 'mixed'. It includes evil as well as order. From this evidence, the challenge is to justify concluding that the universe traces to a personal being who is intelligent, good, benevolent, fair, and so on.

But we need to be clear whether the challenge is to justify inferring a personal source of the universe who is *infinitely* intelligent, infinitely good, benevolent, and so on, or a lesser being. If the former, then Cleanthes is prepared to admit defeat. For he agrees that the evidence does not warrant such an inference. But he does not think that anything of great religious significance is lost in the concession. As he puts the point, 'I scruple not to allow ... that I have been apt to suspect the frequent repetition of the word, *infinite*, which we meet with in all theological writers, to savour more of panegyric than of philosophy, and that any purposes of reasoning, and even of religion, would be better served, were we to rest contented with more accurate and more moderate expressions' (DNR: 105). This is quite in keeping with the tough-mindedness we have seen in Cleanthes right from the start; stick to the facts, no exaggerations beyond the evidence, no flattering ('panegyric') descriptions. One important dimension of this will not have been lost on readers at the time, including Hume's friends who advised suppressing the book, no more than on us now. It is that standard theism exceeds the evidence available to us.

That said, and briefly dismissing two views that he believes to lie outside the scope of experience, Cleanthes takes up Philo's challenge. First, he clears the ground on which the position he is ready to defend will stand. This means dismissing Demea's refusal to allow analogical descriptions of the deity. To refuse analogy in religious language robs it of a base in experience, thus, to an evidentialist like Cleanthes (and Philo, and Hume), robbing it also of any factual or literal meaning. It also means dismissing standard theism, because of its commitment to an infinite conception of the deity. This latter dismissal is two-pronged: the first is that standard theism cannot (except merely logically) be squared with the facts of evil, while the second is that no experience of ours warrants concluding that an infinite deity exists. Interestingly, Cleanthes does not accept Philo's concession on the former point, the mutual logical consistency of God and evil.

Cleanthes' rejection of standard theism is not trumpeted, but it is clear and unmistakable none the less. What, then, does experience support, both in the sense of what can be defended against the argument from evil and what can justifiably be inferred from the available, 'mixed', evidence? In Cleanthes' judgement, this:

> But supposing the Author of nature to be finitely perfect, though far exceeding mankind; a satisfactory account may then be given

of natural and moral evil, and every untoward phenomenon be explained and adjusted. A less evil may then be chosen, in order to avoid a greater: Inconveniences be submitted to, in order to reach a desirable end: And in a word, benevolence, regulated by wisdom, and limited by necessity, may produce just such a world as the present.

(DNR: 105)

By the term, 'moral evil', Cleanthes means evils for which persons are responsible, in the moral sense of the word 'responsibility'. It is more or less the same as what theologians and religious people mean by the word 'sin'. 'Natural evil', by contrast, is evil for which no person is responsible, in the moral sense of responsibility. For example, a natural disaster would be a natural evil.

His final draft of 'the religious hypothesis' (DNR: 40) thus presented, Cleanthes invites Philo's criticism: 'I would gladly hear, at length, without interruption, your opinion of this new theory' (DNR: 105). Let us refer to this 'new theory' as limited theism, inasmuch as it is committed to a limited, that is, a finite, deity, not the infinite God of standard theism.

Experience and speculation

Having thus ruled out, as unsustained by experience, the idea of an infinite deity, how does Cleanthes' alternative fare by the same measure? Cleanthes does not offer any new evidence over and above the various facts of order cited in his previous arguments. What, then, are we to make of his present proposal? Is the notion of a finitely perfect author of nature experiential at all? Is it just pure speculation, thus subject to the same abrupt dismissal that, in Part X, Cleanthes himself meted out to Demea's suggestion of a 'hereafter' solution to the problem of evil? The answer is yes and no. Let us start with the no.

The key point in exoneration of Cleanthes for offering no new evidence is Philo's concession at the end of Part X. Philo conceded that, purely in terms of order in the world, a Cleanthes-like position is warranted. And Cleanthes' introduction of his version of limited theism comes immediately after that. So we must see Cleanthes here as simply building on his earlier position, now conceded by Philo. In the context of the conversation as it is at this stage, he does not see himself as having to start again from scratch. He sees his task now, given Philo's concession of the concept of design in nature, as that of adjusting his prior position to accommodate the additional data, those facts of seemingly pointless evil set forth in Part X. So he does not see his position as in need of new facts, new evidence, so much as fine-tuning. And that is what he offers; in effect, a clarification of the concept of deity.

But this exoneration will only go so far. For instance, we are entitled to ask, what justifies this particular adjustment in the concept of deity? Why this and not another adjustment instead? Or, why not an ultimate dualism of good and evil forces at work, or, better, in competition, in nature; in effect a version of the medieval doctrine of Manichaeanism? Or some other adjustment entirely? Perhaps Philo's trial-and-error hypothesis of a trainee god or gods from Part V (DNR: 71)? But who is to say which adjustment to make? Where is the evidence on which to decide the question? There does not seem to be any. And certainly none is offered here by Cleanthes.

Thus, it is appropriate to now remind Cleanthes of his own dismissal of Demea in Part X: 'Whence can any hypothesis be proved but from the apparent phenomena? To establish one hypothesis upon another is building entirely in the air; and the utmost we ever attain, by these conjectures and fictions, is to ascertain the bare possibility of our opinion; but never can we, upon such terms, establish its reality' (DNR: 101–2). That was apt then. It is no less so now. But other misgivings arise about limited theism as well, and let us briefly look at some.

Is limited theism really a form of theism at all?

The surpassability problem

Being finite, the god of limited theism is surpassable in knowledge, power, and goodness, even if not actually surpassed in reality (assuming for the sake of the argument that this finite god exists). For an infinite deity, if one existed, would automatically surpass a finite deity in those respects, and presumably in others.

But this creates a dilemma for limited theism. On the one hand, if it is claimed that the god of experimental theism is not surpassable or surpassed in fact, then, either way, the God of standard theism is implicitly denied. For the God of standard theism would by definition surpass the deity Cleanthes is now conjecturing. But, on the other hand, if it is allowed that the god of experimental theism is surpassable or actually surpassed (by the God of standard theism, say), then experimental theism is no longer monotheism but polytheism. For either the possibility or the actuality of more than one god is thereby being granted. But a monotheistic theory cannot grant either one; of its nature, it is a one-deity theory. Thus, relative to standard theism, Cleanthes' position is either atheism or polytheism. Presumably, neither would be welcome. Thus, his 'new theory' seems to face a serious identity crisis.

However, it may be argued that this atheism-or-polytheism interpretation of Cleanthes' 'new theory' is quite wrong. The gist of such an argument is that Cleanthes' concept of deity simply commits to less than the standard theistic concept, while leaving open the possibility that it is the fuller, not the lesser, concept that is in fact instantiated.

In the context of Cleanthes' design argument, that is indeed a well-taken point. For there, if the evidence warrants positing a deity, it is the lesser deity of experimental theism, not the greater deity of standard theism. But the evidence in the design argument does not rule out the greater; it is just that the greater concept of deity is significantly underdetermined by the evidence of design. For instance, from the evidence before me I may justifiably conclude that the person who built this doorframe had a good eye for detail and carefully matched the panels. But I have no basis in that evidence to conclude that he is adept at building canoes or making frescoes. He may be. But, on the evidence available to me, I am not entitled to conclude or believe it. Likewise with the deity-indicating evidence of design; it does not warrant the concept of God in standard theism, but none the less it goes part of the way to that concept.

But we have no reason to think that the same applies to Cleanthes' 'new theory'. To see this, suppose that Cleanthes is right that a limited deity, through no fault of its own, could not have done better. He would then have shown that a limited deity has a morally sufficient reason to actualize the actual world. But this makes absolutely no progress whatever towards showing that an infinite deity also has or could have a morally sufficient reason to actualize the actual world. For we have no reason whatever to suppose that the non-logical factors preventing the finite deity doing better apply, either at all or in the same way, to the infinite deity of standard theism. The reason is that the difference between finite and infinite beings is itself an infinite difference. Thus, no increase in the power (say) of the former could ever bring it up to the power of the latter; the difference between finite and infinite is in kind, not just degree. An argument in the reverse direction might sometimes work; that is, if a more powerful, knowledgeable, benevolent being could do no better than this, then arguably a less powerful, knowledgeable, and benevolent being could also have done no better.

Unlike the design argument, then, which, in opening the way to the hypothesis of a deity as the ultimate cause of means–end order in nature, goes part way to the concept of an infinite deity, Cleanthes' argument in response to the problem of evil does not.

The polytheism problem

Here is an objection to the second horn of the dilemma. The god of limited theism, while surpassable, is in fact unsurpassed. Thus, there is no other god. Thus the surpassability clause in limited theism does not entail polytheism.

This objection does not blunt the point, however, as the following illustration shows. Suppose polytheism is true. There are multiple deities. For convenience in this illustration, suppose there are seven deities in all. One day all seven of them are out riding in a car. The car crashes, and six of the gods are killed, leaving only one. Is theism now true? The reason to think so is the obvious one, namely, following the accident, there is now one and only one god. But surely it is not true. The difference between monotheism and polytheism that makes a difference is not the number of gods in practice. After all, if atheism is true, the number of gods in practice is none, but there is still a difference between monotheism and polytheism. The difference that matters is the number of gods that each of those theories countenances. In the former case, the number is one and no more, even in theory, while the number in the latter case is any number greater than zero.

Verdict on Cleanthes' 'new theory'

The upshot is that it is not clear what Cleanthes' concept of a finite deity actually amounts to. Thus it is proportionately not clear what his proposed 'new theory' amounts to as a defence against the empirical argument from evil. Thus it cannot be reckoned successful in establishing that some version of monotheism remains plausible in the face of an abundance of inscrutable evil.

Hume's articulation of the basic presuppositions in the standard debate on the problem of evil (*Dialogues*, Part XI)

Philo makes three points in response to limited theism. The first, which runs through the second and third points as well, and which he then repeats after concluding the third, expresses a basic presupposition in the philosophical debate on the problem of evil ever since. It is this: suppose a person of intelligence and insight more or less like ours were told, prior to having any experience of our world, that its ultimate source was 'a very good, wise, and powerful Being, however finite' (DNR: 105). That person, Philo assures us, would form 'a different notion of [our world] from what we find it to be by experience' (DNR: 105). Surely Philo is right. In particular, this person would never 'imagine . . . that the [world] could be so full of vice and misery and disorder, as it appears in this life' (DNR: 105–6), a point that Philo also suggested earlier (DNR: 103).

The basic device in this thought-experiment is a before-and-after comparison. Essentially the idea is this: begin with as fully thought-out a conception as possible of a world whose ultimate source is the will of a deity; then examine carefully the actual world of experience; now compare the two; the more the pre-conception and the actual experience match, the better for the religious hypothesis, whereas the less they match, the worse for that hypothesis. This basic thought-experiment is virtually everywhere to be found underlying the post-Humean philosophical debate on the problem of evil.

Philo's second point is a variation on the first. Again, suppose a person with a pre-reflective concept of the world as the work of a deity. When he or she is old enough to think about the world, to take the measure of his or her experience of it, he or she does so already believing it has a divine origin. Such a person, Philo thinks, will not lose his or her religious belief to experience, if the belief is solidly grounded. Why not? The world is too ambiguous. And such a person would recognize his or her own inherent limitations and so would grant 'that there may be many solutions of these phenomena, which will for ever escape his comprehension' (DNR: 106). In a word, scepticism will tend to preserve faith when faced with various harsh truths of our experience. This is the second time that Philo has suggested scepticism as a benefit to the believer; recall that he did so in Part X also (DNR: 103).

Philo's third point is his assessment of the effect on natural religion of the inference problem. It is that persons, 'left to gather . . . belief . . . [in] a supreme intelligence, benevolent and powerful . . . from the appearances of things . . . will . . . [never] find any reason for such a conclusion' (DNR: 106). As Philo sees it, the 'mixed' evidence of our experience is too much for any natural religionist argument aimed at proving the existence of a deity with moral attributes. Note here that Philo has dropped the qualification he made when first articulating the inference problem of evil, namely, his serious doubts about attributing to the deity any moral attributes *resembling the human* (DNR: 100). Now he is no longer adding the qualifier, 'resembling the human'. Of course, in practice, the distinction between the two is virtually without difference, as we saw. For, what other meaning do we ever attach to such attributes?

Philo concludes this aspect of his response to limited theism by repeating his thought-experiment: 'Is the world considered in general, and as it appears to us in this life, different from what a man . . . would, *beforehand*, expect from a very powerful, wise, and benevolent Deity? It must be strange prejudice to assert the contrary' (DNR: 107). His conclusion is that, 'however consistent the world may be, allowing certain suppositions and conjectures, with the idea of such a Deity, it can never afford us an inference concerning his existence. The consistence is not absolutely denied, only the inference' (DNR: 107).

Philo turns next to discussion of the causes of evils, especially natural evils, in the world.

The hypothesis of indifference *(Dialogues*, Part XI)

After setting before Cleanthes his point that, beforehand, no reasonable person would predict that a world designed and made by a powerful, wise, and benevolent deity would turn out to be just like our world, Philo suggests that most evils seem to depend on four circumstances (DNR: 107). In this suggestion, Philo's example of evil is pain and suffering. These four circumstances are suggested cautiously, however, for who can know in regard to such matters? As Philo acknowledges, '[a]ll that belongs to human understanding, in this deep ignorance and obscurity, is to be sceptical, or at least cautious' (DNR: 107).

The four circumstances

The four circumstances are these: pain as a cause of action (DNR: 107); 'the conducting of the world by general laws' (DNR: 108); the weaknesses of various sorts in all living things (DNR: 109); and flaws and faults in the workings of nature (DNR: 111). In suggesting and discussing these things, Philo is continuing with the line of thought that is basic in the standard debate on the problem of evil ever since, namely, that any reasonable person would expect a world made by a good and powerful deity to be unlike *this* world in various obvious respects.

Briefly, let us look at the four suggestions in turn, and then all together. Obviously, pain and discomfort are spurs to action. I feel hunger or fatigue, and respond accordingly. I (my body) needs nourishment and adequate rest, and hunger pangs and aches of a certain kind, respectively, are its warning signs. But, Philo wonders, why could not a lessening of feelings of pleasure, as opposed to actual feelings of pain, not achieve the same purpose? If we were designing a world with sentient beings in it, and if we were all-good and all-powerful, would we not choose such a mechanism, in preference to pain, to achieve the desired ends of necessary nourishment and rest? Furthermore, instead of exceptionless laws of nature, would we not, as circumstances warranted, intervene incognito to adjust things for the good? Or, would we not have made plants and animals hardier and, in the case of human beings in particular, more industrious? (DNR: 110). Or, lastly, if we were sufficiently good and powerful, would we not have designed, and then actualized, a universe without accidents or malfunctions, or with many fewer than in the actual world? For instance, were it within our power, would we not have so designed living organisms that the cell mutations that develop as cancers never occur? To be sure, these mutations do not usually threaten the existence of a whole species, but they do cause misery, suffering, and death to many individual members of species (DNR: 112).

What is the moral of the foregoing considerations? It is that the world could have been different in significant ways from how it is, and, in being different in those ways, better. It seems that it could, but we cannot know for sure. So we must be modest and diffident in our suggestions. Possibly, things could not have been different or better in a world designed by a deity than they are in the actual world. In this way, Cleanthes to the contrary notwithstanding (DNR: 105), logical consistency is granted between the ills of this world and the religious hypothesis, including the hypothesis of an infinite deity. In effect, as noted before, this is a sceptical defence of the religious hypothesis against a logical form of the argument from evil. But, allowing that, surely there are enough ways in which we would expect a divinely made world to be different from (and better than) the actual world to rule out *concluding* that this world is of divine origin. That is, surely the natural religionist conclusion is unwarranted, insofar as a deity with moral attributes is concerned (DNR: 113).

The hypothesis of indifference

Philo concludes this phase of his argument against natural religion with the following, dramatic description: 'The whole presents nothing but the idea of a blind nature, impregnated by a great vivifying principle, and pouring forth from her lap, without discernment or parental care, her maimed and abortive children' (DNR: 113). Nature seems blind and indifferent, red in tooth and claw, utterly impersonal and void of feeling in the relentless functioning of its processes of generation and decay. He goes on: 'The true conclusion is, that the original source of all things is entirely indifferent to all these principles, and has no more regard to good above ill than to heat above cold, or to drought above moisture, or to light above heavy' (DNR: 113–14). He places the point in this context: that, as far as we can see, there are four hypotheses to choose among in accounting for 'the first causes of the universe' (DNR: 114). They are, first, that the original cause is perfectly good, second, that it is perfectly evil, third, that it is a mix of good and evil, and fourth, that it is neither good nor evil.

But the 'mixed phenomena' in the total evidence, the mix of good and evil we find in the world, seems to decisively rule out the first two hypotheses. Furthermore, the regularity we find in nature seems to rule out the third. That is, if nature really did trace to a competition between two basic forces, good and evil, then we would expect less uniformity and regularity throughout nature than we find to be the case in fact. The best fit with the facts of our experience, namely, the 'mixed phenomena' spoken of, together with the regularity and uniformity we find throughout nature, seems to be the fourth hypothesis, the hypothesis of indifference (DNR: 114). I take the name, 'the hypothesis of indifference', from the Hume commentator and philosopher of religion, Paul Draper. Rounding out this discussion, Philo maintains that similar points apply to moral evil (DNR: 114).

The culmination of the whole discussion in the Dialogues

Philo has responded sceptically to natural religion from the start. And he remains as much a sceptic here at the end of Part XI as in the beginning. How can that be? Have we not just seen him offer four hypotheses that might make sense of the ultimate principles in nature, and give strong preference to one? How is this to be squared with scepticism?

Philo's response to natural religion runs on two tracks. He emphasizes the limits and weaknesses of human reason, our deep inability to make ultimate sense of things. Given that, his view is that it is best to not even try. Why set out on a journey that you know, at the start, you cannot finish? That is the sceptical track, the deeper and more pronounced of the two. But suppose that, against our better (sceptical) judgement, we *did* engage in speculation about the ultimate nature and source of the universe, and suppose that we kept such inquiries restricted to observational data, what is the most plausible hypothesis? It is in this context that Philo proposes the hypothesis of indifference. His endorsement of that hypothesis, then, as 'the true conclusion', is conditioned accordingly. That is, *if* we go ahead with an inherently futile investigation into the ultimate nature and origin of the universe, or of order and regularity in nature, then the hypothesis having the best fit with the total experiential evidence is that the basic forces and operations of nature are wholly and utterly impersonal.

Philo's answer, then, to the question of the ultimate source and basic principle of the universe is that he does not know. Nobody can know. But, if we speculate none the less, his best guess is that nature is blind, that it is brute nature all the way down. If forced to speculate, his best guess is that the operations and functions of nature are through and through naturalistic and indifferent to us, our hopes, fears, and happiness. In the circumstances, what might cause us to go ahead with speculation? The power and depth of our curiosity itself, as we will see in both the next chapter and the Afterword.

In essence, Hume's *Dialogues* ends here. This mix of scepticism about the whole enterprise of natural religion and of the indifference (to us) of the forces at work in the universe is the culmination of its discussion. That mix is the essence of Philo's, and Hume's, position, insofar as the relationship between faith and reason is concerned. We will see in the next chapter how this position can be expressed fairly naturally in the language of a very mild deism. Before that, however, we must say goodbye to Demea.

And then there were two

Demea now sees clearly that, while his thinking and Philo's followed the same path, they never had the same destination in mind. Think of two roads, Route 24 West and Route 78 West, for instance, to name two in my part of New Jersey, that, for a time, are one and the same, yet their destinations are not the same and after a while they go their separate ways. Demea, aggrieved, feeling betrayed, protests, 'I joined in alliance with you, in order to prove the incomprehensible nature of the divine Being, and refute the principles of Cleanthes, who would measure every thing by a human rule and standard. But I now find you running into all the topics of the greatest libertines and infidels . . . Are you secretly, then, a more dangerous enemy than Cleanthes himself?' (DNR: 114–15).

Here Demea shows two dimensions in his naïveté. First, he has not until now seen that his own purpose and Philo's are at odds. But, second, he still persists in thinking of his own as the only true voice of religion, or of theistic religion, at any rate. Disappointed, unsettled, and ill at ease, now that his eyes are at last open, he leaves (DNR: 115).

Chapter 10

'True religion'

(*Dialogues*, Part XII)

Introduction

Part XII is the longest of the *Dialogues*' twelve parts. It is also the most puzzling and controversial. The heart of the puzzle is Philo's concession to Cleanthes regarding the cause of natural order. He has conceded this twice already, as we saw, once each in Parts V and X. But here in Part XII, the concession is so fulsome and seems to go so deep that it raises the question whether, after all, it is Cleanthes, not Philo, who principally speaks for Hume.

In light of Philo's concession, what, in the end, are we to make of his scepticism? Does he abandon it? Likewise, what are we to think now about his hypothesis of indifference? And what about the naturalism we saw him develop through Parts VI, VII, and VIII, as an alternative to the design hypothesis? And also, in each case, vice versa. That is to say, in light of them, how are we to take the concession? These questions map out our task in this chapter. To answer them is to decide what, in the end, to make of Hume's philosophy of religion itself.

The answer to all of these questions is essentially the same. It is that there is far less to Philo's concession than meets the eye. It does not supersede his scepticism. Indeed, I will suggest that it *is* his scepticism by another name. And neither does it supersede or even conflict with his naturalistic or indifference hypotheses. Of course, in all three cases, appearances are to the contrary. In the end, there is a balance among the four – his concession to deism, his scepticism, his naturalistic hypothesis, and his hypothesis of indifference (his moral atheism) – that reflects what Philo ironically (and perhaps mischievously) calls 'true religion' (DNR: 121).

Appearance and reality in Philo's concession of design in nature

Finding common ground

Part XII opens on Cleanthes and Philo seeming to move to common ground. Perhaps Demea's abrupt departure has made it painfully plain that the disagreements have been deep and sharply expressed. Cleanthes tends to blame Philo for this development: 'Your spirit of controversy . . . carries you strange lengths, when engaged in an argument; and there is nothing so sacred and venerable . . . which you spare on that occasion' (DNR: 116). While it does not seem fair to put all blame on Philo, this rebuke is milder by far than some of Cleanthes' earlier jibes, a mere scolding by comparison. And this time he even includes a possibly mitigating circumstance, Philo's 'abhorrence of vulgar superstition' (DNR: 116).

Philo responds in kind. He disclaims any intent to undercut natural religion, here described as inferring a deity from 'the inexplicable contrivance and artifice of nature' (DNR: 116). He goes further. In terms that recall Cleanthes' 'irregular' argument of Part III, Philo himself now strongly affirms design in nature: 'A purpose, an intention, a design strikes everywhere the most careless, the most stupid thinker' (DNR: 116). And, insofar as the ultimate source of such design is concerned, he asks, 'to what pitch of . . . obstinacy must a philosopher . . . have attained, who can . . . doubt of a supreme intelligence?' (DNR: 117).

Cleanthes adds two points to this lavish concession. First, he wants to have it on record, so to speak, that Philo now agrees to the original analogy on which he (Cleanthes) constructed the first version of his design argument, namely, the 'comparison of the universe to a machine of human contrivance' (DNR: 118; see DNR: 45 for the original reference). Such agreement on Philo's part would be tantamount to disowning his own criticisms of the analogy, for he would be agreeing to Cleanthes' position as it was before he criticized it. And second, Cleanthes wants to commit Philo to repudiating scepticism, which Cleanthes persists in seeing as Pyrrhonistic through and through: 'I think it absolutely impossible to maintain or defend . . . [no system at all]' (DNR: 118). In sum, he wants to leave no doubt that Philo concedes him everything he deems important in his position.

These first three pages of Part XII leave us (me at any rate) with three impressions above all: first, that Philo's concession is excessive and too fulsomely expressed; second, and contributing to the first impression, that no new evidence whatsoever has been offered to warrant capitulation to Cleanthes' position; and third, that this exchange between Philo and Cleanthes is less about the truth and falsity of the design hypothesis than about re-establishing an amiable and sociable atmosphere. This third impression is that Philo and Cleanthes, Philo especially, seem to be acting in a way that is fairly common among friends or friendly acquaintances when an informal conversation has become too sharp, sharper than was intended or expected. And that, together with the lack of new evidence to warrant Philo's apparent change of mind, is reason to suspect there may be less to Philo's concession than it seems. After all, let us not forget Hume's interest in seeming less an enemy of theistic religion than he really is.

Let us now take up the questions I raised in the Introduction. First and foremost among them is the question whether Philo abandons scepticism itself.

That Philo does not repudiate scepticism

'So little . . . do I esteem this suspense of judgment . . . to be possible' (DNR: 118). Thus Philo. There is a lot at stake in this remark. At face value, it seems to repudiate scepticism itself. But appearances can be deceiving, here as elsewhere, and there is less to this remark than meets the eye.

Half a page on in the same speech, Philo says this: 'No man can deny the analogies between the effects: *To restrain ourselves from enquiring concerning the causes is scarcely possible*' (DNR: 119, my emphasis). The underlined statement is the key to unlock what Philo is really getting at in his seeming concession – 'So little . . . do I esteem this suspense of judgment . . . to be possible' – to Cleanthes' dismissive view of scepticism.

We are struck by, and marvel at, the order and regularity in nature at all levels. How natural, then, in our curiosity about that order, to inquire into its source. Indeed, 'to restrain ourselves from enquiring . . . is scarcely possible'. My suggestion is that it is just this naturalness of curiosity about order in nature that Philo is highlighting, when he tells us that he 'esteem[s] . . . suspense of judgment in the present case to be [scarcely] possible'. And there is no incompatibility between scepticism and curiosity.

But there is deep irony here. For while he acknowledges the naturalness of our curiosity about the ultimate source of order in the universe (DNR: 118), Philo also thinks that such curiosity points 'quite beyond the reach of our faculties' (DNR: 37). In both respects, he speaks for Hume himself. Reflected in this lack of fit between curiosity and its resolution or satisfaction there is what Hume, in the *Enquiry concerning Human Understanding*, calls 'the whimsical condition of mankind' (EHU: 160). We cannot but speculate and inquire. But, equally, we cannot in principle satisfy our curiosity. And therein lie the irony and poignancy of the human condition. Thus, far from abandoning scepticism here in Part XII, Philo is deepening the lesson it teaches us about ourselves, our essentially 'whimsical condition' in particular.

I will examine other aspects of the relationship between Philo's concession and his scepticism in the next sub-section and again on pages 206–12.

Philo's hollowing out of his concession

Early in Part XII, Cleanthes tries to tie Philo, by virtue of his concession, to the original design hypothesis and to a repudiation of
scepticism. Cleanthes' words, partly quoted above, are these: first,
'I shall further add . . . to what you have so well urged . . . a strong
analogy . . . to a machine of human contrivance' and, second, 'it . . .
[is] absolutely impossible to maintain or defend . . . no system at all'
(DNR: 118). Philo's immediate response is to suggest that, in the end,
the whole dispute between Cleanthes and himself throughout the
Dialogues is just verbal, a mere quibbling over words based on misunderstandings. As he puts it: 'So little . . . do I esteem this suspense of
judgment in the present case to be possible, that I am apt to suspect
there enters somewhat of a dispute of words into this controversy, more
than is usually imagined' (DNR: 118–19).

At one level, this seems to confirm Cleanthes' interpretation of
the concession, and as such it seems to be playing completely into his
hands. But, as I noted just above, there is less to Philo's concession
than it seems, or than Cleanthes thinks. For there is a second interpretation too, which Philo himself develops as Part XII progresses. The
former largely serves public relations purposes of Hume's own, while
the latter, somewhat masked by the former, reflects Philo's (thus
Hume's) scepticism as it has been developed in the book from the
beginning.

On both interpretations, the dispute over natural religion is
presented as 'merely verbal' (DNR: 120). On both interpretations, the
outcome of the dispute looks just the same. That is the point I wish to
emphasize here; that there is no practical or apparent difference
between the two descriptions, inasmuch as, either way, we are left with
an unresolvable disagreement. And this means that Hume is able to
show us, even if he somewhat disguises and muffles his claim to show
us, that the outcome of the dispute over natural religion is essentially
what the sceptic says. In this way, Philo begins the process of undercutting his concession, thus of denying to Cleanthes the victory that
he thinks has just been offered to him.

To suggest that, in the last analysis, the disagreements between
Cleanthes and himself come down to mere squabblings over words

implies either that the gap between their respective positions is narrow or that, in principle, the gap between them is unbridgeable. If the former, then Philo's concession (indeed his whole dispute with Cleanthes over natural religion) would not really amount to much, when misunderstandings and the like are cleared away, for it takes only a small step to cross a small gap. But if the latter, then there is no point in even trying to bridge the gap, and a debate aimed at doing so becomes merely words. These, respectively, reflect the two levels of interpretation I mentioned just above. Either way, the effect is that the gap between the two sides, whether small or large, is not worth further disputation.

Granting 'a great analogy' between 'the works of nature' and man-made things ('the productions of art'), Philo accepts a proportionate likeness between their respective causes (DNR: 119). So far so good. But he immediately goes on, 'there are also considerable differences' between those two classes of effects. So, 'we have reason to suppose a proportional difference in the causes' (DNR: 119). That a deity exists 'is plainly ascertained by reason', Philo allows (DNR: 119). But, 'if we make it a question, whether . . . we can properly call him a *mind* or *intelligence*, notwithstanding the vast difference, which may reasonably be supposed between him and human minds; what is this but a mere verbal controversy?' (DNR: 119).

In these lines, Philo is suggesting that, although the differences between the causes of natural and man-made order, respectively, are vast, any hesitation to use the same mentalistic language to describe both would be a mere haggling over words, a difference of no consequence. In this we see the old and the new Philo together. The old, the unremitting critic of the design hypothesis, is reflected in the emphasis on the vastness of the differences, while the new, the maker of the concession, is reflected in the suggestion that, vast though the differences are, to withhold the same description of both is merely a verbal quibble. To make sense of Philo here, thus of Hume, means finding the right mix between old and new.

We find the key to the solution on the next two pages. Philo assures us that '[a]ll men of sound reason are disgusted with verbal disputes' (DNR: 119), and then offers a very instructive example of the similarity that, 'vast difference' (DNR: 119) notwithstanding, warrants the same description of both causes. The example is his likening of the respective structures of 'the rotting of a turnip . . . and . . . human thought' (DNR: 120), obvious differences notwithstanding. These two points together show us what Philo is up to.

He tells us that the only remedy for verbal disputes is 'clear definitions . . . and . . . the strict and uniform use of those terms which are employed' (DNR: 119). But what if there are certain kinds of verbal disputes where even this remedy does not work? And what if the dispute between Philo and Cleanthes over the design hypothesis is of that very kind? Then that dispute would be 'a controversy, which admits not of any precise meaning' (DNR: 120). That is to say, the controversy itself, and not just a particular candidate-solution to it, would be factually meaningless, thus futile to engage in. And that is what Philo will now try to show. If he succeeds, he will, by extension, show the futility of natural religion too.

Philo distinguishes between issues of 'quantity or number' (DNR: 120) and issues 'concerning the degrees of any quality or circumstance' (DNR: 119). The former, he tells us, are 'susceptible of . . . exact mensuration' or measurement, while the latter are not (DNR: 120). Parenthetically, this distinction is in the approximate neighbourhood of another distinction, one that is fundamental, and controversial, in Hume's moral philosophy, namely, his distinction between facts, on the one hand, and values, on the other.

On the strength of the distinction between matters of quantity and matters of quality, Philo proposes to show that 'the dispute concerning theism . . . is merely verbal . . . [and, at the same time] . . . *incurably* ambiguous' (DNR: 120, emphasis added). This is a radical claim. On it, curiosity about the great issues of theism and atheism may be virtually unavoidable for reflective people, yet to pursue that curiosity into philosophical theory building is doomed from the start.

To prove his point about the futility of the debate itself, Philo proposes a simple thought-experiment. First, we ask a theist if there is not 'a great and immeasurable, because *incomprehensible*, difference between the human and the divine mind' (DNR: 120, my emphasis). He will surely agree, especially if he is pious (like Demea). It is interesting that Cleanthes does not protest this point, as he did an equivalent version of it in Parts I and II (DNR: 40–1, 45). Then, second, we ask an atheist if there is not 'a certain degree of analogy among all the operations of nature . . . [on the one hand] and the structure of human thought [on the other]' (DNR: 120). The example Philo gives us of an 'operation of nature' is a startling deflation of the analogy. The example is of 'the rotting of a turnip' (DNR: 120). Thus, what we can expect the atheist to agree to is that it is possible to describe the rotting of a turnip and the structure of human thought in such ways that there is some resemblance between them.

Let us try. The rotting of a turnip is a complex, stage-by-stage process that has a structure and occurs over time. Likewise human thought. That too is complex, stage-by-stage, structured, and occurs over time. Or, let us make up our own example: there is a resemblance between you, the reader of these words, and the sound of a dog whistle. What is it? Both of you now occupy space-time coordinates. There is a resemblance, but, outside of a very narrow context, it is hardly very enlightening.

At any rate, this virtually empty agreement by the atheist in hand, Philo then suggests that, in our thought-experiment, we ask him or her 'if it be not probable, that the principle which first arranged and still maintains, order in this universe, bears not also some . . . analogy to . . . the oeconomy of human mind and thought' (DNR: 120). What kind of analogy? A 'remote and inconceivable analogy' (DNR: 120). How could anybody, atheist or not, deny it, so little is involved in the description, thus in the atheist's concession too?

So now we have the theist agreeing that the difference between the (infinite) divine and (finite) human minds is beyond measure and comprehension, while the atheist agrees that there is some remote likeness between the human mind and various natural processes. On the strength of these virtual truisms, Philo asks, in mock triumph: '[w]here then . . . is the subject of . . . the dispute concerning theism?' (DNR: 120). He explains as follows: 'The theist allows, that the original intelligence is very different from human reason: The atheist allows, that the original principle of order bears some remote analogy to it' (DNR: 120). Each is agreeing to a point the other would emphasize. All that remains, Philo assures us, is to work out the degrees of the likenesses and the differences. But those are questions of quality, where no exact resolution is possible. Thus, to pursue the question is futile.

Taken at its face value, Philo's argument here is largely intellectual sleight of hand; the quickness of the tongue deceiving the mind. On that level, the point of Philo's exercise is to find a description of the difference between the two sides in the dispute that, for prudential reasons, allows him to make a concession to the theistic side. But at the same time, the effect of accepting that the debate over natural religion is in the end 'entirely verbal' (DNR: 121, n.1) is indistinguishable from the effect of accepting Philo's scepticism regarding that debate. Thus, Philo's concession comes to very little, far less than Cleanthes thinks. The description on which it stands, his description of the agreement between theist and atheist, ensures that. I will come back to this topic on p. 207.

In this way, what Philo has so fulsomely seemingly given, he takes away, leaving only the hollowed-out shell of the concession remaining. This he calls 'true religion' (DNR: 121), in contrast to 'vulgar' or common 'superstition' (DNR: 121), which he abhors (DNR: 116). But vulgar superstition is Philo's estimate of religion as it is in practice. Thus his abhorrence is of that.

True religion and vulgar superstition

'The proper office of religion'

Cleanthes disagrees, as he must, with Philo's description of how little is supposedly in dispute between theists and atheists. But there is no vehemence or passion in his disagreement. In the circumstances, it is astonishingly mild. He is content to inform Philo that his own 'inclination ... lies ... a contrary way' (DNR: 121). In light of the trivialization of natural religion, of the root differences between believers and unbelievers, and of his own concession to Cleanthes' position that Philo has just set before him, it is quite astonishing to find Cleanthes content to express his disagreement meekly as a difference in inclination. This is not the aggressive, sharp-tongued Cleanthes of earlier on. What are we to make of it? Surely, that Hume's cover-up is in full swing. For if Hume allows Cleanthes to call Philo's bluff, to expose the hollowness of the concession, or the vacuousness of the similarity between causes that Philo is prepared to agree to, then the full depth and sharpness of the difference between the two characters will be plain for all to see.

Cleanthes proposes that religion, 'however corrupted,' by which he means however riddled with superstition, is still better than no religion at all (DNR: 121). In his view, morality requires religion; specifically, he thinks it needs the idea of reward and punishment after death for the righteous and unrighteous respectively (DNR: 121). The conversation now settles to a discussion of the true nature and function of religion. In the circumstances, this is an extraordinarily misdirected response from Cleanthes, for the real, and deep, issue of substance is Philo's proposed reduction of both the natural religionist debate and the theistic side in it to so little.

On the subject of vulgar or popular religion, Philo asks how the various religious pogroms and persecutions in history can be said to be good (DNR: 122). Cleanthes responds by narrowing the rightful scope of religion, 'the proper office of religion,' to 'regulat[ing] the heart of men, humaniz[ing] their conduct, infus[ing] the spirit of temperance, order, and obedience . . . and only enforc[ing] the motives of morality and justice' (DNR: 122). His claim is that it is only when religion gets more ambitious than this, and 'acts as a separate principle over men,' that persecutions result.

Subject to a very important qualification, Philo agrees. His qualification is that 'all religion . . . except the philosophical and rational kind' has greater ambitions and pretensions than those just sketched out by Cleanthes as the proper role and function of religion (DNR: 122). We know from Hume's biographer, E.C. Mossner, that this was Hume's own view too (Mossner 1954: 306).

The question now is which version of true religion is right: Cleanthes', which aims at detaching the history of religious persecutions from religion proper, but which shares with so-called vulgar superstition the notions of a hereafter and a post-mortem reward-and-punishment system; or Philo's (also Hume's own), which restricts true religion to a meagre, distant, vague, and ultimately incomprehensible, analogy between the human mind and the ultimate source of order in the universe? On the latter account, true religion, understood as the truth in religion, comes to the same thing as Philo's (and Hume's) sceptical deism.

Both Philo and Cleanthes agree that religion, as we find it in common practice, is not true religion, that is, not an ideal manifestation of religion. But is Philo's version religion at all, in any meaningful sense of the term?

Philo maintains that Cleanthes' idea of reward and punishment in a hereafter, which most people will think, or at least hope, belongs in the distant future, has little motivational force in practice, at least in comparison to the attraction of the more immediate rewards and punishments in everyday life (DNR: 122). Thus, he argues, even if Cleanthes were right about a hereafter, it would not have the desired effect upon morality. In a reflection of Hume's own thinking about the nature of morality, Philo maintains that experience shows us morality prospering when people's 'natural honesty' guides their conduct (DNR: 123). And experience also shows us, he maintains, that 'the highest zeal in religion and the deepest hypocrisy' go together (DNR: 124). In the latter regard, recall from our first chapter Hume's remark to Boswell that, 'when he heard a man was religious, he concluded he was a rascal'. In that same conversation, Boswell quotes him to say that 'the Morality of every Religion was bad' (Boswell 1947: 76).

Philo's point is that true religion, at least what he persists in calling true religion, has very modest intellectual pretensions; it recognizes the great limitations on our capacity to know the truth, especially in regard to ultimate questions. Furthermore, it does not try to either deduce morality from first principles or guide it by pure reasoning. It recognizes the primacy of feeling and sentiment in morality. By respecting and heeding the basic facts of human nature, essentially that we are beings who, at bottom, live by feeling and habit, true religion (in Philo's version of it) allows morality to be free of the dead hand of theory and ideology. It is in this way, largely indirectly, that true religion 'regulate[s] the heart of men'.

Experimentalism compromised

Philo's so-called true religion represents a departure from experimentalism. For nowhere in practice do we find the kind of behaviour and practice he is describing identified as religion. What he seems to be doing here is arguing from some prior, idealized conception of religion to the inadequacy of religion as we find it in practice. But experience gives us actual religion; mostly superstition, perhaps, but actual religion none the less. Experience does not give us the yardstick by which Philo is now judging religion in practice, or, at least, experience of *religion* does not. Experience does not give us so-called true religion. Thus Philo is here departing from strict experimentalism.

'Terror is the primary principle of religion'

Cleanthes, now recognizing how far afield from popular religion Philo's concept of 'true religion' really is, warns him to be careful not to '[a]llow . . . your zeal against false religion to undermine your veneration for the true' (DNR: 126). But even now, in warning Philo, his tone is mild by comparison to earlier in the book, for instance, his taunting of Philo in Part I or his devastation of Demea's cosmological argument in Part IX.

Cleanthes sees popular religion, rid of its extremisms, as both true religion and valuable to society. He reminds Philo of religion's power to bring comfort (DNR: 126). Philo agrees that popular religion is comforting, but, by then going on to identify fear and dread as the principal inspirations of religion, 'terror is the primary principle of religion' (DNR: 128), he reminds us how far the world is from what we would, beforehand, expect a world designed by a benevolent deity to be. (We may recall Philo's use, to powerful effect, of a similar tactic in Parts X and XI (DNR: 98, 103, 107) while pressing theism's problem of evil.) The actual world of Philo's description here in Part XII causes us to 'brood upon the terrors of the invisible world', thus plunging us 'still deeper in affliction' (DNR: 128). Religion's comfort, then, is comfort in the face of a dreadful world, which is hardly what, 'beforehand . . . [we would] expect from a very powerful, wise, and benevolent Deity' (DNR: 107).

What concept of deity is reflected in popular religion? Surely it is the concept of a deity responsive to our needs or pleas. But that presupposes that the deity has feelings like ours, whereas, in fact, it is 'an absurdity to believe that the Deity has human passions' (DNR: 128). This echoing of Philo's earlier attacks on anthropomorphism represents a further retraction of his concession. It is the hypothesis of indifference in other words. Because it is absurd to think the cause of natural order has feelings like ours, it is absurd to think it cares about us, or is capable of caring about us.

But 'philosophical theists' entertain no such views of the ultimate source of order in the universe (DNR: 129). Neither do 'philosophical sceptics' (DNR: 129). In effect, these are one and the same. It is they, among whom Philo would include himself, who grasp both the truth about religion and the truth of religion, the latter being very limited. But just what is it that they grasp, this so-called true religion?

The five 'ifs'

True religion, as understood by Philo, amounts to no more than the following combination of hypothetical, heavily restricted, points;

> *If* the whole of natural theology ... resolves itself into one simple, though somewhat ambiguous, at least undefined proposition, *that the cause or causes of order in the universe probably bear some remote analogy to human intelligence*: *If* this proposition be not capable of extension, variation, or more particular explication: *If* it affords no inference that affects human life, or can be the source of any action or forbearance: And *if* the analogy, imperfect as it is, can be carried no farther than to the human intelligence; and cannot be transferred, with any appearance of probability, to the other qualities of the mind: *If* this really be the case, what can the most inquisitive, contemplative, and religious man do more than give a plain, philosophical assent to the proposition, as often as it occurs; and believe that the arguments, on which it is established, exceed the objections which lie against it? Some astonishment indeed will naturally arise from the greatness of the object: Some melancholy from its obscurity: Some contempt of human reason, that it can give no solution more satisfactory with regard to so extraordinary and magnificent a question.
>
> (DNR: 129; emphasis on the word 'if' is mine throughout)

If the whole issue is boiled down to the single proposition that there is a remote likeness between the cause or causes of natural order and the human mind; if we can give no fuller interpretation to that likeness; if we can transfer it to no other topic; if the analogy provides absolutely no guide or theme to life, or any hint about what is good or evil, permissible or impermissible; if it merits no attitude or practice of worship; if no other religious practices are appropriate either, no confessions of sinfulness, no asking for forgiveness, no prayers, petitions, professions of love of the deity, and so on; if it gives no reason whatsoever to think that the cause of natural order has any concern for us, or interest in us; if the analogy is restricted exclusively to the concept of intelligence, and even then offered very tentatively; finally, if all the foregoing conditions are accepted, then the inquisitive, reflective, religious (in Philo's sense) person can accept it, on the preponderance of the evidence.

Repeating a point he made earlier in Part XII (DNR: 118–19), Philo acknowledges that '[s]ome astonishment . . . will naturally arise from the greatness of the object' (DNR: 129), issuing in 'so extraordinary and magnificent a question' (DNR: 129). But, also repeating, both the question's obscurity and our native inability to make any further headway with it are equally respected: 'Some melancholy from its obscurity: Some contempt of human reason, that it can give no solution more satisfactory' (DNR: 129).

Scepticism, deism, naturalism, irony

In order to pull together the main threads of Hume's philosophy of religion, let us revisit the question of how we are to think of Philo's concession on the design hypothesis, given his scepticism and his naturalistic hypothesis, and vice versa.

Deism and scepticism

In the first chapter I suggested there might be a tension between Philo's (thus Hume's) scepticism and his deism. Let us pick up the topic again. At face value there is a deep and significant tension between the two. The fundamental reason is that deism is a substantive position, whereas scepticism undercuts affirmation of any such position. How, then, can we think that Hume is both deist and sceptic? I will suggest five ways.

First, the deistic analogy that Philo is willing to concede is so weak and tenuous that it is not the affirmation of it which would violate scepticism, but rather the denial. The reason is that to deny something so vacuous and uninformative would require more solid evidence than accepting it. Considering how little we know, how could we rule out all similarity between the causes of order in man-made things and in natural things? To do so would require us knowing more than we do, or ever could. We simply do not know the causes of natural order. How, then, can we be sure there is no resemblance between them and the causes of order in man-made things? Given scepticism, we neither can nor ever could. Philo's concession comes to no more than that.

Second, as we saw earlier, Philo has characterized the dispute over the design hypothesis as 'merely verbal' (DNR: 120). And if we agree that real disputes are those that, in principle anyway, can be resolved by the introduction of new evidence or the re-assessment of old, then merely verbal disputes are not real disputes in that sense. Verbal disputes that remain when the relevant terminology has been clarified are resolved by force of will, not intellect. Knowing there is no decisive evidence, or even preponderance of evidence, we choose one side or the other. That being so, to characterize a dispute as merely verbal, after the relevant terminology has been clarified, is to adopt a stance towards it akin to scepticism.

But, as I suggested earlier, Hume did not wish to broadcast such a characterization of his point. Instead, as we saw, he has Philo represent the 'merely verbal' nature of the dispute between theists and atheists as though there is really very little substantive difference between them in the end. But that is hardly so, and Hume surely knew that believers and dissenters *are* separated by substantive differences on certain issues. For instance, there is life after death, or not. A person has (or is) a non-physical soul, or not. And so on. But, on Hume's scepticism, we are in principle unable to know which side in these various disagreements is right. So, in the end, our disputations over them are only words. That, I am suggesting, is the real meaning, as opposed to the public relations meaning, of his point that, in the last analysis, disagreements between theists and atheists are 'entirely verbal' (DNR: 121, n.1).

Third, and closely connected to the second point, the relationship between Philo's (Hume's) scepticism and deism may be seen as a bi-level relationship, as follows. The basic level is scepticism about the powers of our minds to make headway with such questions as come up in natural religion. Decisive evidence is, in principle, unavailable either way. Thus we ought not to engage in such inquiries. But our curiosity about such matters as 'the creation and formation of the universe' (DNR: 36) is deep and natural. So, if, against our better (sceptical) judgement, we *do* inquire, then the best we can come up with is a vague idea of a remote likeness between the respective causes of order in natural and man-made things, completely without practical implications. On that level of ill fated but perhaps inevitable inquiry, a weak deism is the best we can do.

Here is an analogy. I start to build a house on land to which I have no legitimate ownership-claim and on which I have no permission to build. I have a very strong desire to build, and ambition to finish the job, but no permission. I erect a frame. Unfortunately, its foundation turns out to be unsteady, the frame itself decidedly wobbly, and the project incapable of improvement or further development. This is simply not a good place to build a secure house. But there is no other, better land available to me. The prudent thing would be to have never tried to build a house here in the first place. Prudence notwithstanding, however, this woebegone house-frame now exists. That is a fact. But the frame neither has solidity in its own right nor legitimacy where it stands. In practical terms, that is, insofar as shelter or dwelling is concerned, it is no better than no house at all.

Fourth, in accepting 'some remote analogy', Philo introduces no new evidence to support doing so. Nor does he suggest any ways in which his previous criticisms are deficient. Thus, all of those criticisms stand. The effect is to emphasize further how virtually empty of content the analogy is to which he now offers a concession. Without going into details here, let us very briefly recall to mind some of those, still unanswered, criticisms: that no knowledge or meaningful discourse is possible outside the scope of experience; that the universe is a one-of-a-kind thing, and so not suited to analogies; that the orderly nature of the cause of natural order itself needs explaining; that for all we know natural order may have multiple causes; that if the cause of natural order is a deity, it may be a minor deity, now deceased; that natural order may have resulted from a long trial-and-error period; that we have a lot of experience of mind and intelligence emerging from generation, while we have no experience whatsoever of the reverse; and so on.

Philo's concession to the design hypothesis without new evidence, and without any indication that he now regards his earlier criticisms as misguided or ineffectual, is not just a deviation from evidentialism – the second I have suggested in this chapter – it is opposed to it. We do not have enough to go on to offer a hard-and-fast interpretation of what this means, but one possibility is that Hume is again drawing attention to the strength and persistence of our disposition to think that order in nature reflects design, the strength and persistence of what we saw J.C.A. Gaskin call 'the *feeling* of design' (my emphasis), notwithstanding our inability to say anything very substantive about it. Again, what Hume is showing us here is a fundamental truth about our own human nature, our essentially whimsical condition.

In Chapter 3, I asked, who, between Cleanthes and Philo, is the truer evidentialist? The answer, clearly, is Philo. Does that verdict survive his concession against the weight of evidence? If there is as little to the concession as I have been suggesting, yes. In light of Philo's not retracting or softening a single one of his earlier criticisms, while yet offering a concession to Cleanthes, Hume is showing us in just which direction the *evidence* points, thereby further showing us the weakness of the design hypothesis and, more widely, natural religion itself.

Fifth, Philo's fullest statement of concession to the design hypothesis (DNR: 129) comes immediately after he has said that it is the *philosophical* theists (as opposed to the vast majority of theists) and the *sceptics* who would be especially favoured by the deity, if there is one, for it is they who best adhere to true religion (DNR: 129). It is they who see what, in the end, is warranted in religion, thus it is they who, most of all, avoid dogmatism and superstition. And, as we saw, Philo confines what is warranted in religion to the heavily qualified, 'five "ifs"', proposition quoted above.

In sum, Philo's (and Hume's) deism comes to the following combination of points: there is a cause (or there are causes) of order in nature; but we know so little that we know of no compelling reason to deny a vague and distant resemblance between that cause (or those causes) and the cause of order in man-made things. That is the full extent to which anything positive can be said on the subject. The analogy on which this conclusion stands is so weak that it does not warrant thinking of the cause (or causes) of natural order as a person, or a mind. All that is warranted is some likeness between it and the human mind. But a rotting turnip meets that condition. In short, beyond the virtually empty single proposition that 'the cause or causes of order in the universe probably bear some remote analogy to human intelligence', we can say nothing positive at all on the subject.

Given both the context in which it is made and the stringent restrictions imposed on it, any substantive content that Philo's concession might be thought to have is virtually dissolved in the very making of it. Furthermore, recall that, in Part I, Philo refers to deism as a heresy stemming from an exaggerated and unjustified belief in the powers of the mind (DNR: 41). Thus, the more our understanding of the powers of the mind is cut back, so too our understanding of the supposed first cause of natural order. As I said in Chapter 1, if there is a tension between this gutted deism and scepticism, it is tension of a very low order.

Deism and naturalism

By definition, deism and naturalism conflict with one another. The former reflects some kind of supernaturalistic account of certain occurrences in the natural world, while the latter disavows supernaturalism entirely. In Parts VI, VII, and VIII, we saw Philo develop a version of naturalism. He did not endorse it in the end, leaving it instead as a hypothesis that, for all we know, might be true. How does that naturalistic hypothesis fit, if it does fit, with the heavily restricted and qualified design hypothesis that Philo is prepared to accept?

The answer is that it fits better than we might, at first, expect. The reason, again, is the virtual emptiness of the design hypothesis that Philo is prepared to accept. The thing to note in particular is that, in his 'five "ifs"' concession speech, Philo never refers to 'the cause or causes of order in the universe' as a deity of any kind, nor as a person, nor as outside the natural order. We have to project those dimensions on to his final version of the concession from earlier remarks.

Does Philo's concession rule out the possibility that the cause or causes of order in the universe could be natural, and not supernatural, things? No. The final draft of the concession (DNR: 129) is so vague and minimal that we cannot even be sure that the cause or causes Philo is referring to are forces or principles in the physical universe or not. Our reason to think they are not, that they may be non-natural, and specifically supernatural, is circumstantial, not direct.

Of course, none of this subtracts from the fact that, by definition, naturalism and deism exclude one another. But, as we cannot be certain that Philo's concession is of a cause outside the natural world, we cannot be certain that what we are calling his deism excludes naturalism. In effect, then, we cannot be certain that what we are calling his deism is really deism at all. That is how vague and minimal the concession is in the end.

This conceded hypothesis falls well short of Cleanthes' view that the design hypothesis is 'a sufficient foundation for religion' (DNR: 71), on any normal understanding of the term 'religion'. What Philo calls true religion is really a kind of philosophy, having virtually nothing in common with religion as we find it to be in practice. It is more moral humanism than religion, as the latter is usually understood. Hume's deism, in other words, is not a religious position at all, in any normal sense of the word 'religion'. And so we must be careful, when interpreting as deism his concession of some remote likeness between the causes of order in natural and in man-made things, respectively, not to read more into it than he intended.

Let us recall two examples of this that, in the end, come to the same thing, namely, the hypothesis of indifference and moral atheism. If naturalism is true, then the cause of natural order is indifferent to us. But indifference to us is fundamental to Philo's weak deism too; it follows from his denial of any moral properties to whatever is originally the cause of natural order. In that respect, Philo's deism has the same practical effect as naturalism. But the denial to the cause of natural order of any moral properties is moral atheism. Thus, as we saw before, Philo's deism is closed to any form of theism. Relative to theism, Philo's deism is atheistic; relative to religion as practised, it is no different in outlook than naturalism.

In conclusion: faith and reason

In Part I, Cleanthes taunted Philo that he wanted to erect faith on scepticism (DNR: 34), an essentially fideistic idea disdained by Cleanthes as naïve and foolish. Yet, here at the end of the *Dialogues*, it seems to be Philo who has the last laugh, his concession notwithstanding. How? As follows.

In the context of the *Dialogues'* discussion, all that now remains of the design argument is a meagre hypothesis with no religious significance. But the design argument is the mainstay of natural religion. So the natural religionist seems to be left with no better rational support for religious belief. Philo's characterization of this situation is that, '[t]o be a philosophical sceptic is, in a man of letters, the first and most essential step towards being a sound, believing Christian', and, '[a] person . . . with a just sense of the imperfections of human reason, will fly to revealed truth' (DNR: 130). But, so characterized, this is fideism, thus making Cleanthes the object of his own jibe.

As just described, the position at the end of the *Dialogues* reflects what Immanuel Kant (1724–1804), the great German philosopher, whose *The Critique of Pure Reason* was inspired by Hume, and who agreed with Hume's destruction of natural religion, saw as the necessary clearing away of reason in religious matters in order to make room for faith. The difference, though, is that Kant means it, whereas Hume (here speaking through Philo) does not.

Afterword

Where is Hume in Hume's *Dialogues*?

The question, 'where is Hume in the *Dialogues*?', is really a cluster of questions. Who speaks for Hume in the book? Does Hume conceal his thinking? If he does, how well, why, and what ought we to think of it? Why does he write in dialogue form in the first place? Very briefly, let us take up these questions here.

In taking them up, though, it will be useful to keep the following, ironic, consideration in mind. It is that these questions are fuelled in part by the fact that Hume's book achieves one of its principal objectives as a dialogue, namely, verisimilitude, which is to say, realism or truth-to-life. We accept that there is real conversation, real discussion, in the book among characters who plausibly advance plausible positions. None of those characters, and certainly neither of the two most prominent in the discussion from start to finish, Cleanthes and Philo, is there only as the designated loser in the debate. But to achieve such realism in a dialogue involves a significant muting of the voice of the author, such that no single character obviously

speaks in that voice. Ironically, then, a by-product of Hume's success in achieving such realism is the set of questions with which I began this Afterword.

The *Dialogues'* realism is announced right at the start by the narrator, Pamphilus. His point is that certain philosophical topics are naturally suitable to dialogue form because 'human reason can reach no fixed determination with regard to [them]' (DNR: 30). And the subject of natural religion seems to fall readily into that category.

Finally, on a historical note, Hume was familiar with the Earl of Shaftesbury's (1671–1713) thinking on the subject of realism in dialogue writing, and on this, as on aspects of his moral theory, Hume was influenced by Shaftesbury.

Who speaks for Hume?

The question of who speaks for Hume in the *Dialogues* needs sharpening. A natural interpretation would be, 'who alone speaks for Hume?' Taken that way, we would expect to find some characters in the book who simply do not reflect the views of the author at all. Think, for instance, of Hylas in Berkeley's *Three Dialogues between Hylas and Philonous* or of Euthyphro in Plato's dialogue that is named for him. But I do not take the question of spokesmanship that way here. Instead, I take it as the question, 'who principally speaks for Hume?', and my answer is Philo.

Aside from a footnote in Part XII (DNR: 121) in which, perhaps, he speaks in his own voice, Hume neither speaks for himself in the *Dialogues* nor does he unambiguously speak through one of his characters. The Canadian philosopher, Ian Hacking, puts it well in a recent issue of *The New York Review of Books*: 'In Plato, or Galileo, or Berkeley, you know the master message; one character, perhaps helped by a couple of sidekicks, is advancing the truth, while the other major characters put the most powerful objections, and are remorselessly ground down. Only Hume's dialogues about religion leave room for ambiguity' (NYRB: 22). As a consequence, judgement about spokesmanship must be made on circumstantial, not direct, evidence.

For pretty obvious reasons, Demea may be ruled out at once. He professes a strong belief in the God of standard theism, and insists that his belief can be proven in the strictest sense. Each is enough to eliminate him from consideration as the voice of Hume in the *Dialogues*.

A serious case can be made out for Cleanthes. He is an experimentalist, like his creator. Also like Hume, he thinks that extreme or Pyrrhonistic scepticism cannot withstand the practice of daily life. Furthermore, it is he who introduces Hume's fundamental distinction between *a priori* and *a posteriori* reasoning, and who then puts it to devastating use against Demea's cosmological argument. Cleanthes accepts the design hypothesis, and we know that Hume himself goes along with a version of it. The narrator in the book said that Cleanthes has an 'accurate philosophical turn' of mind (DNR: 30) and that he is the winner in the debate (DNR: 130). Furthermore, it is to him that Philo concedes, such as that concession is. All in all, Cleanthes' claim to spokesmanship merits serious consideration.

In the end, though, the claim is best denied. To see why, and also why Philo is the main voice of the author, let us look again at some of the foregoing points. True, Cleanthes, like Hume, thinks life overwhelms Pyrrhonistic scepticism. But Cleanthes thinks that our inability to be Pyrrhonists in practice is evidence that Pyrrhonism is false, while Hume does not think that at all. On the contrary, Hume's view is that the Pyrrhonist *wins* on the evidence. Thus, when Hume mitigates his scepticism, by reminding us that we cannot be Pyrrhonists in our everyday lives, he means to show us a fact about us, not about the balance of evidence pertaining to scepticism. And that view, fundamental to Hume's entire philosophical outlook, is represented in the *Dialogues* only by Philo.

It is true that Hume endorses a version of the design hypothesis. But Cleanthes' design hypothesis is robust, one deemed sufficient for religious belief, whereas Hume's own is neither. Furthermore, Cleanthes advocates a form of theism, with a concept of deity that includes caring about us. By contrast, Hume inclines to a wisp of deism, keeps the door open to polytheism and naturalism, and advances the idea that the ultimate cause of order in nature is utterly indifferent to us as individuals. Hume's deism is a bare shell of the position, with no religious value or content. And all of these are the views of Philo in the book, not Cleanthes. Furthermore, Philo is no less, perhaps more, an experimentalist than Cleanthes, and no less committed to the *a priori/a posteriori* distinction.

A proponent of Cleanthes' spokesmanship will likely ask how I know that Philo's deism, not Cleanthes' theism, is Hume's own view. And likewise for the hypothesis of indifference, and the openness to polytheism and naturalism. There is no direct proof. As I said above, it is a circumstantial case based on closeness of fit across a range of issues. There is also Hume's own testimony. In a letter (10 March 1751) to his friend Gilbert Elliot, he wrote, '[h]ad it been my good fortune to live near you, I shou'd have taken on me the Character of Philo, in the Dialogue, which you'll own I could have supported naturally enough: And you wou[l]d not have been averse to that of Cleanthes' (LCD: 25).

Does Hume conceal his thinking in the *Dialogues*?

Yes. The questions, then, are: how?; why?; how well?; and what ought we to think of it? How does Hume do it? By using dialogue form to cause ambiguity about which character speaks for him. In itself, the dialogue form is neither concealment nor reflective of an intent to conceal. Plato wrote dialogues. So did Berkeley. And spokesmanship in their cases is not controversial.

A philosophical dialogue resembles a play, in one respect, a treatise in another. The latter resemblance is in the fact that a philosophical dialogue makes (or tries to make) a substantive contribution to a philosophical debate. But the *Dialogues* is more than either one, and also, in a sense, more than both together.

A play, even a 'philosophical' play, for instance certain plays of Tom Stoppard's, does not suffer as a play if we do not know for sure, or even care, who speaks for the playwright. Quoting Hamlet again, 'the play's the thing' (Act II, Scene II). But a treatise does. Now Hume's *Dialogues* is more than a play. But it is also more than a treatise. By this I mean that it is a serious work by a major philosopher, on topics that he discusses, in his own name, in other writings. How does that make it more than a treatise? By virtue of the fact that, being the work of a major philosopher, we want to know not just what points and arguments are made in it, but also where that philosopher himself stands on the issues on which he is writing. We want to know, legitimately, how this work fits with his other philosophical writings. Consequently, interested in that, it is not enough for us that a philosophical play or a philosophical treatise by that philosopher sets before us good points on one, or two, or all sides of the issues discussed. For the points alone, in their own right, are not the whole of it. Essentially, what I am trying to get at is this: we can legitimately approach the *Dialogues* in any (or all) of the following ways, none being reducible to the others: as a play, as a philosophical play, as a treatise, as a work of a major philosopher, David Hume, thus as a valuable text from the point of view of 'Hume studies'. The concealment within the text affects the fourth of these aspects especially.

In addition to concealment within the text, there is Hume's concealment of the text itself, his suppression of the book until after his death. This plausibly suggests that, within the book, he had failed to cover his tracks as well as he wished. For, even if we disagree that Philo is the principal spokesman for the author, preferring the theistic Cleanthes instead, we can still see, surely, that Philo's criticisms of Cleanthes' views are serious and remain unanswered. Then there is the negative, deflationary tone and effect of the book as a whole. Thus, even if Hume had successfully built into the book sufficient deniability for himself on the former account, he would still have scant deniability in respect to the book overall.

The next question is 'why?' The answer is simple. It is that, while the *Dialogues* is a controversial book, as are other writings of Hume's, its author was not a controversialist by nature. His writings provoked, but he was no provocateur, in the usual sense of the term. He tells us so himself in this letter, written in 1766, 'I could cover the floor of a large room with books and pamphlets wrote against me, to none of which I ever made the least reply, not from disdain (for the authors of some of them I respect) but from my desire of ease and tranquility'(Mossner 1954: 286).

The answer to our next question, 'how well does Hume conceal his views?', is contained in the answer just given. Looked at one way, namely, in light of his friends' judgement that he could not safely publish the book in his lifetime, his concealment is not very good. But looked at another way, namely, in light of the on-going dispute about spokesmanship, his concealment was good enough.

What ought we to think about Hume's effort to conceal his true thinking? For instance, is it an attempt to mislead his readers? And if so, what ought we to think of that? At one level, of course, Hume *is* trying to mislead his readers. And all things being equal, that may be morally dubious. But all things are not equal. Hume perceived a threat to himself, if his views became widely known at the time. And surely we do not think he had an obligation to publish views that could be expected to cause himself harm.

The question, 'what ought we to think of Hume's concealment?', has a wider implication as well. For it raises the question of our overall estimation of Hume's book. Let us end with that.

The nub of the concealment is Philo's concession. That is the principal cause of the book's internal tension, and reflects its deepest ambiguity. But that tension and ambiguity are significant parts of the book's greatness. So, to make up our minds about Philo's concession is, to a large extent, to make up our minds about the book itself.

I suggest looking at the concession, thus the book, like this. In Hume there is no glib dismissal of certain deep questions that lead some thinkers to transcendent answers, although we find in him far less respect for the answers themselves. (For a famous/notorious instance of the latter, see the final paragraph of the *Enquiry concerning Human Understanding* (EHU: 165).) What are we to think about order in nature? Could blind forces really cause it? Our curiosity here is natural. A feeling of design comes readily to mind. But then, pulling against that curiosity and that feeling, undercutting them, there is the narrow scope of our understanding. So how can the curiosity make headway, or the feeling receive corroboration? They can't. These two things, curiosity about order and scepticism about the powers of our understanding, reflect warring dispositions, with Hume's book a dramatic enactment of their conflict. Perhaps, then, we ought to see Philo's concession as Hume's showing us, but not telling us, that here, on these deep questions, he is genuinely of two minds, at once inclining two contrary ways.

Bibliography

Works by Hume

Dialogues concerning Natural Religion, ed. J.C.A. Gaskin (New York: Oxford University Press, 1998). 'Oxford World's Classics' edition.

The Natural History of Religion, ed. J.C.A. Gaskin (New York: Oxford University Press, 1998). 'Oxford World's Classics' edition.

'My Own Life', in Gaskin's 'Oxford World's Classics' edition of the *Dialogues*.

'A Letter Concerning The Dialogues, 10 March 1751' in Gaskin's 'Oxford World's Classics' edition of the *Dialogues*.

A Treatise of Human Nature, ed. L.A. Selby-Bigge, second edition, P.H. Nidditch (New York: Oxford University Press, 1978).

Enquiry concerning Human Understanding, ed. L.A. Selby-Bigge, third edition, P.H. Nidditch (New York: Oxford University Press, 1995). Gaskin, in his 'Oxford World's Classics' edition of the *Dialogues*, includes Section XI of the *Enquiry*.

Other works

Aiken, H.D. (1966) 'Introduction', in his edition of the *Dialogues* (New York: Hafner).

Baier, A.C. (1991) *A Progress of Sentiments: Reflections on Hume's Treatise* (Cambridge, MA: Harvard University Press).

Bell, M. (1990) 'Introduction', in his edition of the *Dialogues* (London: Penguin Books).

Boswell, J. (1947) 'Interview with Hume, 7 July 1776', in Norman Kemp Smith's edition of the *Dialogues* (Indianapolis: Bobbs-Merrill): 76–9.

Box, M.A. (1990) *The Suasive Art of David Hume* (Princeton: Princeton University Press).

Burnyeat, M. and Frede, M. (eds) (1997) *The Original Sceptics: A Controversy* (Indianapolis: Hackett Publishing Company).

Butler, R.J. (1960) 'Natural belief and the enigma of Hume', *Archiv fur Geschichte der Philosophie*: 73–100.

Chappell, V.C. (ed.) (1966) *Hume* (New York: Doubleday).

Draper, P. (1996) 'Pain and pleasure: an evidential problem for theists', in D. Howard-Snyder (ed.) *The Evidential Argument from Evil* (Bloomington: Indiana University Press).

Draper, P. (1996) 'The skeptical theist', in D. Howard-Snyder (ed.) *The Evidential Argument from Evil* (Bloomington: Indiana University Press).

Flew, A. (1997) *Hume's Philosophy of Belief* (Bristol: Thoemmes Press). Reprint of 1966 edition.

Fogelin, R.J. (1993) 'Hume's Scepticism', in D.F. Norton (ed.) *The Cambridge Companion to Hume* (New York: Cambridge University Press).

Fogelin, R.J. (1994) *Pyrrhonian Reflections on Knowledge and Justification* (New York: Oxford University Press).

Gaskin, J.C.A. (1979) 'Hume, atheism, and the "interested objection" of morality', in D.F. Norton (ed.) *McGill Hume Studies* (San Diego: Austin Hill Press).

Gaskin, J.C.A. (1988) *Hume's Philosophy of Religion*, second edition (Atlantic Highlands: Humanities Press International).

Gaskin, J.C.A. (1993) 'Hume on religion', in D.F. Norton (ed.) *The Cambridge Companion to Hume* (New York: Cambridge University Press).

Gaskin, J.C.A. (1998) 'Introduction' to his 'Oxford World's Classics' edition of the *Dialogues*.

Hacking, I. (2000) 'The lives of animals', *The New York Review of Books*, XLVII (11), 29 June.

Livingston, D.W. (1998) *Philosophical Melancholy and Delirium: Hume's Pathology of Philosophy* (Chicago: University of Chicago Press).

Locke, J. (1961) *An Essay concerning Human Understanding* Vol. 2 (New York: Dutton).

Mackie, J.L. (1996) 'Evil and omnipotence', in M. Adams and R. Adams (eds) *The Problem of Evil* (New York: Oxford University Press).

Mates, B. (1981) *Skeptical Essays* (Chicago: University of Chicago Press).

Mossner, E.C. (1954) *The Life of David Hume* (Austin: University of Texas Press).

Mossner, E.C. (1966) 'Philosophy and biography: the case of David Hume', in V.C. Chappell (ed.) *Hume* (New York: Doubleday).

Norton, D.F. (1982) *David Hume: Common-Sense Moralist, Sceptical Metaphysician* (Princeton: Princeton University Press).

Norton, D.F. (ed.) (1993) *The Cambridge Companion to Hume* (New York: Cambridge University Press).

Norton, D.F. (1993) 'An introduction to Hume's thought', in D.F. Norton (ed.) *The Cambridge Companion to Hume* (New York: Cambridge University Press).

Noxon, J. (1966) 'Hume's agnosticism', in V.C. Chappell (ed.) *Hume* (New York: Doubleday): 361–83.

Noxon, J. (1976) 'Hume's concern with religion', in K.R. Merrill and R.W. Shahan (eds) *David Hume: Many-Sided Genius* (Norman: University of Oklahoma Press).

O'Connor, D. (1998) *God and Inscrutable Evil* (Lanham: Rowman & Littlefield).

Pears, D.F. (ed.) (1963) *David Hume: A Symposium* (London: Macmillan).

Pears, D.F. (1976) 'The naturalism of Book I of Hume's *Treatise of Human Nature*', *Proceedings of the British Academy*, Vol. LXII (London: Oxford University Press).

Pears, D.F. (1996) *Hume's System* (New York: Oxford University Press).

Pike, N. (1964) 'Hume on evil', in N. Pike (ed.) *God and Evil* (Englewood Cliffs: Prentice-Hall).

Pike, N. (1970) 'Hume on the argument from design', in Pike's edition of the *Dialogues* (Indianapolis: Bobbs-Merrill).

Popkin, R.H. (1980) 'Introduction', in his edition of the *Dialogues* (Indianapolis: Hackett Publishing Company).

Root, H.E. (1967) 'Introduction', in his edition of *The Natural History of Religion* (Stanford: Stanford University Press).

Smith, N.K. (1947) 'Introduction' to his edition of the *Dialogues* (Indianapolis: Bobbs-Merrill).

Smith, N.K. (1966) *The Philosophy of David Hume* (London: Macmillan).

Stewart, M.A. (1996) 'Hume's philosophy of religion', *Philosophical Books*, 37.

Strawson, G. (1989) *The Secret Connexion: Causation, Realism, and David Hume* (Oxford: Clarendon Press).

Strawson, P.F. (1985) *Skepticism and Naturalism: Some Varieties* (New York: Columbia University Press).

Stroud, B. (1977) *Hume* (London: Routledge).

Stroud, B. (1984) *The Significance of Philosophical Scepticism* (Oxford: Clarendon Press).

Swinburne, R. (1979) *The Existence of God* (Oxford: Clarendon Press).

Williams, B. (1963) 'Hume on religion', in D.F. Pears (ed.) *David Hume: A Symposium* (New York: Macmillan): 77–88.

Wykstra, S.J. (1996) 'The Humean obstacle to evidential arguments from suffering', in M. Adams and R. Adams (eds) *The Problem of Evil* (New York: Oxford University Press).

Wynn, M. (1999) *God and Goodness* (New York: Routledge).

Yandell, K.E. (1990) *Hume's 'Inexplicable Mystery': His Views on Religion* (Philadelphia: Temple University Press).

Index